SLAVERY *and* FREEDOM *in* Sava

SLAVERY *and* FREEDOM *in*

Savannah

Edited by

Leslie M. Harris *and*

Daina Ramey Berry

THE UNIVERSITY OF GEORGIA PRESS

Athens and London

Published in cooperation with
Telfair Museums

This project is made possible by a grant
from the U.S. Institute of Museum and
Library Services.

Library of Congress
Cataloging-in-Publication Data

Slavery and freedom in Savannah / edited by
Leslie M. Harris and Daina Ramey Berry.
  pages cm
Includes bibliographical references and index.
ISBN 978-0-8203-4410-2
  (pbk. : alk. paper)
ISBN 0-8203-4410-9
  (pbk. : alk. paper)
1. African Americans — Georgia — Savannah —
History. 2. Slavery — Georgia — Savannah —
History. 3. Antislavery movements — Georgia
— Savannah — History. 4. Slaves — Emanci-
pation — Georgia — Savannah. 5. Free African
Americans — Georgia — Savannah — History.
6. African Americans — Georgia — Savannah —
Social life and customs. 7. Savannah (Ga.) —
History. 8. Savannah (Ga.) — Race relations.
9. Savannah (Ga.) — Social life and customs.
I. Harris, Leslie M. (Leslie Maria), 1965–
II. Berry, Daina Ramey.
F294.S2S58 2014
306.3'6209758724 — dc23
2013026911

British Library
Cataloging-in-Publication Data available

Contents

Sidebars

Foreword

As the oldest art museum in the South, Telfair Museums in the heart of Savannah's Historic District has a vital role to play in telling the story of urban slavery.

Beginning with the preservation of the former slave quarters at the Owens-Thomas House in the mid-1990s, Telfair Museums has demonstrated its commitment to promoting new understanding of this important topic. The thousands of visitors who walk through our doors each year hear a broad story about the site and all of its inhabitants, including free and enslaved men, women, and children.

We are proud to further expand the public's understanding of American history and culture by exploring the complexities of urban slavery and freedom in the American South with this valuable publication, *Slavery and Freedom in Savannah*.

Material generated by prominent national and international scholars for this book will provide essential information from which we will further develop the histories of Telfair Museums' two National Historic Landmark buildings—the Owens-Thomas House and Telfair Academy of Arts and Sciences. This publication will also offer students, academics, and lay historians the opportunity to discover a deeper, more complete story about our collective past.

Coeditors Leslie M. Harris and Daina Ramey Berry have thanked the numerous people involved with this project in their acknowledgments. I extend my heartfelt appreciation to those individuals as well. I would also like to recognize the Institute of Museum and Library Services, which awarded the Telfair a large grant used to provide funding for the October 2011 symposium "Slavery and Freedom in Savannah" and this subsequent book. Other financial assistance for the symposium came from the Johanna Favrot Fund for Historic Preservation of the National Trust for Historic Preservation, the City of Savannah, and the Friends of the Owens-Thomas House. Partnering organizations for the symposium included the Second African Baptist Church and Live Oak Public Libraries. Finally, I'm grateful for our ongoing partnership with the University of Georgia Press. Their professionalism and attention to detail have secured in this publication a significant and useful document that will be turned to for years to come.

LISA GROVE, Director/CEO
Telfair Museums

Preface

With the preservation of the Owens-Thomas House slave quarters in the mid-1990s, Telfair Museums began introducing visitors to a broader spectrum of its former inhabitants than before—white and black; men, women and children; enslaved and free. This new effort in interpretation began a process of telling a more complete story, "the whole story," as Alice Walker would say, about the house and *all* of its inhabitants. *Slavery and Freedom in Savannah* focuses on the lives and labor of the enslaved people who built, maintained, and serviced the house, and contextualizes the Owens-Thomas House within the social environment of its neighborhood, where more than 50 percent of the residents were people of color—enslaved and free. Special emphasis is given to the Telfair family and their enslaved servants in an effort to bridge and contextualize their story as part of Telfair Museums' history.

For over a half century, Telfair Museums' architecturally significant Owens-Thomas House has been interpreted as the home and stylish showplace of two former owners: Richard Richardson, the merchant and banker who first commissioned the residence, and later George Welshman Owens, plantation owner, alderman, mayor, Georgia state senator and representative, and U.S. congressman. Attention was also paid to the most famous guest at the house, the Revolutionary War hero the Marquis de Lafayette, who stayed there in 1825 when the house was between owners and run as an upscale boardinghouse. The Telfair Academy of Arts and Sciences (now Telfair Museums), following the bequest of Margaret Gray Thomas, opened the Owens-Thomas House to the public for tours in 1954. Tours focused primarily on the architecture and decorative arts, with limited information about the families who owned and lived in the house and nothing about the enslaved household workers. In 2005 and 2006, the museum received two National Endowment for the Humanities consultation and planning grants, which allowed the institution to move forward with its reinterpretation efforts. In 2010, the museum received a Museums for America grant from the Institute of Museum and Library Services, which supported the "Slavery and Freedom in Savannah" symposium presented in October 2011 and the publication of this book, which includes material presented at the symposium.

I believe that the truth about any subject only comes when all the sides of the story are put together, and all their different meanings make one new one . . . the whole story is what I'm after.
—Alice Walker,
  "Beyond the Peacock"

The Johanna Favrot Fund for Historic Preservation of the National Trust for Historic Preservation, the City of Savannah, the Second African Baptist Church, Live Oak Public Libraries, and the Friends of the Owens-Thomas House also supported the symposium.

Slavery and Freedom in Savannah will broaden public understanding of American history and culture by exposing audiences to the complexities of urban slavery and freedom. Providing the foundation for the entirety of the reinterpretation project, the new research generated by nationally and internationally prominent scholars provides a crucial informational base for future interpretation and exhibits at the Owens-Thomas House. The complete picture of this largely unstudied form of slavery in Savannah—a microcosm of urban slavery throughout the nation—unfolds through the Telfairs' own historic assets and stories.

TANIA SAMMONS, Senior Curator
Decorative Arts and Historic Sites

Acknowledgments

This book has benefitted from contributions of time, energy, and resources by many different people and institutions. We would like to thank the staff of Telfair Museums, especially Telfair's director and CEO, Lisa Grove; Cyndi Sommers; Paulette Thompson; Harry DeLorme; and especially Beth Moore, who performed crucial work in obtaining the images for the book. Steven High, a former Telfair Museums director and CEO, and Vaughnette Goode-Walker, a former Telfair Museums staff member, provided critical early support for this book project. We thank Allison Dorsey, professor of history at Swarthmore College, for introducing us to Vaughnette and thus connecting us with this project. Tania Sammons, senior curator of decorative arts and historic sites for Telfair Museums, deserves special mention for her whole-hearted dedication to this project, her integrity, and her willingness to answer all manner of questions about the Owens-Thomas House and Savannah's history.

The writers represented in this book have contributed their best efforts toward making this a work of the highest quality. We couldn't have asked for better intellectual collaborators in this important effort. We thank them for their patience in answering endless questions from two scholars who were learning about the fascinating city and people that many of them have dedicated their lives to understanding.

Archivists in Savannah were unfailingly supportive. We are grateful to Luciana Spracher, director of the City of Savannah Research Library & Municipal Archives; Lynette Stoudt, senior archivist of the Georgia Historical Society; and the staffs at the Bull Street Branch of the Live Oak Public Libraries of Chatham, Effingham, and Liberty Counties, and at the Bryan-Lang Historical Library of Camden County, Georgia. Thanks go to Chyna Bowen, Nedra K. Lee, and Jermaine Thibodeaux for their research assistance.

Our wonderful local hosts in Savannah were Vaughnette Goode-Walker; Deborah L. Mack of the Smithsonian Institution's National Museum of African American History and Culture; Diane and Ervin Houston; and Tina B. Brown. We are grateful as well to Bill Strothers, who welcomed us to Ivanhoe Plantation in Camden County, Georgia. We thank the Telfair Museums Owens-Thomas House Advisory

Committee for the 2011 *Slavery and Freedom in Savannah* symposium: Ronald Bailey, Michael Benjamin, Verdise Bradford, Pastor C. MeGill Brown, Constance Coleman, Jeanne Cyriaque, Shirley James, Charles J. Johnson Jr., Candy Lowe, Deborah L. Mack, Jerome Meadows, Danielle Meunier, Tanya Milton, Paul M. Pressly, Preston Russell, Leon Spencer, Lynette Stoudt, Richard Shinhoster, John Tuggle, Robin B. Williams, and Darlene Wilson. And many thanks to the Institute of Museum and Library Services, the City of Savannah, the National Trust for Historic Preservation, Live Oak Public Libraries, and the Second African Baptist Church for their support of this project.

The staff at the University of Georgia Press has managed this project with energy, patience, and grace. Many thanks to Derek Krissoff, who as senior editor worked with us closely during the early stages of this book project; and to Lisa Bayer, director of the Press; Jon Davies and Beth Snead; and especially John Joerschke, who carried us across the finish line. We are especially grateful to our copy editor, Kip Keller. Steven Moore's index provides a wonderful map to this book.

As we were completing this volume, we learned of the tragic death of one of our authors, Mark Finlay, an esteemed historian and citizen of Savannah. We dedicate this volume to his memory, and to the people of Savannah. We hope this work and Mark's example inspire Savannahians to carry on their investigations of the region's rich historical legacy.

Introduction

Leslie M. Harris and Daina Ramey Berry

We are amid a renaissance in the study of slavery and emancipation in the United States. One of the prime areas of research encompasses the lives and contributions of African Americans, enslaved and free, in urban areas.[1] *Slavery and Freedom in Savannah* brings together the latest scholarship on one of the most important port cities of the South, from its founding through the early twentieth century. This book positions slavery and emancipation, along with their aftermath, as a central set of events that left no one in the city untouched and that cast shadows into the twentieth century.

Most histories of slavery have been concerned with understanding plantation slavery. This is not surprising, since for more than four centuries nearly all enslaved people of African descent who labored in North America did so in rural communities. Plantation slavery was the chief driver of the transatlantic and domestic slave trades in the United States and throughout the Americas. Because of the centrality and economic successes of plantation slavery, historians have sometimes assumed that slavery in cities was insignificant and that slave labor was ill suited to urban economies. But a reexamination of slavery in North American cities reveals the importance of urban communities — especially port cities — to the slave economy, and the adaptability of slave labor and slave mastery to metropolitan regions. Urban slavery was part of, not an exception to, the slave-based economy of North America and the Atlantic World.

Savannah exemplifies the centrality of cities to slave-based economies, and the centrality of slavery to cities. Urban communities such as Savannah incorporated slave labor into their economic, social, and political frameworks, often from the very beginning of their existence. Thus, the founders of the Georgia colony, led by the British general James Edward Oglethorpe, requested and received black laborers, no doubt enslaved, from the neighboring colony of South Carolina to help construct the city. This request came despite the restrictions on slavery in Georgia intended to create a colony that would forgo large, slave-reliant plantations in favor of smaller farms that would provide opportunities for ordinary British citizens seeking a new life in North America. But colonists and trustees alike were ultimately unable to imagine a colony—much less a world—without slavery. By the 1750s, slavery was an important component of the colony's economy, and on the eve of the Revolutionary War, Georgia colonists were among the most vociferous defenders of the continuation of slavery and the slave trade, amid patriots' attempts to undermine the British war effort by embargoing the British slave trade. Indeed, no southern region hoping to build an economy dependent on agriculture could imagine itself a success without slave labor. By the mid-1770s, Georgians had committed to slavery, and Savannah was the port through which many of their American and transatlantic slaves arrived.

But blacks did not simply accept white Georgians' decision to continue slavery after the American Revolution. Freedom-seeking blacks established maroon communities in rural areas around Savannah in the chaotic aftermath of the war. Although the communities were successful for a time, supporters of slavery ultimately crushed them as threats to the surrounding slave system, which was struggling to reassert itself.

That struggle was resolved with the successful emergence of the slave-based cotton economy of the nineteenth century. Savannah grew to be the third-largest antebellum southern exporter of cotton, behind the behemoth of New Orleans, Louisiana, and Mobile, Alabama. Although not the largest city in the South, Savannah was key to the success of the southeastern Cotton Kingdom. The city flourished because of its location amid fertile coastal rice plantations, cotton plantations to the west, and Atlantic access to markets for raw materials, slaves, and finished products. Rice and indigo were other important crops that carried over from the eighteenth-century economy, the former reaching its peak production on the eve of the Civil War. Although antebellum Savannah was not as populous as Baltimore, New Orleans, or Charleston, its slave-produced wealth is still evident in the gracious squares of the planned city.

In Savannah as throughout the South, labor became associated with black slaves. Whites competed with blacks for skilled and unskilled jobs. Employers with the ability to pay had little difficulty in—and sometimes preferred—owning or hiring slaves; as a result, white workers fought for, and often lost, the ability to dominate trades within Savannah.

Free blacks occupied a middle ground between white workers and enslaved blacks in

Savannah, forming a small, precarious, yet vibrant community. Though required by law to have white guardians and prevented from owning real estate, some free blacks nevertheless ran small businesses; owned property in collaboration with their white guardians, who held the deeds in their own names; and led some of the largest black church congregations in the South, composed of free and enslaved blacks. But these fragile freedoms were always subject to whites' interpretation and enforcement of laws that designated blacks as less than whites.

The history of Savannah and its hinterlands highlights the struggles for control and autonomy between owners and enslaved people in slave-labor-based communities throughout the South. Both slave owners and enslaved people adjusted to the conditions of the city in a variety of ways. The arrangement of living quarters demonstrates the variability of experiences necessary to the success of slavery in the city. Domestic slaves owned by wealthy families might live in proximity to their owners, in their attics or basements, or in separate urban slave quarters, as was true of the residents of the Owens-Thomas House. Other enslaved individuals, couples, and families lived "independently" in shacks they rented, perhaps seeing their owners only intermittently, for example, when it was time to hand over the wages they may have earned in skilled occupations around the city, if their employers did not pay their owners directly. Slave owners who hired out their slaves may not have had enough space on their city lots to house them, or may not even have lived in Savannah. These types of conditions have led some scholars to call such forms of slavery "nominal." But the autonomy that owners allowed enslaved people could be limited at any time; and all wages earned by such slaves were ultimately the property of their owners. Additionally, the city's white constables, as well as the slave owners themselves, formed a broad network of control over enslaved people, bolstered by increasingly detailed slave codes. Among the community of white laborers, free blacks, and slaves, the lines of slavery and freedom—and just as importantly, of race and status—might blur in the day-to-day rhythm of work and home, but whites easily redrew those lines to maintain control over the wealth that enslaved people produced.

The bold resistance to enslavement exemplified by Revolutionary-era maroon communities did not cease in the antebellum era. From running away to outright rebellion, enslaved people expressed their dissatisfaction with the system of slavery broadly as well as with specific abuses inflicted on them by individual owners. In contrast, elite slave owners, as exemplified by the Owens and Telfair families, viewed themselves as benevolent employers who were duty-bound to enslave blacks; in their eyes, abuses were rare, though not nonexistent. And on those occasions when they lost control of their enslaved property, Savannah slaveholders sent their workers to the Chatham County Jail to receive punishments ranging from incarceration to public whippings, thus reinforcing the city government's involvement in maintaining the system of slavery.

Indeed, Savannah's economic dependence on and whites' belief in the correctness of slavery never wavered in the antebellum years. By the time of the Civil War, Savannah's economic success and political position made its capture central to the Union army's plan to crush the slaveholding republic. Although the city's beautiful architecture was largely preserved, Sherman's troops destroyed slavery and reordered, at least temporarily, the relationships between blacks and whites. In the face of strong and sometimes violent white opposition, blacks briefly gained access to the vote and political office, and expanded on antebellum institutions such as churches and schools. For the next forty years, blacks sought to negotiate their new roles as members of the paid working class, hoping to carve a space in which to exercise their full rights as citizens. They made every effort to remember the years of enslavement while fighting against new forms of racial subordination, which were often associated with mob violence. But by 1900, the gains that blacks had made during Reconstruction had been replaced by legal segregation; whites limited blacks' access to the political realm, employment, and a host of other rights and privileges of citizenship. In response, Savannah's blacks became part of regional and national efforts to continue the march toward freedom and autonomy for African Americans, work that did not see fruition until the mid-1950s, when a series of Supreme Court decisions struck down segregation.

Savannah is a prime location for understanding both the centrality of slavery and race to the national and world economy, and the importance of the city to southern landscapes and the southern economy. Tourists from all over the world have been fascinated with coastal Georgia in general and Savannah in particular. They visit to see the state's oldest city, which has been hailed as a model for eighteenth- and nineteenth-century city planning.

Yet cities such as Savannah hold in their physical structures sometimes overlooked clues to their early history. We have been pleased to work with the Owens-Thomas House, a historic site that is part of Telfair Museums, to provide a broader context for the house's existence and to facilitate greater knowledge about all the people who at one time or another inhabited the house and contributed to its upkeep and preservation. The house was built by the famed British architect William Jay between 1816 and 1819 for Richard Richardson, a cotton merchant, banker, and slave trader, and his wife, Frances Lewis Bolton. The Richardsons lived there for only three years; upon Frances's death, Richard sold the house, which was then occupied by Mrs. Mary Maxwell, who operated an elegant boardinghouse there for six years. In 1830, George Welshman Owens bought the house, and it remained in the Owens family until 1951, when his granddaughter Margaret Thomas bequeathed it to the Telfair Academy of Arts and Sciences — today's Telfair Museums. The beauty of the early iron gates, tabby-constructed exterior walls, interior arched bridge and symmetrical stairway, courtyard garden, and carriage-house slave quarters enchants visitors, but also inspires deeper questions about the complex relationships among those who inhabited the dwellings, as well as about their connections to the enormous plantations owned by the Owens family.

Our work with the Owens-Thomas House builds upon some twenty-plus years of collaboration among museum professionals, academic historians, and historical archeologists, in which major U.S. landmarks and historic sites have begun to tell more fully the history of nonwhites and nonelites. For much of the twentieth century, most of these experts believed that nonwhites and nonelites did not have a history worth recovering. Sites such as the Owens-Thomas House were concerned only with the fine objects the wealthy had left behind, and visitors—largely white—fantasized about owning the mansion, the comfortable bedrooms, and the luxurious dining rooms; they never imagined themselves as the enslaved and free laborers who made such living possible. Similarly, historians and others presented slavery as a positive experience for the enslaved. Indeed, house tours often used the word "servant" rather than "slave," if slavery and servitude were referred to at all. Through such museum presentations, the brutality of slavery was minimized and the place of blacks as present-day servants to whites was reinforced as the best role to which blacks should aspire.[2]

These ideas about the history of slavery began to shift in the 1950s, and we live today among new, more complicated ideas about the meaning of slavery for our institutions and for our history. More and more teachers are able to share with their students, from grade school through college and beyond, an understanding of slavery that includes the perspectives of both the slave owner and the enslaved. More and more people understand that slavery was a system of forced labor regimented through the use of brutality against African Americans. Yet we understand as well that African American labor, culture, and experience has contributed so much to the world around us, that African Americans were foundational to U.S. economic and political success.

This "new" history, inspired by the scholarship and activism of African Americans throughout the nineteenth and twentieth centuries, began to take hold in the halls of academe in the 1960s and then to spread into the museum world. In 1987, the Smithsonian Institution's landmark exhibition *Field to Factory: Afro-American Migration, 1915–1940* recast the role of museums in interpreting African American history. In 1991, the Museum of the Confederacy, in Richmond, Virginia, mounted what is believed to be the first major exhibition on slavery, *Before Freedom Came: African American Life in the Antebellum South*; and between 2005 and 2007, the New-York Historical Society mounted the two-part exhibition *Slavery in New York* and *New York Divided: Slavery and the Civil War*. Even more sweeping were the National Park Service's efforts throughout the 1990s and continuing today to reinterpret historic sites by moving away from a view of American history emphasizing the success of largely white actors in a land of the free and toward a more complex view of how freedom and wealth were also rooted in the displacement of Native Americans, built on the backs of enslaved people, and extracted from the undercompensated labor of European and non-European working-class immigrants to North America. The influence of these national institutions has inspired public and private historic sites at the state and local levels to reassess their assumed audiences and to collaborate with scholars in an effort to ensure their interpretations and brochures take a more encompassing view of the histories they tell.[3]

Thus, reinterpreting historic sites to include slavery and a broader range of experiences is part of a broad and important movement of historical recovery in the United States—one that has momentum and will continue. The path has not been without controversy. For example, the reenactment of a slave sale at Colonial Williamsburg in the 1990s inspired fear that such an event would not be respectful. But those who witnessed the performance were surprised and moved at the ability of the museum to thoughtfully depict the complex spectacle that was a slave auction. In addition, and just as importantly, Colonial Williamsburg continues to uncover the history of slavery at that site in Virginia and in the surrounding area, using archaeology, historical records, and material culture to contribute to the historical interpretation used by museums there and to our knowledge of the history of slavery.[4]

The reinterpretation of such sites does not erase prior histories, but builds on them to deepen our knowledge of the past that was created by multiple groups in this country, sometimes at odds with one another, sometimes working together, even if under duress, but all part of the fabric of our past and foundational to an understanding of our present. Thus, something that for most of the twentieth century was rejected by museums has been slowly but surely embraced. The opening of the National Museum of African American History and Culture on the Mall in Washington in 2015, long discussed and long awaited, will be a fitting summation of many of these efforts even as it continues to spur those of us at the local level to hone our understanding of our histories—all our histories.

Slavery and Freedom in Savannah is the story of a house, a neighborhood, a city, and a community. The nine chapters, twenty-five sidebars, and numerous illustrations provide readers a better understanding of the role of slavery, emancipation, race, and class in this southern urban community and its hinterlands. But the implications and legacies of Savannah's history, as well as the process of historical recovery this volume represents, should reach far beyond the city's geographic boundaries.

SLAVERY *and* FREEDOM *in* Savannah

The Transatlantic Slave Trade Comes to Georgia

James A. McMillin

Georgia is often touted as the only British North American colony to outlaw slavery. True, the colony's founders, the Georgia Trustees, rejected slavery soon after the colony came into being in the early 1730s, but their ban only delayed the expansion of slavery, for a little more than a decade. After the trustees removed restrictions on slavery, the slave population grew rapidly, increasing from four hundred in 1751 to some sixteen thousand on the eve of the Revolutionary War. The overwhelming majority of these enslaved laborers were Africans. Convinced that slavery was critical to the colony's economic development, Georgia planters and merchants imported thousands of black captives, both directly from Africa and indirectly through South Carolina and the West Indies. Most of the forced migrants entered Georgia through the colony's principal commercial port, Savannah. By the Revolutionary War, slavery was a central element of Georgia's economy.[1]

In 1732, King George II of England granted a distinguished board of trustees, led by the British general and member of Parliament James Edward Oglethorpe, a twenty-one-year charter for the colony of Georgia. The British government and the trustees intended for the new province, located between the Savannah and Altamaha Rivers and stretching west to the Pacific Ocean, to provide a buffer between the Spanish in Florida and British South Carolina. By settling the borderland with white farmer-soldiers instead of planters and slaves, they hoped to shield South Carolina's rich plantation economy from Spanish invaders and Native Americans.[2] They had other motives as well; the sponsors envisioned the colony as a haven for England's "worthy poor" and European Protestant refugees.[3] The immigrants would "gain a comfortable subsistence" by producing silk and wine, which were in great demand in England, and would buy imported British manufactured goods, thus increasing "the trade, navigation, and wealth of these our realms."[4] Convinced that only white Protestant yeoman farmers could accomplish these goals, the

1

James Edward Oglethorpe and the Georgia Plan

Richard West Habersham, James Edward Oglethorpe at Belgrade in 1718, 1885. Courtesy of the Georgia Historical Society, A-1361-327.

In late 1732, the ship *Anne*, carrying 114 persons from the London area, dropped down the Thames and was soon rolling in the swells of the open sea. Many of the voyagers were failed, hard-bitten, sometimes hard-drinking small merchants, artisans, laborers, along with their wives and children. The well-to-do James Edward Oglethorpe, former member of Parliament, military officer, compassionate reformer, and visionary, led the expedition. He was also hotheaded and violent. On one occasion he wounded two political opponents with a sword, and on another he killed a man in a bawdy house.

Together with other prominent Englishmen, Oglethorpe had convinced King George II to grant them a charter to establish a colony in Georgia to be governed by a board of trustees that included him. Such a colony would offer the "worthy poor" a second chance to pursue commercial opportunities for the benefit of the British Crown; and it would establish a military buffer to protect England's southern colonies in North America from the Spanish in Florida. In sum, the colonists from one of the world's largest metropolitan centers were expected to become farmers and citizen-soldiers on a hostile and desolate frontier, a rather utopian scheme.

After a fifty-eight-day voyage, the colonists struggled up forty-foot Yamacraw Bluff on the Savannah River in early 1733. The river's name became that of the first settlement in Georgia, the last of the original thirteen colonies and the only British colony that almost from its founding banned black slavery. Oglethorpe believed that slaves would jeopardize the work ethic of white yeoman farmers, threaten the colony with the possibility of insurrections, and discourage white immigration.

As they adjusted to their new surroundings, the colonists tried to reconcile the "paradise" promised to the reality found. In the spring of the first year, Oglethorpe returned from a brief visit to Charles Town (Charleston), where he had sought aid for the colony, to find the settlers discontented, disobedient, and ill. He believed their condition stemmed from heavy rum drinking and the employment of slave artisans from South Carolina, whose presence encouraged shiftlessness among the settlers. He immediately sent the slaves back and stove in the barrels of rum.

Oglethorpe subsequently prevailed on the trustees in England to ban slavery in Georgia, and Parliament enacted similar legislation in 1735. From the outset, the cornerstone of the trustees' and Oglethorpe's plan for Georgia was the prohibition of slavery—for military, moral, and social reasons. They knew that slave "rebellions" had occurred in other British colonies, and they did not want "insurrections" to lead to the "ruin and loss" of Georgia. Furthermore, they were convinced that slave labor would produce "idleness" and "luxury" among the white settlers, undermining their effectiveness as soldiers, farmers, and merchants. In the opinion of Oglethorpe and the trustees, banning slavery would encourage more whites to relocate to Georgia, since they would not face competition from slave labor.

Oglethorpe condemned black enslavement as "an abominable and destructive custom," and on at least one occasion he quickly expelled Carolinians who brought slaves onto the Georgia side of the Savannah River to work a plantation. But Oglethorpe himself hired or borrowed hundreds of black slaves from Charles Town who worked under white guards to fell trees, build a ring of fortifications around the town, and lay out Savannah's streets in a unique, grid-like pattern of public squares. Additionally, Oglethorpe was a stockholder and, briefly, director of England's slave-trading Royal African Company. His antislavery beliefs were limited, at best, to this colony, which he hoped would be different from the others. But even he found it impossible to do without slavery in building Georgia.

On this point, Georgia's proslavery faction agreed, repeatedly complaining in letters and petitions to the trustees and the British government that without slave labor the colony would never enjoy the prosperity of the South Carolinians. After Oglethorpe departed for England for the last time, in 1743, this faction became larger and more strident. By the end of the decade, the trustees recognized that their policy of excluding black slaves from Georgia faced defeat. Finally, on January 1, 1751, the British government legalized slavery in Georgia.

The importation of slaves surged. Within a few years, the population of Savannah and the Georgia Lowcountry had grown to four thousand whites and two thousand African American slaves. In 1755, years after Oglethorpe had returned to England, the Georgia Assembly passed a slave code designed to "keep slaves in due Subjection and Obedience." A slaveholding, rice-producing planter elite was emerging. The colony no longer resembled the one James Edward Oglethorpe had envisioned. Rather, it had become more like its neighbor South Carolina.

In 1785, three years before his death, Oglethorpe met with John Adams in England. Though history is silent on their private conversations, we know that they shared the view that slavery was a heinous institution.

WALTER J. FRASER JR.

3

trustees banned Catholicism, slavery, and rum, and created a land system that limited individual property ownership.[5]

The trustees accomplished some of their goals. Oglethorpe maintained peaceful relations with the Creeks and Cherokees, and in 1742 he led British soldiers in a successful defense of the colony against a Spanish invasion. He founded and laid out Savannah, one of America's most beautiful and well-designed cities. During the first ten years of colonization, the trustees sent eighteen hundred tradesmen and artisans from England and Scotland, and religious refugees from Switzerland and Germany, to Georgia. Another twelve hundred immigrants came to the colony at their own expense during the decade. But just about everything else went wrong. The trustees ran short of money and from time to time could not provide settlers with the food and supplies they had been promised. Oglethorpe was a poor administrator and, to some, overbearing. Settlers resented not having a voice in local government, as well as the land-ownership policies and the bans on rum and slaves. To make matters worse, the colonists produced only small amounts of silk and wine, and little else. Although the Lutheran Salzburgers who settled at New Ebenezer, inland on the Savannah River, prospered on a limited scale, many early immigrants either died or moved on. By 1751, of the three thousand whites who had migrated to the colony, only nineteen hundred remained.[6]

More than anything else, the trustees' land and slave policies stymied economic growth and immigration. Each colonist sponsored by the trustees received fifty acres; those who paid their own way could acquire more, but individual ownership was limited to five hundred acres. The allotments could not be sold, and only male heirs could inherit land. Since most of the land around Savannah was unsuitable for small subsistence farms—much less for raising silk worms or grapes—many settlers were assigned land that they could neither farm nor sell. A shortage of labor and capital made matters worse. To clear land, make necessary improvements, and construct buildings, landowners needed capital and hardworking, affordable laborers. This was especially true for those who wanted to cultivate rice. Lacking capital, most settlers could not afford to pay free workers, who were in short supply. Once the land restrictions were lifted in the late 1730s and large quantities of inexpensive land became available, wage laborers became even scarcer. Like other North American colonists, Georgians preferred to work their own land rather than someone else's.[7]

Soon after they arrived in Georgia, settlers began complaining about the trustees'

Africans and Indians in Colonial Georgia

By 1733, the year of Georgia's settlement by the British, slavery had already profoundly shaped the region between Charleston and St. Augustine. Beginning in the sixteenth century, Spanish and French colonialism exposed Native populations to devastating new diseases, and the British settlers who established the Carolina colony in 1670 demonstrated an insatiable demand for slave labor. In intertribal wars, Indians traditionally captured enemies, but South Carolina planters and traders encouraged Native societies to take unprecedented numbers of them and amplified the violence of warfare by offering firearms in return for Indian slaves. As a result, the Savannah River Valley became home to a succession of slave-raiding Indian societies, including the Westos, Savannahs, and Yamasees. Between 1670 and 1715, southern colonists acquired at least twenty-five thousand and perhaps as many as fifty thousand Indian slaves: some remained in South Carolina, toiling alongside African slaves, but most were exported to British colonies in New England or the Caribbean. Disease and slave raiding exacted a terrible toll on Indian populations across the Southeast, threatening to destroy even those allied with South Carolina.

Responding to the threats that the Indian slave trade posed, a coalition of Indian nations led by the Yamasees declared war on South Carolina in 1715. The Yamasee War transformed the colonial South and later became a critical factor in the decision to establish the Georgia colony. Native warriors killed about 7 percent of South Carolina's white population, drove the remaining settlers and their African and Indian slaves to seek refuge in fortified Charles Town, and terrified colonial officials into reconsidering the wisdom of enslaving Indians in a region where Native power was so considerable. After the final peace was brokered in 1718, Native people restructured their societies. Survivors of formerly independent chiefdoms banded together, creating new confederacies, which were multiethnic and sometimes multilingual. Dynamic and populous, nations like the Creeks and Cherokees emerged as power players in the colonial South, negotiating more favorable alliances with Britain, France, and Spain. South Carolinians, fearful of another Native revolt, turned almost exclusively to African slavery. Meanwhile, Spanish Florida attempted to thwart the growth of Carolina's plantation economy by offering freedom to slaves who escaped from British colonies. Especially receptive were newly arrived Kongolese slaves, many of whom had practiced Catholicism in Africa.

Seeking to stabilize this violent borderland region, Britain planned Georgia as a buffer between South Carolina and Florida and a

Unknown artist, Oglethorpe with Creek Indians. *Courtesy of Hargrett Rare Book and Manuscript Library, University of Georgia Libraries.*

peaceful mediator with Indian nations. Upon his arrival in February 1733, Georgia's founder, General James Oglethorpe, cultivated an alliance with a local group of Creek and Yamasee Indians called the Yamacraws. Their chief, Tomochichi, permitted the Georgia colonists to settle Savannah. Although he maintained local authority, Tomochichi was a liminal figure among the Creeks; the most important early mediator between Georgia and the Creeks was Coosaponakeesa, or Mary Musgrove. Born around 1700 to a Creek woman from a powerful family and a British trader, she was educated in South Carolina. Coosaponakeesa, her kinsmen Chigelli and Malatchi, and the Creek politicians who succeeded them negotiated land treaties, military alliances, and trading terms with Georgia, and the two polities maintained fairly peaceful relations until the onset of the American Revolution.

Slavery played a major role in diplomacy between Georgia and its Indian neighbors.

Georgia's attempt to ban African slavery encouraged some colonists to resort to Indian slavery, which persisted in the colony even after the African ban was reversed in 1751. In the interim, Creeks, in their capacity as military allies, captured runaway South Carolina slaves, including some of the participants of the Stono Rebellion of 1739. Following the legalization of African slavery in Georgia, the European and African population of Georgia boomed, soon surpassing the Creek population of roughly twenty thousand. On Georgia plantations, the descendants of African and Indian slaves intermarried and had children, giving rise to a significant numbers of "mustees"—an Anglo corruption of the Spanish term *mestizo*, which Georgians applied specifically to those of Afro-Indian descent.

Creeks initially rejected Georgia's obsession with race. The society that they had fashioned from the remnants of ancient chiefdoms was already diverse and multiethnic, and an individual's place within it was based mostly on kinship ties. Most African Americans entered Creek country kinless, as runaways, captives, or slaves of resident traders. Those who managed to marry Creeks or become adoptees of clans shed their status as slaves and moved into the category of people who belonged. One such slave was a woman named Suckey, taken from Georgia during the Revolutionary era by a Creek warrior. Suckey eventually married David Randon, a Creek who was also likely her captor; she and the couple's five children all became Creek citizens. By the late eighteenth century, increasing numbers of African-descended people had entered the Creek Nation, but fewer and fewer achieved Suckey's status. As racial ideology gained currency among Indians and the United States grew increasingly threatening and powerful, Creek society became less inclusive. By 1800, some Creeks began to hold black slaves in transgenerational bondage and established their own plantations. The memory of that older, kin-based society endured, however; the Creeks who dissented most sharply from the new racial order moved into Florida, where they became known as Seminoles.

CHRISTINA SNYDER

policies, especially the slavery ban. A group of Savannah settlers who became known as the Malcontents bombarded the trustees with letters, petitions, and pamphlets demanding slaves.[8] Aware that slave-produced rice and indigo were bringing great wealth to planters just across the Savannah River in South Carolina, the Malcontents persistently argued that the semitropical climate and the scarcity of affordable labor made black slaves "essentially necessary" to the economic success of the colony.[9] Oglethorpe and his fellow trustees vigorously opposed the Malcontents in the late 1730s and early 1740s, but the trustees themselves were not antislavery activists. Indeed, Oglethorpe had participated in the British slave-trading Royal African Company. And even during the time of the ban, slaves came to the colony. The trustees themselves had brought in slaves to assist with the building of Savannah. Other slaves were imported illegally, often from South Carolina.[10] Still, Oglethorpe and his fellow trustees insisted that legalizing slavery would undermine their carefully designed, idealistic plan for Georgia and that eventually the colony would become merely an extension of South Carolina. It would also, as Oglethorpe accurately predicted, "occasion the misery of thousands in Africa . . . and bring into perpetual Slavery the poor people who now live there free."[11]

The proslavery settlers made little headway in legalizing slavery until the English victory over the Spanish in 1742, which effectively ended the Spanish threat to Georgia and South Carolina and seriously weakened the trustees' most practical argument for excluding slavery. A year later Oglethorpe returned to England for good, and he soon lost

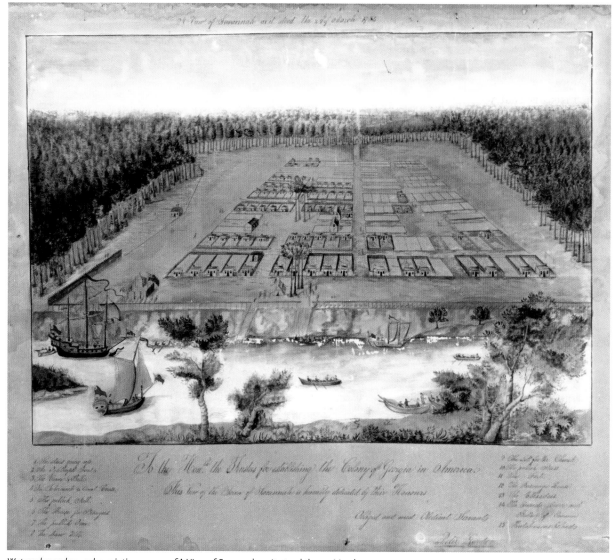

Watercolor and gouache painting, a copy of A View of Savannah as it stood the 29 March 1734.
The original engraving is commonly attributed to Peter Gordon but was actually made by
P. Fourdrinier based on a sketch by London draftsman George Jones.

interest in Georgia. Without Oglethorpe present to oversee the colony, more slaves were introduced into the colony, and by the mid-1740s it was clear that the trustees would not be able to uphold the slavery ban.[12]

In 1747 Savannah's foremost merchant, James Habersham, prepared a new, detailed economic development plan for the colony, which made a strong case for legalizing slave labor, insisting that without it Georgia could not compete with South Carolina. The plan was created at the request of the Reverend Johann Martin Bolzius, the leader of the Salzburger community at New Ebenezer; Bolzius had previously supported Oglethorpe's suppression of slavery.[13] The English revivalist George Whitefield, Habersham's former boss and friend, also supported repealing the ban. In a 1748 letter to the trustees, Whitefield, who had founded the Bethesda Orphanage near Savannah, warned, "Georgia never can or will be a flourishing province without negroes are allowed."[14] Having invested in a South Carolina plantation, Whitefield was well aware of the profits that slave labor produced. Bolzius too pleaded with the trustees on behalf of slavery in Georgia: "If their Honours are please to comply with the supplications and desires of the other Colonists for introducing Negroes . . . , we and our friends in Germany will say not a word against it."[15]

The incessant demands for slaves, the removal of the Spanish threat, Oglethorpe's departure, financial problems, and slow economic development finally wore the trustees down, and in the early 1750s they gave up on their idealistic plan, repealed the bans on slavery and the importation of slaves, and returned Georgia to the king.[16] By the time the slave-trade ban ended in 1751, Georgians already held four hundred slaves.[17]

When the legal trade began, Georgians or agents on their behalf imported two groups of Africans from Charles Town, South Carolina, through the practice of transshipment, the transferring of goods in transit from one vessel to another.[18]

Charles Town merchants, seeing opportunity in Georgia, began to sell Africans in Savannah and Sunbury.[19] Some slaves were transported overland to Georgia, but most arrived via small ships or coasters. The consignments were usually small, but a group of sixty Africans who had recently arrived in Charles Town from the Gold Coast (modern Ghana) was shipped to Savannah in 1765.[20] During the twenty-five years of the colonial legal trade, known as the royal period, Charles Town merchants reexported an estimated 4,129 Africans to Georgia, most of them arriving after 1764. The largest number of reexportations occurred in 1773 and 1774, when 2,396 slaves were transshipped to Georgia.

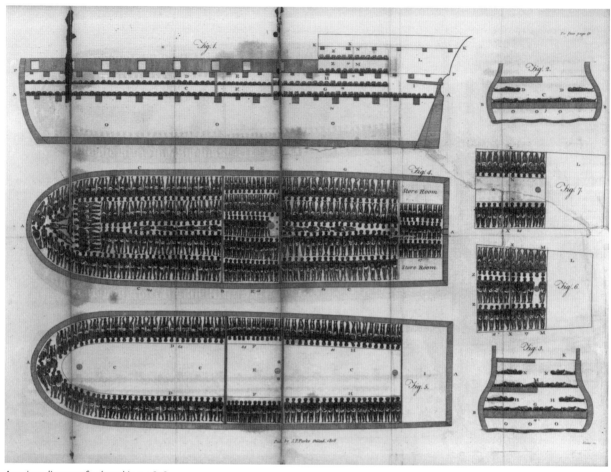

American diagram of a slave ship, c. 1808.
Courtesy of The Granger Collection, NYC—
All Rights Reserved.

South Carolina merchants and factors sent more Africans to Georgia than to any other North American colony. Between 1750 and 1776, 6 percent of the captives delivered to Charles Town were reexported to Georgia.[21]

Georgia's first known legal shipment of slaves from outside the North American mainland occurred in 1755, when the brig *Cumberland* arrived from Jamaica with eight slaves.[22] The slaves probably had recently been disembarked by one of several slavers that transported African captives to Jamaica in early 1755.[23] Over the next fourteen years, more than 125 vessels disembarked slaves in Georgia from the West Indies; however, the trade was sporadic. No shipments arrived from the West Indies in 1758 and 1759, and only one in 1761. Since most of the vessels that transshipped slaves between the West Indies and Georgia were small and mainly carried freight, the ships usually disembarked fewer than ten slaves. But there were four large transshipments: sixty slaves arrived from St. Kitts in 1763; seventy from Montserrat and fifty from Jamaica in 1765; and seventy-three from St. Kitts in 1767.[24]

The conditions of enslaved and free blacks in colonial Georgia were described by Olaudah Equiano, one of the most well-known black men of the eighteenth century. In the narrative that secured his fame (published in 1789), Equiano describes several visits he made to Savannah, both while enslaved and as a free man. Equiano most likely served as an enslaved sailor on the *Prudence* when it transported seventy slaves from Montserrat to Savannah in 1765. A few days after he arrived, he heard George Whitefield deliver a sermon to a large crowd in the city. Equiano was "very much struck and impressed" with Whitefield's "fervor and earnestness."[25] It was also during this visit to Savannah that Equiano was nearly beaten to death by "Dr. Perkins" and his white servant for interacting with slaves in Perkins's yard. During another visit to the city a few months after, a silversmith reprimanded Equiano. Later that year Equiano was able to purchase his freedom in the West Indies, but when he returned to Savannah he encountered further trouble following an altercation with a slave owned by a Savannah merchant named Read. Unhappy with the exchange, Read demanded that Equiano be flogged "without judge or jury."[26] His troubles did not end with that incident. Equiano and his enslaved friend Mosa were arrested by night watchmen for burning a candle in Mosa's house after nine. Other whites attempted to kidnap Equiano, thinking they could sell him back into slavery. Not surprisingly, when Equiano "took final leave of Georgia" in 1767, he wrote, "The treatment

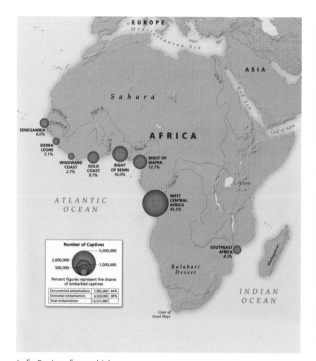

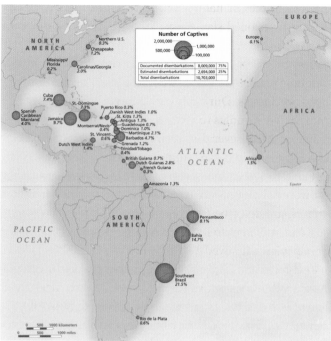

I had received in it disgusted me very much against the place; and when I left it . . . I determined to never more revisit it."[27]

Most of the vessels that transshipped slaves from the West Indies to Georgia were registered in the West Indies, including the *Prudence*, which was owned by Equiano's former master, Robert King, but several Savannah merchants, including Habersham, Basil Cowper, William and Edward Telfair, and Joseph Clay, operated ships that participated in the slave trade.[28] From 1755 through 1764, at least 1,081 slaves were transshipped from the West Indies to Georgia, with more than half arriving from Jamaica and St. Kitts. Between 1766 and 1775, another 1,791 arrived in Savannah and Sunbury; of these, 261 were transshipped from St. Kitts, 136 from Jamaica, and 230 from Grenada. The West Indies was listed as the origin of another 494, and "Unknown" as that of 360 forced immigrants.[29] No doubt some seasoned slaves—enslaved laborers who had been born in the West Indies or had spent more than six months there—were sent to Georgia to be sold. But seasoned slaves were difficult to sell because Georgia planters believed most were either infirm or recalcitrant; it is assumed here that less than 1 percent of the slaves transshipped from the West Indies to Georgia were seasoned slaves.[30] The indirect trade with the West Indies reached its zenith in 1767, when nearly six hundred people arrived in forty-two vessels. During the royal period, an estimated 2,872 slaves were transshipped from the West Indies to Georgia.[31]

Before 1766, several circumstances discouraged the direct shipment of slaves from Africa to Georgia. As mentioned previously, until 1750 the colony was sparsely populated, and although settlers had been clamoring for slaves, few could afford to purchase them; nor were settlers producing much in the way of staples that could be exported. In 1751, Habersham described the colony's dismal output: "I suppose we shall hardly make Rice this Year sufficient to Load a Ship of 500 barrels to London, and if a Small Portion of our Hands were employed in the Cultivation of Inicoe [indigo], it wou'd go but a little way in loading a Ship."[32] Habersham and his partner, Francis Harris, owned and operated a merchant house in Savannah, but they, like the other merchants and factors in town, were dependent on Charles Town merchants for importing the manufactured and dry goods they sold and for exporting Georgia's products.

In 1751, Savannah lacked just about everything needed for the slave trade. It had only one municipal dock, few warehouses, and no lazaretto, or pesthouse (a place for quarantining newly arrived immigrants of all races to protect the colony from infectious diseases). The Savannah River (the colonial city of Savannah was located seventeen miles from the coast) was too shallow for large oceangoing vessels. When Equiano visited Savannah in 1766, the ship he was on had problems navigating the river, forcing him to use "boats" to obtain cargo. It was dangerous work: Equiano was "frequently beset by alligators," who tried to get into his boat.[33] Moreover, Savannah merchants lacked the capital to finance slave sales. These circumstances were exacerbated by the onset of the French and Indian War in 1756. Fighting between Great Britain and France increased the cost of transportation between Georgia and the other North American colonies, the West Indies, and Europe, and the higher costs substantially reduced or eliminated the profitability of rice and indigo.[34]

When the war ended in 1763 there were more than thirty-six hundred slaves in Georgia.[35] Although African and West Indian slaves were being transshipped to Georgia and

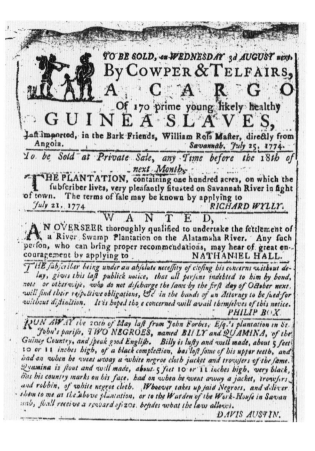

sold, nearly all slaves in the colony either had been bought in Charles Town and then sent to Georgia or had accompanied South Carolina owners immigrating to the colony. Between 1750 and 1763, most slaves ended up on Lowcountry plantations, working to produce rice in freshwater inland swamps along the Midway, Newport, and Savannah Rivers. In 1763, additional prime rice-growing land became available between the Altamaha and St. Mary's Rivers, and more slaves were sent there to cultivate the staple. Subsequently, rice production rose rapidly, increasing from 7,702 barrels in 1763 to 23,540 in 1773. Other exports, including indigo, corn, deer and beaver skins, naval stores, and

Table 1. Estimated African slave imports into Georgia from South Carolina, the West Indies, and Africa, 1751–1776

Years	South Carolina	West Indies	Africa	Total
1751–55	68	8	0	76
1756–60	798	150	0	948
1761–65	372	923	0	1,295
1766–70	144	1,495	2,895	4,534
1771–75	2,747	296	2,302	5,345
1776–80	0	0	266	266
Total	4,129	2,872	5,463	12,464

Sources: *Georgia Gazette*, Clay & Co. Papers, and Telfair Family Papers, Georgia Historical Society, Savannah, Georgia; Elizabeth Donnan, ed., *Documents Illustrative of the History of the Slave Trade to America*, 4 vols. (Washington, D.C.: Carnegie Institution of Washington, 1930–35), 4:616–25; W. Robert Higgins, "The South Carolina Negro Duty Law" (master's thesis, University of South Carolina, 1967), 149–265; Darold D. Wax, "'New Negroes Are Always in Demand': The Slave Trade in Eighteenth-Century Georgia," *Georgia Historical Quarterly* 58, no. 2 (Summer 1984): 193–220; Betty Wood, *Slavery in Colonial Georgia, 1730–1775* (Athens: University of Georgia Press, 1984), 88–109; Julia Floyd Smith, *Slavery and Rice Culture in Low Country Georgia, 1750–1860* (Knoxville: University of Tennessee Press, 1985), 93–112; Gregory E. O'Malley, "Beyond the Middle Passage: Slave Migration from the Caribbean to North America, 1619–1807," *William and Mary Quarterly* 66, no. 1 (January 2009): 125–72; Voyages: The Trans-Atlantic Slave Trade Database, http://www.slavevoyages.org.

timber, were also on the rise, and by the middle of the decade Georgia's economy had improved to the point that it could absorb entire cargoes of African captives.[36]

The first slave ship to come directly from Africa, the sloop *Mary Brow*, arrived on April 9, 1766, with 78 captives embarked at Saint-Louis, Senegambia. That year another six ships, with 487 slaves, reached Savannah. Four of the vessels arrived directly from Africa; two stopped in the West Indies first, where some of the slaves were disembarked. Over the next five years (1767 through 1771), twenty-one slavers delivered 2,824 enslaved laborers to Savannah.[37] In 1772 and 1773, difficulties with Great Britain curtailed the slave trade, and only two ships arrived, with 282 captives. But unlike several other colonies in 1774, Georgia quickly resumed its slave trade. Indeed, in that year more captives (1,475) arrived directly from Africa than in any other year of the royal period.[38]

In the fall of 1774, the First Continental Congress (to which Georgia did not send a representative) agreed to stop importing British goods, including slaves, beginning on December 1, 1774. The boycott met with limited success in Georgia. Many Georgians opposed the ban, especially merchants, who argued that the constraints adopted by the Continental Congress did not apply to Georgia because the colony wasn't represented in that body. In a letter dated April 7, 1775, the Savannah merchant Joseph Clay assured a West Indies firm that the city was still open for business: "As to your ports they are all open and there is not the least reason to expect they will be otherways & and of Coarse Negros may be Brought in."[39] Georgia's ports, alone among those in the colonies, remained open to the slave trade on a limited basis in 1775 and 1776. When the British snow *Prince Tom* arrived in Savannah in July 1775 with 180 Africans, officials allowed the vessel's captain, Benjamin Mason, to disembark only the 40 slaves intended for the Savannah River plantation of Benjamin Stead. "Afraid it may appear improper abroad," officials ordered the snow to depart with the remaining 140 slaves. When a ship arrived with 200 captives from Senegambia later that year, the crew was not allowed to unload them.[40] But in 1775 the snow *Amelia* disembarked 197 slaves in Georgia, and in 1776 the *Nelly* delivered its cargo of 266 captives to the colony. The arrival of the *Nelly* marked the end of the colonial slave trade to Georgia.[41]

From 1766 through 1776, thirty-six slavers arrived directly from Africa with 5,180 captives. Another 469 slaves arrived on six ships from Africa that had stopped first in the West Indies or another North American colony. Overall, an estimated 5,649 slaves were transported by these vessels from Africa to Georgia. Combining these 5,649 slaves with the 4,129 Africans transshipped from South Carolina, and the 2,872 transshipped from the West Indies brings a total of 12,650 Africans. This number is less than the 13,600 captives imported into Virginia, or the 28,850 into South Carolina, during the same period. But in the 1770s more Africans arrived in Georgia than Virginia. Also, because newly arrived Africans made up such a large percentage of the 16,000 slaves in Georgia in 1776, they would have been far more evident in the Georgia Lowcountry than in the Chesapeake.[42]

During the royal period, slave ships arriving directly from Africa carried an average of 144 captives. On May 23, 1770, the *Sally* delivered the largest cargo—340 Africans who had embarked in Sierra Leone. The vast majority of the vessels were small, 150 tons or less; all the ships were registered in Great Britain, and nearly all the voyages began in England: eighteen from London, eleven from Liverpool, two from Lancaster, and two from Bristol.[43]

Although planters preferred "prime Men & Women . . . not exceeding twenty-five years of age," extant records of Savannah cargoes suggest that they did not always receive what they wanted.[44] In 1774 the *Philip and Daniel* arrived with 172 African captives; 66 percent of them were males and 34 percent females. Of these, 51 percent were adults and 49 percent were children. According to Cowper and Telfair, who handled the sales, there were too many "Old Men & Women" and "Small Boys & Girls" in the cargoes.[45] Because detailed records of Georgia slave voyages are limited, determining the sex ratio of each cargo that arrived in the colony is not possible. But based on the historian Betty Wood's analysis of colonial Georgia plantation inventories and lists—she found that "men heavily outnumbered women"—it is safe to assume that far more males than females were transported to Georgia.[46]

The time of year that slave ships arrived influenced the prices received for their cargoes. Slaves sold best from March through July, when the labor demands of rice cultivation were the greatest. After that, sales slowed and prices dropped, especially during the winter months. Planters were reluctant to purchase Africans who had not had time to adjust to the change in climate from tropical Africa to subtropical coastal Georgia.[47] Disappointed by slave sales from the sloop *Daniel* in the fall of 1774, the merchants Cowper and Telfair advised an English firm "to send no vessels to the continent after [the] middle [of] September as the weather considerably affects the Slaves."[48] Accordingly, thereafter 31 percent arrived during the spring, 35 percent in summer, 27 percent in the fall, and 8 percent in the winter.[49]

Planters were just as exacting when it came to the origin of Africans. They exhibited preferences for and prejudices against the African regional origins of their slaves.[50] Above all else, they favored captives from the coastal regions of Senegambia (or Gambia) and the Gold Coast. According to the Savannah merchant Joseph Clay, others were acceptable, including those "from the Windward Coast say from Senegall to the Gold Coast inclusive," but Africans from the Bight of Benin, Bight of Biafra, and Angola were to be avoided.[51] The Charles Town merchant and planter Henry Laurens, who sold slaves to

Georgia planters and owned rice plantations in the colony himself, made his customers'—and his own—convictions quite clear in a letter of 1756: "The slaves from River Gambia [Senegambia] are preferr'd to all others save the Gold Coast," while "there must not be a Callabar among them."[52] (Calabar is the name of a town and a river in southeastern Nigeria.) In another letter he advised that "Gold Coast are best[;] next To Them The Windward Coast are prefer'd to Angolas."[53] Clay's and Laurens's preferences were based on characteristics supposedly embodied by regional types. South Carolina and Georgia rice planters preferred servile, tall, healthy, male, dark-skinned, young, and blemish-free Africans familiar with rice cultivation. They considered these prime slaves. The coastal regions of Senegambia and the Gold Coast were the areas of West Africa most closely associated with these characteristics. When Senegambia and Gold Coast slaves were not available, or too expensive, planters would buy captives from Sierra Leone, the Windward Coast (modern Liberia and Côte d'Ivoire), and Angola. Those from the Bight of Benin and Bight of Biafra (the coastal regions of modern Togo, Benin, Nigeria, Cameroon, Equatorial Guinea, and Gabon) were to be avoided. Viewed as recalcitrant, small, slender, weak, often yellowish in color, and possessing an alarming penchant for suicide, Whydahs, Ibos, Bite, Bonny, and Calabars brought the lowest prices.[54]

The origins of South Carolina and Georgia slave shipments reflect the biases of merchants and planters. According to the historian Philip D. Morgan, during the 1760s and 1770s South Carolina traders and planters imported slaves mainly from five regions: Senegambia, Sierra Leone, the Windward Coast, the Gold Coast, and west-central Africa. The two regions at the top of Laurens's hierarchy, Senegambia and the Gold Coast, accounted for one-third of the imports. In Georgia, the origins of slaves shipped either direct from Africa or with one intervening stop were more in line with Clay's hierarchy. From 1766 through 1776, 33 percent were listed as coming from Senegambia, 26 percent from Sierra Leone, 17 percent from Africa, 10 percent from the Windward Coast, 9 percent from west-central Africa, 5 percent from the Gold Coast, and 0 percent from the Bight of Benin, the Bight of Biafra, or southeastern Africa. Nearly three-fourths of the captives came from Senegambia, Sierra Leone, the Windward Coast, and the Gold Coast. Only three cargoes, totaling 510 captives, or 9 percent, originated to the east and south of the Gold Coast. Despite the demand for slaves from the Gold Coast, only one large shipment (257 captives) arrived from that region. Similarly, just 6 percent came from the Windward Coast, which some merchants and planters referred to as the "rice coast." The supply and cost of Gold Coast and Windward Coast captives on the coast of Africa, and competition for these slaves in other American markets, determined their availability in Georgia.[55]

Identifying the origins of the African slaves that were transshipped from the West Indies is difficult at best. Most extant custom records list only the West Indies port from which the slaves were shipped. Newspaper advertisements for slave sales are also vague as far as specific African origins; most identify the captives simply as "New Negroes" recently arrived from the West Indies. Accordingly, the regional origins of only about 10 percent of the nearly 3,000 Africans who were transshipped to Georgia from the West Indies are known. Of these, 100 African captives were listed as from Senegambia, 20 from Sierra Leone, 122 from the Windward Coast, and 60 from the Gold Coast. When the documented origins of the West Indies transshipments to Georgia and the two major sources of slaves, the slave trade to Charles Town and Savannah, are combined, a pattern of regional African origins emerges. In the royal period, 60 percent are listed or assumed to come from Africa, 15 percent from Senegambia, 12 percent from Sierra Leone, 6 percent from the Windward Coast, 4 percent from west-central Africa, 3 percent from the Gold Coast, and 0 percent from the Bight of Benin, the Bight of Biafra, or southeastern Africa. For the African captives whose regional origin is known, 38 percent came from Senegambia, 30 percent from Sierra Leone, 14 percent from the Windward Coast, 10 percent from west-central Africa, 8 percent from the Gold Coast, and 0 percent from the Bight of Benin, the Bight of Biafra, or southeastern Africa. This is what is documented, but it should be noted that because the origin of 90 percent of the people transshipped from the West Indies is not known, the pattern is probably somewhat skewed. If the regional origins of the Africans imported into Jamaica and the Leeward Islands (at least half the slaves brought to Georgia from the West Indies were reexported from these sites) are taken into account, a higher percentage of captives would have been brought from the Gold Coast, the Windward Coast, the Bight of Benin, and the Bight of Biafra, and a lower percentage from Senegambia, Sierra Leone, and west-central Africa.[56] Taking this into account suggests that the African population of Georgia included captives from every major slaving region except southeastern Africa.

Managing the sales of these Africans benefited both Savannah merchants and factors. During most of the 1770s, this was especially true in Georgia, where "great Quantities of Lands Uncultivated" led to quick sales of slaves at high prices.[57] Although Savannah merchants do not appear to have invested directly in slave voyages, they received generous

Table 2. Origins of African slave imports into Georgia from South Carolina, West Indies, and Africa, 1751–1776

Region	Percentage of slaves of identifiable origin						
	1751–55	1756–60	1761–65	1766–70	1771–75	1776–80	Total
Senegambia	0	0	39	44	36	0	43
Sierra Leone	0	0	0	24	45	0	29
Windward Coast	0	0	9	20	0	0	14
Gold Coast	0	0	51	1	2	0	2
Bight of Benin	0	0	0	0	0	0	0
Bight of Biafra	0	0	0	0	0	0	0
West-central Africa	0	0	0	11	9	0	10
Southeastern Africa	0	0	0	0	0	0	0
Total	0	0	99	100	100	0	98
Number for whom origins known	0	0	127	3,051	1,536	0	4,714
Total estimated number of imported Africans	76	948	1,295	4,534	5,345	266	12,464

Sources: *Georgia Gazette*, Clay & Co. Papers, and Telfair Family Papers, Georgia Historical Society, Savannah, Georgia; Elizabeth Donnan, ed., *Documents Illustrative of the History of the Slave Trade to America*, 4 vols. (Washington, D.C.: Carnegie Institution of Washington, 1930–35), 4:616–25; W. Robert Higgins, "The South Carolina Negro Duty Law" (master's thesis, University of South Carolina, 1967), 149–265; Darold D. Wax, "'New Negroes Are Always in Demand': The Slave Trade in Eighteenth-Century Georgia," *Georgia Historical Quarterly* 58, no. 2 (Summer 1984): 193–220; Betty Wood, *Slavery in Colonial Georgia, 1730–1775* (Athens: University of Georgia Press, 1984), 88–109; Julia Floyd Smith, *Slavery and Rice Culture in Low Country Georgia, 1750–1860* (Knoxville: University of Tennessee Press, 1985), 93–112; Gregory E. O'Malley, "Beyond the Middle Passage: Slave Migration from the Caribbean to North America, 1619–1807," *William and Mary Quarterly* 66, no. 1 (January 2009): 125–72; and Voyages: The Trans-Atlantic Slave Trade Database, http://www.slavevoyages.org.

commissions on the cargoes of slaves that they handled in Savannah. According to the firm Cowper and Telfair, Savannah merchants charged a 5 percent commission on the gross sale of slaves. In 1773, the sale of the 115 captives disembarked by the brig *Francis* totaled £4,850, for which Cowper and Telfair and another firm received a total of £242.50. They were pleased with the results: "The average Considering their Quality is amazing & I think will Encourage Others to adventure this way." And they did; Cowper and Telfair vended two more cargoes the following year.[58] Their commissions in 1774 for the sale of slaves brought by the sloop *Daniel* and the bark *Virginia* totaled £448.32. They also charged the sponsors of the voyages for advertising and conducting the sales, paying duties, and nursing, feeding, housing, and clothing slaves before they were sold. In addition, they collected interest on the credit they extended for slave purchases.[59]

Profit was not the only reason merchants trafficked in slaves; selling black laborers gave slave vendors a leg up on the competition. Unwilling to jeopardize their labor supplies, planters maintained sound relationships with merchants who sold slaves and in most cases paid slave vendors before other creditors. In a letter of 1774, a merchant with Clay and Company described the advantage that merchants who sold slaves had over those who did not: "We are very apprehensive that the large Quantity of New Negro's sold this Year will absorb the coming Crop and make the Planters at least many of them backward in discharging their Store Debts as they will in general support their Credit with the Negro Merchant even if they are obliged to do it at the expense of the Dry Good Merchant."[60] Moreover, slave sales and credit payments brought planters into merchants' stores, where they bought dry goods and manufactured products. Most importantly, as Edward Telfair pointed out, it enabled them to "carry a very considerable part of the Export of this province."[61]

Close ties with planters and exceptional profits also opened social and political doors for merchants. During most of the colonial era, an elite group of planters and merchants dominated South Carolina and Georgia society and politics. Although a commercial career did not guarantee entry into the group (gentlemen viewed merchants as newcomers until they "acquired a stake in the country"), it did in many cases enable merchants to amass land and slaves and form close ties with planters.[62] Participation in the slave trade—which merchants and factors discreetly referred to as the "African Trade" or the "Guinea Trade" to avoid offending societal sensibilities—presented no obstacles to joining the upper class. Lowcountry planters welcomed them into their families, social clubs, churches, and the colonial legislature. In Charles Town, prominent members of firms that sold slaves included George Austin, Samuel Brailsford, Miles Brewton, John Hopton, Henry Laurens, Thomas Middleton, and Roger and Thomas Loughton Smith. The slave trade came much later to Savannah, but by 1776 the slave traders Joseph Clay, James Habersham, John Graham, and Edward and William Telfair were among the emerging elite of Georgia society.[63]

Edward Telfair's rise to prominence was not unlike that of several other Georgia and South Carolina merchants. Born in Scotland in 1735, Telfair worked in Scotland, Virginia, and North Carolina before embarking on a career in 1766 as a merchant in Savannah. Along with his brother William, Edward formed a partnership with another Scot, Basil Cowper. Cowper provided the funding, and the Telfairs contributed, as the historian Paul M. Pressly describes it, the "business acumen and a voracious appetite for dominating the market."[64] The firm of Cowper and Telfair prospered, and by the time of the Revolutionary War it was one of the leading merchant houses in Georgia.[65] Besides trafficking in slaves, the firm purchased planters' crops, contracted for the shipping and insurance, and negotiated with buyers. It sold planters dry goods and British manufactured products, supplied smaller, rural firms, and provided credit. The company owned and operated vessels that engaged in the coastal, West Indies, and Atlantic slave and provisioning trade; its employees repaired and performed maintenance on many of the ships that docked in Savannah.[66] In 1774, Cowper and Telfair exported more goods to England than any other Georgia firm.

Both Telfairs married late, and well. At the age of forty, William married Elizabeth Bellinger, daughter of the wealthy South Carolina planter Edmund Bellinger. Edward wed the daughter of another prosperous South Carolina planter, William Gibbons, who had relocated, with his large holding of slaves, to Georgia along the Savannah River to cultivate rice. Edward was thirty-nine and Sally sixteen when they married.[67] Through marriage, wealth, and property in land and slaves, Edward Telfair became a member of the elite group that governed Georgia. He was elected to the Commons House of Assembly in 1768, the Provincial Congress in 1774, and the Continental Congress in 1778. He served on the Council of Safety and the Committee of Intelligence and signed the Articles of Confederation. After the Revolutionary War, he served several terms as governor of Georgia. He was one of ten men to receive an electoral vote for president in the first U.S. presidential election.[68]

Between 1767 and 1776, Cowper and Telfair handled fifteen sales of African cargoes in Georgia—more than any other firm, partnership, or individual. The partnership of John Inglis and Nathaniel Hall sold nine slave cargoes. Other slave-dealing firms included John Inglis and Company, Joseph Clay, Clay and Habersham, George Baillie and Company, Johnson and Wylly, George Cuthbert, Alexander Wylly, Gordon and Netherclift, John Graham and Company, and Read and Mossman.[69]

Substantial capital was required to finance the sale of African cargoes. Planters often did not pay for slaves until the harvest after they acquired them. If the harvest failed, merchants usually had to wait another year or longer for payment. In 1793, Edward Telfair was still attempting to collect for a shipment of slaves that had arrived in Savannah two decades earlier.[70] In 1755, Henry Laurens of South Carolina (who operated on a much larger scale than any Savannah firm) warned a young man considering entering the trade that "we are often in advance more than [£]10,000."[71] Knowledge of the local market was essential to success. Slavers depended on merchants and factors to keep them abreast of local conditions, a sensitivity to which could mean the difference between profit and loss. Merchants and factors advised shippers of slave buyers' preferences for and against African ethnic groups. They also consulted on when to send cargoes and what sort of slave prices, and politics, to expect on arrival. An astute appraisal of the local market and buyers facilitated the quick selling of cargoes at profitable prices and the receipt of punctual payments.[72]

If sales were delayed, Africans suffered. When slave ships arrived at the mouth of the Savannah River after a five- to ten-week Middle Passage, captains were required to proceed first to Tybee Island, where in 1767 a lazaretto (or pesthouse) had been built for quarantining Africans. At the pesthouse, a doctor examined the captives; if no diseases were found, officials released the slaves, but if they detected smallpox or other diseases, they extended the quarantine for forty days after all the victims had recovered. When the slaves were released, the slave ships proceeded up the Savannah River to Savannah. Small groups of slaves were sold on the vessels that brought them to Savannah; large groups were housed and sold in slave yards. A number of merchants and firms had slave yards, including Cowper and Telfair, John Graham, and Inglis and Hall. Other sales were held on nearby plantations; at the City Exchange on Bay Street at the corner of Bull Street; and in Yamacraw, on the west side of Savannah.[73]

If slaves were not bringing acceptable prices, merchants would hold them off the

Slave ship manifest of the schooner Dolphin, *August 24, 1794. Inward Foreign Slave Manifests, 1789–1798; Collector of Customs, Savannah, Georgia, 1789–1913; Records of the U.S. Customs Service, Record Group 36; National Archives and Records Administration, National Archives at Atlanta.*

market until conditions improved. They delayed as well the selling of slaves who had not recovered sufficiently from the ravages of the Middle Passage. In 1774, extended confinements led to the death of many Africans before Cowper and Telfair could sell them. During a transshipment from the West Indies, nine of the sixteen Africans consigned to the firm died, and one more captive died soon after the vessel arrived in Savannah. Out of a cargo arriving directly from Africa, the firm was consigned thirty-two Africans, but fourteen died during the Middle Passage and quarantine.[74] The Sierra Leone captives from another vessel suffered an "amazing Loss" before they could be sold. The merchants estimated that the deaths had reduced the sponsors' proceeds by "near two thousand pounds Sterling." Cowper and Telfair blamed the deaths on "inveterate scurvy," "a long passage," and "Long detention of the Ship, by touching at different Islands in the West Indies."[75] West Indies clerks and ship crews may have mistreated the captives. While

Equiano "was . . . employed by his master," he "was often a witness to cruelties of every kind, which were exercised on [his] unhappy fellow slaves." He noted:

> I used frequently to have different cargoes of new negroes in my care for sale; and it was almost a constant practice with our clerks, and other whites, to commit violent depredations on the chastity of female slaves; and these I was, though with reluctance, obliged to submit to at all times, being unable to help them. When we have had some of these slaves on board my master's vessels to carry them to other islands, or to America, I have known our mates to commit these acts most shamefully, to the disgrace, not of Christians only, but of men. I have even known them gratify their brutal passion with females not ten years old.[76]

Despite the abuse and the "Great Mortality" suffered by many of its victims, the transatlantic slave trade supplied Georgia with hardworking, affordable enslaved laborers that planters and would-be planters sought.[77] The forced migration of more than twelve thousand African captives transformed the province, especially the Lowcountry. Attracted by the wealth that rice was producing in South Carolina, Georgia planters used Africans to establish and operate a slave-based plantation economy patterned after South Carolina's. The transformation took only one generation; by the end of the royal period, the Lowcountry had become a slave society and Africans the "dominant element in the slave population."[78] Their toil enriched both rice planters and merchants, who rose to the top of society and government in colonial Georgia. During the Revolutionary War, the slave trade was disrupted, but the economy established during the colonial period meant that slavery in Georgia was too deeply rooted to be displaced.[79]

"The King of England's Soldiers"
Armed Blacks in Savannah and Its Hinterlands during the Revolutionary War Era, 1778–1787
Timothy Lockley

The Revolutionary War was never simply a struggle between the British on the one side and Americans on the other. Americans themselves were deeply divided about whether a war to achieve independence from Britain was a good, moral, or legal thing to do, and friends, neighbors, and even families split between those loyal to Britain and those supporting the American patriots. Neither was the war of concern only to whites. Southern black people hoped that the war would mean the end of slavery. In December 1778, it was a black man, Quamino Dolly, who guided British troops through the surrounding swamps in their successful effort to capture Savannah. When a joint Franco-American force attempted to recapture the city the following October, their efforts were thwarted because reinforcements from Beaufort, South Carolina, led by sympathetic blacks "plunged through swamps, bogs, and creeks which had never been attempted before but by bears, wolves, and run-away negroes."[1] About 400 slaves worked on the fortifications of Savannah during the siege, while others, particularly women, worked as cooks and laundresses for the troops. A further 150 enslaved men were organized into two companies and "armed and equipt as infantry." The loyalist governor James Wright later commented that the black soldiers had "contributed greatly to our defence and safety" during the joint Franco-American assault on the city.[2]

Black troops continued to serve with the British until the evacuations of Savannah (July) and Charleston (December) in 1782. Most frequently, black recruits served as drummers, but a significant number were also used as general laborers, and a few served as musketeers in the infantry.[3] As patriot forces gradually pushed loyalists back to their urban strongholds of Charleston and Savannah in 1781 and 1782, British commanders created a cavalry unit from black volunteers. As late as December 1782, one South Carolina planter complained to the patriot governor about the activities of upward of a hundred mounted

"Black dragoons who have been out four times within the last ten days plundering & robbing . . . Last night they came as high as Mrs Godins where they continued from 11 o'clock till 4 this morning, & carried off everything they could . . . all her cattle, sheep, hogs, horses."[4]

Although precise figures do not exist, one historian estimates that roughly ten thousand slaves from Georgia were dislocated during the war.[5] Of these, a relatively small number of loyalist blacks left Charleston and Savannah with the British. Far more stayed behind to face the wrath of masters. During the war, with planters and overseers often absent either on active service or at political meetings, and the regular slave patrol system in abeyance, many slaves left their plantations and visited relatives and loved ones or travelled to Savannah to look for paid employment. Moreover, both loyalist and patriot forces took slaves from plantations as spoils of war, and these slaves trailed behind the armies with the equipment and supplies. After the war, planters expended much effort, often in vain, in trying to track down the slaves who they thought should have been on their properties.

Unknown Artist, Sir James Baird Attacks the American Rear. Capture of Savannah. 1778. Publisher: J & F Tallis, London & New York. This image, probably from the mid-nineteenth century, depicts Quamino Dolly leading British Troops on Savannah. Courtesy Ed Jackson.

Some Lowcountry slaves took advantage of the confusion caused by the war to flee into swamps. This was the point at which runaway slaves became maroons, intending to create their own distinct communities completely separate from white society. One of the largest of these communities formed on islands in the Savannah River, about eighteen miles upstream from Savannah. These islands are located within a large kink of the river, where it diverts from a direct north-south route to meander northeast toward Purrysburgh before gently heading back northwest. The main channel of the river forms the eastern side of an oval-shaped area of land that is roughly nine miles from north to south and six miles from west to east at its widest extent. The western boundary is formed by Abercorn Creek and Mill Creek (formerly known as Clark Creek), which eventually rejoins the main channel at the top of the oval shape. Big Collis Creek and Bear Creek split this land north to south, and Little Abercorn Creek links Abercorn Creek and Bear Creek to create three principal islands. Numerous smaller islands bounded by small shallow

The Haitian Revolution's Savannah Connection

Monument dedicated to Haitian soldiers' participation in the American Revolution, Savannah. Photograph: David J. Kaminsky.

In the summer of 1791, nearly fifteen years after the United States declared its independence from Britain and only two years after the start of the French Revolution, the French colony of Saint-Domingue erupted in its own bitter and bloody twelve-year revolutionary struggle. Thousands of bondpeople rose up against the Caribbean island's white and mixed-race slaveholding class in a bid to secure freedom and national independence. After defeating imperial armies from France, Britain, and Spain, the revolutionaries ultimately triumphed. In January 1804, Saint-Domingue became Haiti, the first independent black republic outside Africa. The Haitian victory sent aftershocks throughout the Atlantic world. Even as the revolution inspired fear among slaveholders throughout the Americas, it gave hope for freedom to those suffering under slavery and European imperialism.

In the United States, white citizens rarely made the connection between their struggle for freedom and that of slaves, though the language of slavery had often been invoked by the founding generation to express their perceived mistreatment by the British government. But the Haitian Revolution had an important, though rarely told, connection to the U.S. struggle for freedom: many of the future Haitian revolutionaries had first gained valuable fighting experience through their participation in the American Revolution.

In December 1778, well-equipped British soldiers led by Lieutenant Colonel Archibald Campbell took the city of Savannah, Georgia, hoping eventually to capture nearby Charleston and then the greater Carolinas. Strong loyalist support in Georgia, coupled with unremarkable resistance by the colonists and a floundering militia and Continental army, made the British army's successful siege of Savannah a foregone conclusion. In early September 1779, black and mixed-race soldiers from Saint-Domingue joined American colonists and French troops in a failed effort to retake the city. The total number of Saint-Domingue troops who sojourned to Georgia remains contested, but estimates place the number at 500–800. The Saint-Domingue fighters, who were known as free people of color (*gens de couleur libre*), constituted the Chasseurs-Volontaires de Saint-Domingue (volunteer light infantry). Led by the French general and admiral Charles-Hector, count d'Estaing, the infantrymen joined regular French metropolitan troops stationed in Saint-Domingue and a host of smaller volunteer units from across the island when they set sail for Georgia in some twenty-five warships.

Arriving in the waters off the coast of Georgia by September 11, 1779, General d'Estaing had moved his troops, which included members of the chasseurs, into Savannah by September 16. Despite pounding the city heavily with cannon fire for weeks, d'Estaing's forces failed to cripple entrenched British defenses surrounding the city. And even though illness ran rampant among his troops and hurricane season was quickly approaching, d'Estaing stubbornly ignored advice from subordinates to call off the siege. Instead, he mounted a highly secretive and bloody ground assault on the morning of October 9 at Spring Hill. He hoped to finish the job quickly and return to the Caribbean and then to France. Poor weather and scattered enemy forces, however, hindered his troops' best efforts. In the morning fog and swamp-like conditions, General d'Estaing was injured and the famed Polish cavalry officer Casimir Pulaski killed; countless chasseurs fought valiantly at the Spring Hill redoubt, though many perished. As fighting intensified into the third week of October, the death count rose on the Franco-American side. The British suffered only minimal losses. Realizing that victory was impossible, d'Estaing ordered a retreat on October 17, 1779. British troops showed no mercy, firing upon Franco-American forces as they hastily withdrew. Members of the chasseurs were assigned rearward positions to guard the retreat of d'Estaing's troops; they were later credited with saving the Franco-American forces from total destruction.

Back on Saint-Domingue, some black soldiers continued to serve in the Chasseurs-Volontaires until the unit disbanded in the early 1780s. But their experiences in Savannah provided them with useful fighting tactics. In a sense, the siege of Savannah was their rehearsal for revolution.

Though historians have yet to identify and account for most of the Saint-Domingue fighters or the scope of their involvement during the siege of Savannah, legend has it that Henri Christophe, a future king of Haiti, was among them, perhaps as a drummer boy. He became a leading figure during the Haitian Revolution, serving as a general under Toussaint Louverture and ruling as king from 1811 until 1820.

A monument honoring the contributions and bravery of the Chasseurs-Volontaires who fought on behalf of Savannahians and the American colonists sits in downtown Savannah in Franklin Square. Dedicated in 2007, the monument pays homage to the long-ignored efforts of Saint-Domingue soldiers to secure American freedom—and by implication, honors their struggle for freedom from slavery as well.

JERMAINE THIBODEAUX

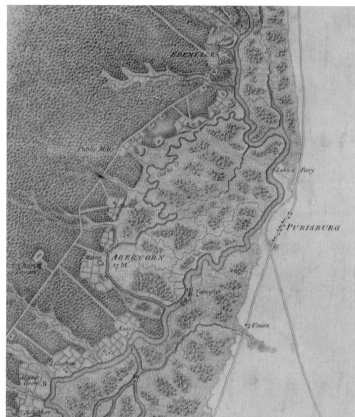

Purrisburg in detail from Sketch of the Northern Frontiers of Georgia, Extending from the Mouth of the River Savannah to the Town of Augusta, *by Archibald Campbell (London: William Faden, 1780). Courtesy of the Library of Congress, Geography and Maps Division.*

creeks also exist. Modern maps tend to overemphasize the main channel of the river at the expense of the other creeks, but a map of 1780 shows more clearly that Abercorn Creek was navigable by smaller boats and could be used as an alternative to the main channel of the river.

These river islands were particularly attractive to maroon groups for several reasons. First, being surrounded by water, they were defensible, and all were heavily forested with cypress trees, which provided natural cover. The ground was often more swamp than terra firma, and in the spring, when river levels were generally higher than normal, the islands became impassable other than by boat. Maroon settlements were most likely located on the highest, and therefore driest, places, and dwellings might well have been raised up on stilts. The islands were also home to alligators, water moccasins, and eastern diamond rattlesnakes, which deterred any casual visitors.

Second, the islands, being roughly thirty square miles in area, were large enough to support a significant population of maroons. Aside from the dangerous fauna mentioned above, the islands were home to turtles and birds, such as geese and ducks, and the creeks offered the opportunity to catch fish. Lowcountry slaves were well accustomed to supplementing their diet by hunting in nearby swamps. The naturalist William Bartram, visiting Jonathan Bryan's plantation about eight miles north of Savannah in 1770, observed that "several of his servants came home with horse loads of wild pigeons (Columba migratoria), which it seems they had collected in a short space of time at a neighbouring bay swamp."[6] For slaves skilled in such techniques, surviving in the swamp for longer periods of time was certainly viable. Small plots of cleared land could be planted with vegetables, corn, and rice, all of which slaves had grown on plantations, and in the virtually frost-free climate the crops could be harvested for much of the year.

Third, the maroons had found a location that was sufficiently distant from white settlement to ensure their isolation. Ebenezer was eight miles to the north, while Purrysburgh was four miles to the east on the South Carolina bank of the main channel of the Savannah River. Neither town was of any size. The 1780 map marked a road that crossed the river at Zubley's ferry, eventually meeting the Savannah–Ebenezer road on the other side of the swamp. No other contemporary map showed this road, and it does not exist now, suggesting that it might have been a military road used solely during the Revolutionary War. One British force had crossed the Savannah River very close to where maroons later took up residence. It is entirely possible that black troops gained firsthand knowledge of the islands while still in the king's service.[7] The twin roads that ran parallel to the river on either side were at least a mile, and often several miles, from the river itself, and the plantations that could be accessed from the roads were few and far between. For the most part, the land between the river islands and the roads, especially on the South Carolina side, was simply an extension of the same low, swampy ground that characterized the islands. Furthermore, the size of the river islands meant that settlements could be constructed and land cleared and planted with crops without sacrificing secrecy. Even when whites were aware of a maroon settlement on the Savannah River islands, they had to find the precise location by searching an inhospitable environment and navigating almost impassable terrain.

Fourth, the river islands were positioned on a boundary between South Carolina and Georgia, meaning jurisdiction over them was unclear. The Savannah River, which forms most of the boundary between South Carolina and Georgia, flows into numerous channels as it nears the sea. The exact demarcation of authority over the marsh lands and islands in the river was unclear; not until the signing of the Treaty of Beaufort, in April 1787, did South Carolina and Georgia come to an agreement on the boundary line.[8] Since any military action against the maroons would involve public expense, each state government probably hoped that the other would take the initiative and thus pay the bill. It is possible that military authorities on both sides were cautious about violating the sovereignty of a neighboring state by sending troops in pursuit of maroons without express permission. The maroons' location in the Savannah River exploited this jurisdictional confusion.

Further confirmation that the Savannah River islands west of Purrysburgh were an ideal location for a maroon settlement: the islands have not been settled or built on in contemporary times. Their remote and inaccessible location meant that even planters of the antebellum era never drained and divided them up, as they did with similar islands nearer Savannah. The pristine landscape became part of the Savannah River National Wildlife Refuge in 1927 and has remained undisturbed by people ever since.

For former slaves who had fought for the British at the siege of Savannah and during the ensuing four years, but had been left behind by the British after the war, finding a secure refuge where they could maintain their freedom was evidently preferable to the alternative—a return to enslavement on a rice plantation. Since so many slaves were missing after the war, or had been removed by the British, planters set about restocking their estates with slaves, partly by direct importation from Africa and partly by transshipment from the Caribbean. One estimate suggests that by 1787 the black population of the Lowcountry had already reached, and most likely exceeded, prewar levels.[9] The slavery experienced by the newly imported was just as harsh, unrelenting, and soul destroying as it had been before the war. The act of 1770 that set out how slaves were to be controlled continued to be the basis of slave law after the Revolution, and indeed remained largely unchanged until 1865; little to no amelioration for the condition of Georgia slaves came out of the American war for liberty.[10] Johann David Schoepf, a German visiting the Lowcountry in 1784, believed that the lives of slaves were "harder and more troublous than that of their northern brethren": "On the rice-plantations, with wretched food, they are allotted more work; and the treatment which they experience at the hands of their overseers and owners is capricious and often tyrannical."[11] Given the regimes that most Lowcountry slaves endured, it is not surprising that a separate maroon community was an attractive proposition.

Later sources confirm that black loyalists first took up residence on the Savannah River islands shortly after the British left in 1782, yet little is known about them until late in 1786. Some whites knew, or suspected, the existence of a maroon settlement near Savannah as early as 1783; James Houstoun's advertisement for two fugitive slaves, Peter and Jupiter, both coopers, stated: "There is great reason to believe they are harboured by the Abercorn negroes."[12] In general, however, it seems likely that the settlements remained secret and hidden from white eyes for four years, and that maroons kept a low enough profile not to arouse attention or anger from neighboring planters. Perhaps four years of tranquility made the maroons overconfident, or perhaps the original group of former soldiers became augmented by new fugitives who lacked the same cautious approach, but by 1786 the maroons were committing "robberies on the neighboring planters" and clearly causing enough trouble to be noticed.[13] On October 3, 1786, the grand jury of Chatham County, Georgia, brought the activities of the maroons into the spotlight by complaining about "large gangs of runaway Negroes" who were "allowed to remain quietly within a short distance of this town, without an attempt of the Militia Officers in the districts where they are . . . to subjugate them."[14]

The grand jury's complaint spurred those in charge of local military units into action. Just over a week later, a combined force of militia units and the Savannah Light Infantry were involved in a skirmish with the maroons. This encounter, which occurred on October 11, 1786, ended inconclusively, with "three or four" maroons reportedly killed while a similar number of the militia were wounded. Later the same day, a new assault on the "out-guards" posted by the maroons was repulsed after "the Negroes came down in such numbers that it was judged advisable to retire to their boats, from which the Negroes attempted to cut them off." Only the discharge of an artillery piece from one of the militia's boats held back the maroons long enough for the soldiers to escape. Clearly, the maroons were well armed, aware of the need to post sentries, and sufficiently numerous—"supposed upwards of 100"—as well as brave enough to counterattack against armed has been published by the Governor of the Danish West India islands, for regulation of the dress, conduct, and expences, of the people of colour, free and slaves, under his government. He forbids them the use of diamonds, embroidered silks, wrought or painted stuffs, chintzes, cambricks, muslins, gauzes, fine linens, all kinds of dimity, fine laces, gold and silver lace, silk shoes, all kinds of ornaments, buckles of Piere de Strace, or such-like stones, all kinds of hair dressing, with or without caps, together with all sumptuous dress whatever.

Montego Bay, September 9. The sloop Ranger, seized on Thursday the 24th ult. by Daniel Flowerdew, Esq. was, on the 31st following, condemned as legal prize at the Grand Court.

ALEXANDRIA, September 14.

ABOUT four o'clock last Tuesday morning Mr. M'Daniel's tavern in Dumfries was destroyed by fire, supposed to be occasioned by a candle being left in the bar. A number of gentlemen were asleep in the house, and narrowly escaped by jumping out of the chamber windows, some of whom were much hurt. The fire had got to so great a height before discovered that many of the gentlemen had not time even to take their wearing apparel with them.

Richmond, September 14. About half past seven o'clock, on Tuesday evening last, a beautiful luminous body, of a globular form, was seen in the S. W. descending with velocity in a N. E. direction. It burst ed without any noise, blazed with great brightness for the space of half a minute, and then disappeared. Its size we cannot pretend to determine, though it appeared (to the eye) about the bigness of a man's head.

Charleston, October 6. Wednesday evening died, Mr. Joseph Vincent Burd, Printer, of this city. He was married on Saturday se'nnight, and whilst at supper, in the midst of jocund festivity, the hand of death came upon him, and in a few days he left a widowed bride, and is himself no more!

Yesterday came up the Catherine, Capt. Murray, from Bristol, in 11 weeks.

On the 2d inst. put in here in distress, the snow Hero, Capt. Walker, from Musquito Shore, bound to London, having sprung a leak, out four weeks.

9. On the 5th ult. at night a schooner, called the Mary, was run away with from the port of Norfolk, Virginia, with her cargo, consisting of rum, coffee, sugar, &c. There were concerned, viz. —— Butts, a native of Rhode Island, James Wilson, and another Irishman, name unknown.

On Saturday the 24th of June the University of Edinburgh conferred the Degree of Doctor of Medicine, after the usual publick and private trials, upon 20 gentlemen, of whom 4 were Americans, 5 Irish, 5 English, and 6 Scotch.

12. The William and Mary, Capt. Wilson, is arrived at Norfolk, in 52 days from London; also the Essex and Samuel, Capt. Mitchell, from Nantz, in York River.

SAVANNAH, October 19.

A NUMBER of runaway Negroes (supposed to be upwards of 100) having sheltered themselves on Belleisle Island, about 17 or 18 miles up Savannah river, and for some time past committed robberies on the neighbouring Planters, it was found necessary to attempt to dislodge them. On Wednesday the 11th inst. a small party of militia landed and attacked them, and killed three or four, but were at last obliged to retreat for want of ammunition, having four of their number wounded. Same

---

guards, but the Negroes came down in such numbers that it was judged adviseable to retire to their boats, from which the Negroes attempted to cut them off, but were prevented by Lieut. Elfe of the Artillery, who commanded a boat with 11 of the company, and had a field piece on board, which he discharged three times with grape shot, and it is thought either killed or wounded some of them, as a good deal of blood was afterwards seen about the place to which the shot was directed. On Friday morning Gen. Jackson with a party proceeded to their camp, which they had quitted precipitately on his approach. He remained till Saturday afternoon, when he left the island, having destroyed in such rough rice as would have made 25 barrels or more if beat out, and brought off about 60 bushels of corn, and 14 or 15 boats and canoes from the landing. He also burnt a number of their houses and huts, and destroyed about four acres of green rice. The loss of their provisions it is expected will occasion them to disperse about the country, and it is hoped will be the means of most of them being soon taken up.

DIED. Mr. David Davies.

On Sunday last arrived the schooner Hope, Daniel M'Intire, Master, from Montego Bay, Jamaica, in 26 days. On the 3d instant, off the Havana, he fell in with the schooner June, Joseph Wade, Master, from Jamaica to Newbern, North Carolina, then 23 days out, and on the 9th parted with them, all well, in lat. 30, 57. N. Capt. M'Intire informs that the Elizabeth, M'Niel, from Jamaica to Charleston, put into the Havana for provisions on the 4th instant.

Monday last Charles Stewart stood in the pillory two hours, and next day was publickly whipped, for house-stealing; he is to receive the remainder of his punishment this week, after which he will be discharged.

The sloop Dolphin arrived here yesterday after a passage of 12 days from New-York.

We are desired to insert the following Extracts from a New-York paper of the 16th of August last:

Philadelphia, August 12. The great landholders, says a correspondent, are continually complaining of the want of emigrations from Europe; but those men know not what they complain of, or what they wish for. Whence, and wit may as easily be made to smile at the follies of monarchies with the citizens of the republick of America. Look at the men who thrive time enough as long to learn. How few of them have assimilated to our manner and government. How bitterly do they deplore, in all their letters to Europe, the distracted state of our country. Deluded creatures! it our American, who have the least understood the real distraction of the war, views the present situation of our country with very different hues; he watches our happiness by the price of labour and grain, and wisely concludes that America never advanced more rapidly towards wealth and independence than she does at present; he views the languor and mistakes of our publick bodies as the effects of a weakness produced by the mighty convulsions of the war, and which will certainly yield, like many of the diseases of the human body, to the healing hand of time. Let Americans be wise—and if they wish to be an united people, let them prefer our old citizens, whose manners, habits, and principles, agree perfectly with the new and democratical forms of government. Nothing can be expected of ours imprudent, says one of our correspondents, than to fee the strangers and foreigners intermeddling in our politicks as soon as they set their feet upon our shores. During the late wars, the state of Pennsylvania was kept in constant hot water by Oliveau, and some others, of equally turbulent and worthless character. At present the state is threatened with a convulsion by a set of new comers, who call themselves "Lately Adopted Sons." One of these, nobly, probably, earned a scanty subsistence in a garret in London, or in the West Indies, during the late war, by writing against the American Rebels, now yields himself as a cutting instrument of the rage of a crazy old man against the Bank of North America. Another, who never saw a paper shilling in his life till he came to America a year or two ago, and who knows nothing of the nature or principles of a paper currency, echoes the bellowings of a party in its favour; a third accuses an eminent lawyer of gross blunders in his profession, and thus insults him with a challenge for laughing at his ignorance and stupidity.

Another correspondent proposes that "the Lately Adopted Sons" should have a patent for inventing the new mode of dealing by inkshed, instead of bloodshed, and that a newspaper should be erected to the memory of the CHIEF JUSTICE, for his still is preventing a breach of the peace, after every possible step had been taken to break it, but without effect.

Entered inward at the Custom-House since Oct. 5.

	From
Schooner Hopewell, Kerr,	Norfolk
Schooner Hope, Smooke,	Baltimore
Sloop Favourite, Fitzpatrick,	Charleston
Schooner Thomas, Webley,	Ditto
Schooner Mayflower, Farrow,	Ditto
Sloop Vigilant, Conyers,	Ditto
Schooner Willing Maid, Johnson,	St. Augustine
Schooner Hope, M'Intire,	Jamaica

Cleared out

	For
Schooner Mayflower, Farrow,	Charleston
Ship Commerce, Adam,	Jamaica
Schooner Industry, Newell,	Charleston

To be sold at the Printing Office,

THE ACTS
OF THE
GENERAL ASSEMBLY,

Passed at Augusta last January and February,

Containing the Import and Tobacco Acts, &c.

879

white soldiers. Realizing the strength of the military forces ranged against them, the maroons decided to abandon their camp and retreat farther into the swamp. When General James Jackson led another sortie against the maroons two days later, he found their settlement empty but well stocked. The maroons had planted several acres of the island with corn and "green rice," giving them a steady food supply that could be augmented by fishing from the "14 or 15 boats" that Jackson captured. All these supplies, amounting to "as much rough rice as would have made 25 barrels or more if beat out, and . . . about 60 bushels of corn," were either destroyed or taken. Jackson also "burnt a number of their houses and huts," thus rendering the site uninhabitable, though since whites had been to the camp, it clearly was no longer suitable as a secret refuge for former slaves.[15]

With their settlement destroyed, the maroons were forced to raid plantations, "from whence they carry off whole stacks of rice at a time to compensate, as they term it, for their incredible magazine of provisions . . . destroyed at their camp." During October and November 1786, they attacked several plantations on both sides of the Savannah River, leading one observer to describe them as "much more troublesome to the citizens than when we routed them."[16] On November 29, 1786, "upwards of twenty of them armed, attacked the house of Mr Wolmar, with an intention of taking his life & robbed him of every valuable he possessed. Fortunately for himself he was not at home." The white authorities could not allow such actions to continue, not just because of the havoc the maroons were wreaking, but also because of the example they were setting for the enslaved population: "The freebooty they reap, and the independent state they are in, have strong charms of allurement, of course, their numbers are daily increasing." The attacks on the maroons in October 1786 had been led by units from Georgia, and therefore the maroons settled in South Carolina, "from whence they frequently make irruptions unto Georgia," but felt free to "range at large" on the South Carolina side: "Nigh one hundred of them armed having been seen a few days since, between Purisburgh & the Union."[17] In early December, General Jackson wrote to the governors of South Carolina and Georgia urging concerted action against the maroons in order "to put a stop to their marauding, as well as to make some severe examples." As if to illustrate what he meant by "severe examples," Jackson casually mentioned that the head of one maroon, killed during a plantation raid, had been "fixed on the western road." Jackson feared that "if something cannot be shortly done, I dread the consequences—they are as daring as any & from their independent state, from the ease they enjoy in S. Carolina, forbode what I dread to express, a capital insurrection." Jackson, who had fought in the Revolutionary War, also warned that the maroons should not be underestimated, since "their leaders are the very fellows that fought, & maintained their ground against the brave lancers at the siege of Savannah, & they still call themselves the King of England's soldiers."[18] The governor of Georgia, no doubt alarmed that runaway slaves "have with arms opposed the Militia that have been ordered out to suppress them," responded immediately to Jackson's letter with an offer of a £10 reward for each maroon captured or killed, but his South Carolina counterpart made no immediate response.[19]

In March 1787, the maroons raided the home of the South Carolina planter John Lewis Bourquin, wounding him in the process, and departed with one of his drivers and "ten barrels of clean rice." Bourquin reported to his representative in the South Carolina legislature that "they have in my hearing threatened the lives of many of the citizens," and he requested that the state take immediate action. In particular, he pointed out that the militia were "not willing to go after them . . . As it will require more than a few days to have them entirely extirpated they say there ought to be provisions ordered to be provided for them by the public." Bourquin also hinted at the connections that most likely existed between maroons and those who remained enslaved. Plantation slaves often supported maroons with food, weaponry, and information. Most plantations were too large to be monitored constantly and therefore slaves were able to contact maroons at night on distant parts of the plantation, especially where there was river access. Bourquin feared that if the maroons were not suppressed, then the real danger would come from "our own indoor domestics," emboldened by white inaction and maroon success.[20]

Galvanized into action, the governor of South Carolina ordered that a hundred "minute men" be engaged, at a salary of one shilling a day, for a full month, with rations and ammunition provided by the state. For each maroon captured or killed, a £10 reward would be payable, matching the proclamation made by the governor of Georgia the previous December.[21] To augment the minutemen, the South Carolina government also recruited twenty Catawba Indians. The Catawba had been used to hunt maroons before, since their "manner of hunting renders them very sagacious in finding an Enemy by their Track," and also because they were able to "hunt the Negroes in their different recesses almost impervious to White people at that season of the year."[22] Once his forces were assembled, the leader of the expedition, Colonel Thomas Hutson, faced an obvious problem: how to locate and destroy the maroons? He must have had some intelligence on the movements of the maroons, since on April 21, 1787, he was able to send three boats to "waylay" a party of maroons in Collin's Creek (probably Big Collis Creek) and succeeded in killing several.[23] It was not until May 6, however, that the main encampment of the maroons was located, "on the lower side of Bear Creek." The camp itself "was 700 yds in length, & about 120 in width" and contained twenty-one houses, enough to house up to two hundred people, though far fewer maroons are mentioned by name in the records. In addition, "the whole of the cleared land was planted in rice and potatoes." This camp was larger than the one destroyed the previous October and is evidence of the speed with which maroons could construct settlements. Surrounding the camp was "a kind of breech work about 4 feet high" constructed out of "logs & cane that came out of the cleared ground," while the single narrow entrance "would admit but one person to pass at a time." One hundred fifty yards down the creek a sentry was posted, and "about two miles below their camp they had fallen large logs across the creek in order to prevent boats passing up (small canoes might pass at high water)."[24] The maroons were well versed in defensive tactics, as one might expect from "the King of England's soldiers" who had successfully defended Savannah in 1779. Moreover, several historians have observed that the use of fortified camps was a common tactic in African warfare, and since much of the enslaved population of the Lowcountry was African, it is plausible to argue that the Savannah River maroons were using traditional knowledge to defend their settlements.[25] Once their defenses had been breached, however, the fighting spirit of the maroons quickly evaporated, and most escaped "into the swamp firing a few shot at random." Six maroons were reported killed and their camp was destroyed. A few days later, the Effingham County, Georgia, militia encountered a group of eighteen maroons "on their way to the Indian nation" and captured nine of them.[26] A week later saw the capture of Lewis, one of the maroon leaders, who was taken to Savannah and put on trial.[27]

Lewis's trial record provides a vast amount of information about the internal organization of the maroon camp and, uniquely, of the personalities of the maroons themselves. For instance, Lewis stated that he joined the maroons in 1785, only after "his Masters White Overseer used him ill," an indication that not all the maroons on the Savannah River islands had necessarily served with the British army.[28] The maroon community was not a static institution. Rather, it grew as children were born or as new recruits arrived, and shrank as members sickened and died, or even returned to plantations. The self-styled leader of the maroons was Sharper, who "was called Captain Cudjoe," most likely after the leader of the Jamaican maroons who had successfully negotiated in 1739 a treaty with British authorities that recognized maroon freedom on the island. Sharper had been taken from a plantation in Colleton District, South Carolina, by British forces under General Provost during a raid into South Carolina in the spring of 1779. Evidently left behind after the British evacuation, Sharper had remained at large in the Lowcountry. At one time he was detained in Sunbury, twenty miles south of Savannah, before at some point taking up residence in the Savannah River.[29] Lewis was second in command of the maroons, calling himself "Captain Lewis," but he and Sharper clearly had an uneasy relationship, with Lewis refusing to follow Sharper's orders on more than one occasion. According to two female maroons who testified at Lewis's trial, the two leaders "frequently quarrelled," with one suggesting that it was because Lewis suspected "he did not get his share of plunder," while the other thought that "Lewis wanted his own people as Sharper took all his men." Sharper and Lewis "disagreed and Separated" after a local white man, John Casper Hirschmann, was murdered by the maroons.

Hirschmann had encountered the maroons more than once, once stopping to talk to them from a boat in the Savannah River. The day before he died, Hirschmann met Lewis and two other maroons in the swamp and "begged" them "to carry him to the Camp . . . as he wanted Victuals of which he was in search." Little is known about Hirschmann's circumstances, but evidently he was not above trading with maroons, and if he was aware of their raids on nearby plantations, it did not prevent him trying to make contact. Lewis made Hirschmann wait overnight at a campfire before taking him to the main camp at first light. Sharper was outraged, saying that "Lewis had no business to bring White people to camp," and ordered Hirschmann be killed immediately. Chicheum, a maroon with possible Native American ancestry, judging by his name, shot Hirschmann and dumped his body "in to a pond." After the murder, Lewis "Separated camp with Sharper."[30]

Other information about maroon life can be gleaned from the record of Lewis's trial. The maroons grew rice and corn on the island, but for meat they raided nearby plantations, taking sheep and cattle with apparent impunity. At least eight of the maroons had guns, which they used mainly for killing livestock but which, of course, could also be used to defend the camp and to threaten adversaries. Lewis stated that he had "called on Mr Thomas Pollhill and told him to take Care of the runaway Negroes, or by'e and by'e, they would Come and hurt him." Raids on plantations not only netted maroons food, but also were opportunities to restock their powder and ammunition, to take clothes—Lewis for example had "a great Coat which he said he got from Lowerman"—and to recruit more slaves. The first skirmish between the maroons and the militia, in October 1786, had prevented "Sharper and Lewis going to fetch more of Mr Guerards hands," though it is not clear whether these recruits were volunteers or were to be pressed into joining the maroons.

The two women who testified against Lewis, Juliett and Peggy, had run away from their plantations together with their husbands within the last year. Phillis, on the other hand, "a stout, strong made wench, . . . about 28 years of age," had fled from James Gunn's Cashall-Hall plantation in 1783, taking her one-year-old son with her. When Captain Dasher captured her in 1787, she still had the boy with her, now named "Sharper," suggesting that his father might have been the maroon leader.[31] Labor among the maroons was clearly gendered: "all the women Stayed in Camp" and planted rice, while the men conducted raids on nearby plantations and organized the defense of the settlement. None of the women had guns, and when the militia attacked, one of Sharper's first orders was to send "all the women in the canes" to hide. When the battle was lost, the maroons scattered and attempted to flee northeast, away from the concentration of white settlement in the Lowcountry and toward land still occupied by the Creeks and Cherokees. Not all made it, but of the ten maroons listed in the newspapers as being captured by the militia, nearly all were women, who may not have been able to travel as quickly as the men, and at least one had a child with her. The only man recorded as being captured was Lewis, but he was traveling south toward "his Master's Mills on Ogeeche," perhaps hoping to blend back into the slave population as an ordinary runaway and not a maroon leader. He was "taken by two negroes belonging to Mr Bird" before he reached his destination, and the fact that he was captured by two slaves is further evidence that racial solidarity had its limits. Even if the two slaves had been sympathetic to those resisting slavery, once the maroons were forced to abandon their island refuge, it was clear that their cause was finished. It is also possible that the increased vigilance of whites, as a result of their fear that the maroons might inspire greater resistance among the enslaved, caused resentment among those remaining on plantations. When maroons raided plantations for food, supplies, and recruits, those most likely to suffer were the slaves, either because masters suspected them of colluding with the rebels, or because there was now simply less food on the plantation.

Lewis's trial for the murder of John Casper Hirschmann and three counts of robbery took place before four justices of the Chatham County Inferior Court. A jury of seven was selected to hear the case, and the trial record indicates that only three people testified: Lewis himself, Peggy, and Juliett, there being no bar in the slave code to black people testifying against other blacks. It did not take the jury long to convict Lewis of all charges, though it seems likely that he did not commit the murder. Even if he had been acquitted of the murder, the outcome would have been same: the robbery charges also merited a death sentence. The justices ordered that "the Negroe Lewis . . . be hanged on the South Common by the Neck until he shall be Dead on the Ninth day of June next at ten o'clock in the Morning; After Which his head to be Cut off and Stuck upon a pole to be sett up on the Island of Marsh opposite the Glebe land in Savannah River." By ordering the mutilation of Lewis's corpse, the justices were following the act of 1770 "for the better governing of Negroes," which ordered that the "manner of death" in capital cases involving slaves should be the one judged "most effectual to deter others from offending in like manner."[32]

The same act stated that all capital sentences had to be approved by the governor, and therefore all relevant documents relating to the trial were sent to Augusta. The state's executive council "approved the sentence" and issued a warrant for the execution of Lewis on the day appointed. A terse report in the local newspaper the following week stated: "Last Saturday Lewis, one of the head-men of the camp of runaway negroes lately broke up, was executed pursuant to his sentence."[33] Two years later Lewis's owner, Oliver Bowen, was awarded £40 compensation by the state for his executed slave. Requests from other slaveholders for compensation for slaves "killed among the Runaway Negroes" were rejected, since the state paid only for slaves executed after a trial, not for those killed by the militia while "in arms against this state."[34] Those unable to produce a trial transcript received no compensation.

The destruction of the maroon camp in the Savannah River in May 1787, and the dispersal of the maroons themselves, seemed to mark an end to the use of those islands as refuges for large numbers of slaves. No doubt individuals, and perhaps small groups, fled into the swamps for as long as slavery persisted in the South. As late as 1823, newspapers reported: "A correspondent in Purysburg informs us, that a number of armed negroes were encamped in that neighborhood, and that several gentlemen had gone in pursuit of them."[35] This was an isolated report, however, and there are no records to suggest that the militia or the state governments had to mount large-scale expeditions against armed slaves on the Savannah River as in 1787. If the maroons numbered "upwards of 100," as reports suggested, the militia killed very few of them. Just £60 was paid out by the South Carolina government, equating to six deaths, and only a small number were reported in the press as being captured. Those who were captured could expect reenslavement, since masters were expected to claim those advertised in the press. If no claimant came forward, the slave would be sold by the state.[36] But it seems likely that the majority of the maroons succeeded in escaping northward and avoided a return to slavery.

After the chaos of the Revolutionary War, the removal of the maroons in the Savannah River marked the completion of a process of reestablishing racial slavery in the Low-country that had been in progress since 1782. The "general asylum" offered by the maroons to prospective runaway slaves was a challenge that could not be ignored. Lowcountry planters were well aware of the situation in Jamaica and in Suriname, where maroon groups had "fixed and fortified the recesses . . . and opposed and harrassed their masters until they were obliged to treat with them; and they are now an actual independent colony." They did not believe that the "runaway negroes" (contemporaries never called them *maroons*) were yet comparable to Jamaican maroons, but "to have despised or neglected" the Savannah River maroons might have led to independent maroon communities becoming so strong that even "the best stationary regiments could not subdue them."[37] The effort put into the destruction of the maroons—two state governments together provided more than a hundred troops and recruited a party of Catawba, all of whom had to be paid or rewarded as well as supplied with food and drink—was considerable. The South Carolina government alone paid out £241 for supplies, with soldiers' pay in addition to that.[38] Such sums are evidence of how seriously the threat posed by maroons was taken in societies where the entire economy was constructed around racial slavery. By eliminating the maroon threat, white authorities reasserted their control over African Americans and ensured that whatever future resistance they encountered from the enslaved, although varied and widespread, would ultimately be insufficient to challenge the institution of slavery until the Civil War.

At the Intersection of Cotton and Commerce
Antebellum Savannah and Its Slaves
Susan Eva O'Donovan

When the topic of antebellum slave labor comes up, it is all too common to picture vast plantation landscapes populated by gangs of black workers making their weary way through fields of growing cotton. That is not an incorrect image. By the end of the antebellum era, close to 70 percent of America's slaves lived in the rural Deep South, and most of them were involved in the production of cotton. Those who were not cultivated the region's other great staples: sugar, tobacco, and rice. Thus, the story of antebellum slavery is largely rural and agricultural. But this is not the whole story. Missing are the slaves who labored in industrial settings. Missing are those who extracted ores from deep underground. Missing are the slaves who lived and labored in southern cities. Most important of all, missing are the legions of mobile women and men who connected all those pieces together and who, at various times and places, were themselves agricultural, industrial, and even urban workers. The history of Savannah helps tell that larger and more complicated story, one that reveals a complex, dynamic world in which the lines between urban and rural, industrial and agricultural, were more fiction than fact, but a story in which cotton still stood at the center.

Savannah has a long history as a city of laboring slaves, and until the early nineteenth century, much of that history was shaped by the making and marketing of the Lowcountry's signature crops—rice, indigo, and Sea Island cotton. Eagerly demanded by European, northern, and West Indian markets, those commodities quickly transformed James Oglethorpe's well-planned city into a bustling commercial outpost in the Atlantic system of trade. Though initially banned from the colony, slaves soon became the lifeblood of Savannah and the surrounding Lowcountry plantations. Besides producing the staples that fueled Savannah's colonial economy, slaves fed and clothed the city's free population, tended gardens, groomed horses, drove wagons, operated rice mills, and made

Above: Picking Cotton Near the Savannah River, Frank Leslie's Lady's Magazine. *Courtesy of the Georgia Historical Society, 1361PR-01-01-01.*

Left: Alfred Waud, Rice Culture on the Ogeechee, near Savannah, Georgia, Harper's Weekly, July 5, 1867. *Courtesy of the Library of Congress, Miscellaneous Items in High Demand Collection, Prints and Photographs Division, LC-USZ62-93554.*

up a large part of the city's artisanal class. As was the case around the Atlantic littoral, gaily dressed enslaved women dominated the local trade in foodstuffs and also figured heavily among the ranks of domestic servants. Many urban slaves were hired out by owners, sometimes to learn a trade, sometimes to earn their keep, and sometimes simply to ensure that surplus workers were kept busy and—from a master's perspective—out of mischief.[1]

Despite a fairly constant traffic between countryside and town, the slaves who lived and labored in and around colonial Savannah occupied a fairly limited geographic space. Hemmed in to the north and the west by the commercial behemoth that was colonial Charleston, eighteenth-century Savannah was the junior partner in a circum-Lowcountry economy. With the exceptions of an Indian trade that delivered hides from deep in the hinterlands and a maritime commerce that ensured Savannah a (minor) place in the Atlantic system, the city and its residents served a narrow arc of sandy-soiled and forested land that reached from Augusta and its environs south toward Darien and, for much of the colonial period, not much farther west than Midway. It was within these bounds that Georgians produced the rice, indigo, timber, tar, turpentine, and droves of hogs and cattle that crossed Savannah's wharves and into the holds of waiting ships. Thus, while responsibility fell largely to slaves to both make and move the city's major colonial exports, they did so within a region that was neither large nor particularly cosmopolitan. That, however, changed with the introduction of short-staple cotton.[2]

American producers were not strangers to upland cotton. Farmers had been cultivating it for years for domestic purposes and by some estimates grew as many as three million pounds annually in the last years of the eighteenth century.[3] But it was not until a series of inventors (Eli Whitney being the most famous) devised the means to separate the plant's notoriously sticky seed from its valuable fiber that it became a viable commercial crop. Wildly popular among interior farmers and planters and eagerly sought by European and northern textile manufacturers, upland cotton swiftly displaced rice, sugar, indigo, and tobacco as the nation's premier slave-grown commercial crop. Availing themselves of slaves no longer wanted by Chesapeake planters, prospective cotton growers surged across the forests and prairies of the American Southeast. As cotton's territory expanded with them, the volume of American exports shot up. In 1801, the United States produced eighty thousand bales. A half century later, output had shot up 625 percent, and American growers harvested nearly five million bales in 1859.[4]

Slavery and Freedom in Savannah's Industrial Corridor

The centrality of slave labor in antebellum Savannah's urban economy became especially clear along the western edge of the city limits, where several industries, transportation networks, and neighborhoods converged. The origins of this industrial corridor can be traced to 1733, when James Oglethorpe agreed to set aside some swampy land west of his settlement for Native Americans; this area became known as the Oglethorpe Ward. White settlers had pushed the natives out by 1757, which permitted increasingly intensive cultivation of the lowlands for cotton and, especially, rice. As enslaved workers cleared timber, leveled land, and constructed complex systems of drainage and irrigation canals, the rice culture of the prosperous Springfield and Vale Royal plantations became fully part of a transatlantic network of commerce.

By the early nineteenth century, however, city officials became increasingly concerned about apparent connections between the stagnant waters that filled rice fields and diseases such as malaria and yellow fever. Under the Dry Culture Act of 1817, the city required certain properties to not grow rice, offering landowners a modest payment in return. The planter Joseph Stiles retooled his plantations, operating a sawmill and a brick-manufacturing facility near the confluence of Musgrove Creek and the Savannah River. Meanwhile, the "canal fever" that had swept New York and other states soon came to Savannah; the Savannah, Ogeechee, and Altamaha Canal Company received its first charter in 1824. Soon, hundreds of slaves (generally leased from planters and investors who stood to profit from transportation improvements) cleared trees, dug the channel, cleared muck, and built the canal locks. In 1831, the canal connected the Savannah River with the Ogeechee, sixteen miles away. Enthusiasm for railroads soon followed: the Central of Georgia Railroad received its first charter in 1833. Once again, enslaved persons did much of the hard labor required to link Savannah with Macon, 190 miles away, building what was, at the time, one of the longest railroads in the world. Although the canal failed to make money at first, its fortunes rose again after 1836 as new investors used slave labor to construct new brick locks, turning basins, and a deeper channel, which conveniently connected the railroad yards with the Port of Savannah. Several new public slips gave hundreds of people from the hinterlands the opportunity to use the waterway for their commercial transactions. The Central of Georgia's site underwent a major expansion in the 1850s: an impressive roundhouse, passenger terminal, freight warehouses, and other buildings were constructed, and still stand. By the late antebellum period, the former Indian settlements and rice fields of the Oglethorpe Ward had been transformed into a vibrant metropolitan industrial corridor.

This intersection of the railroad, canal, and port lured several industries, including a tannery, a rice press, an iron foundry, at least two brickyards, and several mills that sawed raw lumber or worked it into finer pieces such as doors, sashes, shingles, and rice casks. Most of these industries relied upon slave labor: by 1850, the Central of Georgia owned 123 slaves; Robert Habersham's Upper Steam Rice Mill, 65; the Lachlison brothers' iron foundry, 16; and several other brick works and smaller sawmills, a few each. Tellingly, when the landowner William Stiles tried to sell his brickyard, he told potential buyers that his location served the interests of industrial slavery—slaves, he said, would be less "liable to get drunk or into the guardhouse or perhaps drowned" than more itinerant employees. In 1848, Stiles sold another portion of the Vale Royal Plantation to Williams Giles and Robert Bradley of Wilmington, North Carolina. They soon built a massive steam-powered lumber mill at the junction of Musgrove Creek, the canal, and the Savannah River. Newspaper boosters described this as a temple to timber, with massive columns reminiscent of cathedrals, and as the "noblest structure of the kind South of the Potomac." By 1857, creditors reported that Giles's reputation was as "good as gold," with the mill, slaves, and real estate valued at more than $100,000. Indeed, Giles's company owned 65 slaves, and he owned another 23 as an individual.

These developments sparked a population boom in the Savannah industrial neighborhoods. Soon, hundreds of people worked for the railroad, hundreds more in the industries, and hundreds more as the raftsmen, boatmen, teamsters, and draymen who carted goods along the land and water routes that connected the merchants of Savannah with the rest of the world. In contrast to southern coastal cities that had suffered depopulation, observers reported that new houses in Savannah were "rented before the walls are up" in the Oglethorpe Ward, the principal industrial neighborhood. The 1840 census shows this as the most populated and most diverse part of the city, with 999 whites (many of them recent immigrants), 281 free blacks, and 1,046 slaves living in an area where the boundaries among white, black, slave, and free were somewhat fluid. Most lived in densely packed wooden shanties, boardinghouses, and "double tenement negro houses," none of which resembled the large homes and verdant squares that characterized wealthier parts of the city.

The people who lived and worked in the industrial corridor faced innumerable challenges. Work was unsteady, and employers could discharge all or most of their free laborers whenever sales lagged. The enslaved faced different kinds of uncertainties, since they might be leased to other slaveholders, sold to pay off business debts, or moved to plantations hundreds of miles away. Owners often cared little about breaking up families. Work on locomotives and in the steam-powered factories was dangerous; deadly boiler explosions and other tragedies were not uncommon. Huge saw blades could hurl slabs of lumber that would kill a man instantly. Since no sturdy bridge connected some of the mills with the residential neighborhood, a number of slaves died by drowning in the canal or the Savannah River. Life in the neighborhood was hard for other reasons as well. City officials complained of the "most foul and unwholesome condition" of the place, where hogs and cattle ran unattended. The stench of manure, sewage, and cowhides being tanned added to the noxious environment. House fires and the burning of wood for industrial steam engines kept the area under a constant cloud of smoke. Prostitution was common, another activity where boundaries between the races were often blurred. Disputes over wages, card games, and unpaid bills often led to gunfire among local residents, travelers from the hinterlands, and sailors from around the world.

A dramatic episode occurred in the summer of 1861, when as many as fifteen slaves ran away from the Bradley and Giles lumber mill. Officials recaptured many of the escapees hiding among the district's sawmills and brickyards, but not before two men had apparently been murdered and hastily buried in the canal bank. A vigilante group called the Blue Cap Cavalry resolved to avenge these murders, finally capturing a runaway named Toney. After several days of struggle, they lynched Toney on July 17 at the Dean Forest Bridge over the canal. Savannah's newspapers downplayed the event and boasted instead of the city's successes in creating a vibrant industrial economy that produced and transported large quantities of lumber, bricks, cotton, and rice. Nevertheless, the slave-based economy of Savannah's antebellum industrial corridor was about to change.

MARK R. FINLAY

Bulky, heavy, and awkward to maneuver, cotton almost always made the last leg of its journey to northern and foreign mills by boat. National and international shipping soared along the Atlantic and Gulf Coasts as cotton swept the land. Yet cotton's effect on America's ports was not evenly distributed. Those that benefited the most were the ones with easy and direct access to the southern interior. Savannah was one of those fortunate port cities. Perched on the bank of a navigable river that drained both Georgia's and South Carolina's new cotton districts (areas that together produced 75 percent of the nation's crop in 1811), Savannah quickly gained prominence as an exporter of cotton, launching its first steamship to Liverpool in 1818.[5] First bags then bales of the staple soon crowded the city's wharves. Though production rose and fell according to the whims of international credit markets, the net trajectory of those piles of cotton was ever upward. In the decade before the Civil War, exports from Savannah came to surpass a half-million bales annually, and it was in those years that Savannah edged out Charleston as the leading Atlantic port for American cotton, making it third overall in the nation and behind only the commercial giants of Mobile and New Orleans.[6]

As eager farmers pushed ever farther into the southern interior, Savannah's merchants, factors, and shippers followed along in their wake, eager to trade their services for a share of cotton's profits. By the mid-1830s, cotton grown on central and west-central Georgia plantations had begun arriving in the city, much of it conveyed by water and wagon. The completion of the Central of Georgia Railroad to Macon in 1843 was followed in the 1850s by a flurry of railroad building that resulted in a thicket of trunk lines, feeder lines, and local connectors. Cotton grown as far away as western Alabama and middle Tennessee trundled into Savannah and onto waiting boats. By the eve of the Civil War, planters from as far away as Chattanooga, Tennessee, and Huntsville, Alabama, were sending their harvests to Savannah, where, according to one northern visitor, the city's depots and yards "groan[ed] constantly under the immense burden" of cotton.[7]

Cotton, however, does not move on its own. It needs human intervention, and in the antebellum South, the humans who most often intervened were slaves. African Americans moved hundreds of thousands of bales of cotton along the Savannah River and its tributaries, and in Savannah, the number of those all-important laborers jumped along with the expansion of cotton. The city's population of slaves more than doubled in the forty years before secession, leaping from scarcely more than 3,000 in 1820 to 7,700 in 1860.[8] Laboring on the city's wharves as well as on vessels such as the *Talamico*,

Table 3. Export of cotton from the Port of Savannah, 1800–1848

	Foreign		Coastwise		Total	
	Bags/bales	Pounds	Bags/bales	Pounds	Bags/bales	Pounds
1804	20,977	5,733,426	22,865	6,223,578	43,842	11,957,004
1825	64,906	23,366,160	72,789	26,204,040	137,695	49,570,200
1826	108,486	39,054,960	82,092	29,553,120	190,578	68,608,080
1839	—	—	—	—	199,176	71,703,360
1840	—	—	—	—	284,249	102,329,640
1841	—	—	—	—	147,280	53,020,800
1842	142,386	52,258,960	79,868	28,752,480	222,254	81,011,440
1843	193,099	69,515,640	87,727	31,581,720	280,826	101,097,360
1844	130,964	48,456,680	113,611	42,036,070	244,575	90,492,750
1845	182,073	69,187,740	122,471	46,538,980	304,544	115,726,720
1846	77,852	31,140,800	108,454	43,381,600	186,306	74,522,400
1847	119,321	50,114,820	114,830	48,228,600	234,151	98,343,420
1848	127,760	54,936,800	115,473	49,653,390	243,233	104,590,190

Note: Compiled by Luciana Spracher. For a complete list of the references used to compile this table, see the note on tables in this chapter's endnotes on pages 219–20. The statistics for 1804 represent the period January 1, 1803, through September 30, 1804, a period of one and a half years, rather than one year. Initially, cotton appeared in units referred to as *bags*, but the terminology switched to *bales*. Today, the U.S. standard for a bale of cotton is approximately 500 pounds. During the period examined, bags and bales weighed 300–450 pounds.

the *Columbia,* and the *John A. Moore*—all of which plied the Savannah River—slaves handled heavy cargoes of cotton and other goods; they served also as pilots, firemen, and mechanics as river traffic proliferated.[9] Slaves dominated the crews on the tugboats that maneuvered seagoing vessels between the city and the mouth of the Savannah. Thousands of enslaved southerners performed this type of work. Some, often women, worked aboard boats as domestics and cooks. Others piloted and paddled small craft and canoes. Aboard the larger vessels, slaves served as deckhands, firemen, and, occasionally, pilots, a group distinguished, according to one northern visitor to Savannah, by the broad-brimmed

Table 4. Export of cotton from the Port of Savannah, 1850–1860 (bales)

	Upland cotton			Sea Island cotton		
	Foreign	Coastwise	Total	Foreign	Coastwise	Total
1850	142,700	187,099	329,799	8,904	1,641	10,545
1851	145,150	160,642	305,792	8,497	3,145	11,642
1852	116,849	224,958	341,807	7,605	3,656	11,261
1853	135,691	193,352	328,953	6,767	6,577	13,344
1854	98,580	203,363	301,943	3,861	11,667	15,528
1855	178,194	195,714	373,908	6,993	7,474	14,467
1856	177,182	200,426	377,608	8,138	7,346	15,484
1857	152,228	158,791	311,019	6,611	10,028	16,639
1858	159,141	117,680	276,821	8,561	7,447	16,008
1859	253,743	198,523	452,266	8,298	8,489	16,787
1860	331,159	190,137	522,096	6,596	18,245	24,941

Note: Compiled by Luciana Spracher. For a complete list of the references used to compile this table, see the note on tables in this chapter's endnotes on pages 219–20.

black hats that they wore.[10] So popular were slaves as crew members that a number of ships' captains preferred no one else. As the commander of a Charleston-based steamer admitted to a visitor, it was more economical to hire an Irishman, but easier to control a slave. He could beat a slave into submission, but if an "Irishman misbehave[d]," his only recourse was to send him ashore.[11]

Though the population of slave watermen grew as cotton cultivation spread, they were vastly outnumbered by the legions of men (and they were almost exclusively men) who drove slaveholders' wagons. Overlooked and understudied, teamsters, cart men, and those who prodded slow-moving oxen embodied, according to one of their few historians, the commercial character of the antebellum South.[12] They also stood—or moved—at the heart of cotton's overland traffic. Enslaved teamsters delivered loads of freshly ginned cotton from their owners' plantations to riverside quays and local merchants. As railroads stretched into the countryside, enslaved teamsters brought cotton to newly constructed depots. But because there were never railroads enough to carry every bale every step of the way from plantation to port, enslaved teamsters remained on the roads up to and through secession, and often in great numbers. In Savannah, a pair of merchants declared that easily 2,000–2,500 wagons rolled into the city each year, particularly in late winter and "principally from the distance of 100 miles."[13] It was a traffic that showed no signs of slowing even as the nation began to splinter apart.[14]

The growth of Savannah's involvement in the cotton trade did not come at the expense of other facets of the city's commercial life. Indeed, Savannah's emergence as the nation's leading Atlantic port in the South helped intensify older colonial economies. Thus, even as some slaves carried enormous loads of cotton out of the hinterlands and onto the ships that congregated along the city's riverfront, others continued to produce, process, and deliver to market large and profitable cargoes of rice, pine lumber, shingles, and oak staves as well as what one city mayor dubbed "sundries": the wheat, flour, wool, hides, pelts, copper ore, tallow, and beeswax that flowed into town from as far away as the mountains of Tennessee.[15] These were not unimportant commodities. Exports in timber alone more than doubled between 1843 and 1848, jumping from 8 million to 16.5 million board feet, much of it rafted into Savannah along the slave-made Ogeechee Canal and then eagerly bought by northern and foreign ship makers.[16]

Mobile and hard-working slaves were unquestionably the muscle and machinery behind the city's exuberantly growing market economy, but the services enslaved people rendered did not stop there. As had been the case in the colonial era, black women and men performed myriad nonagricultural services. Hundreds of slaves were sent from the city by their owners, for instance, to make up the crews who built all the railway lines and canals that served as arteries of commerce.[17] Others spent their days working within the city: running their owners' errands, scrubbing laundry, tending gardens, and, if on the diminutive side, cleaning Savannah's chimneys. While enslaved in Savannah, William Grimes worked as a horse groom, coachman, and field hand on nearby plantations.[18] Slaves also continued in their long-standing role as urban entrepreneurs, underwriting the city's survival through their domination of the local trade in vegetables, fruit, eggs, poultry, and meat. Some of these hucksters lived within the city limits. Others commuted from outlying villages and plantations. A northern visitor named Emily Burke claimed to have "known women to come one hundred miles to sell the products of their own industry."[19] Still other slaves frequented the city's bustling market as customers sent by slaveholders too busy to buy for themselves. One of the Savannah River's most prominent

Table 5. Export of rice from the Port of Savannah, 1800–1860

	Foreign	Coastwise	Total
1804	7,059 tierces	5,138 tierces	12,197 tierces
1825	2,154 tierces	5,081 tierces	7,231 tierces
1826	4,978 tierces	6,477 tierces	11,455 tierces
1839	—	—	21,332 tierces
1840	—	—	24,392 tierces
1841	—	—	23,587 tierces
1842	5,933 tierces	16,131 tierces	22,064 tierces
1843	10,675 tierces	15,606 tierces	26,281 tierces
1844	10,307 tierces	18,236 tierces	28,543 tierces
1845	11,712 tierces	17,505 tierces	29,217 tierces
1846	5,025 tierces	27,122 tierces	32,147 tierces
1847	10,218 tierces	21,521 tierces	31,739 tierces
1848	7,987 tierces	22,149 tierces	30,136 tierces
1850	11,042 tierces	30,434 tierces	41,476 tierces
1851	7,496 casks	28,106 casks	35,602 casks
1852	9,937 casks	29,992 casks	39,929 casks
1853	5,646 tierces	21,270 tierces	26,916 tierces
1854	7,654 casks	23,094 casks	30,748 casks
1855	5,149 casks	3,071 casks	8,220 casks
1856	7,880 casks	22,027 casks	29,907 casks
1857	6,787 casks	20,749 casks	27,536 casks
1858	7,284 casks	24,061 casks	31,345 casks
1859	6,836 casks	31,294 casks	38,130 casks
1860	6,639 tierces	28,949 tierces	35,588 tierces

Note: Compiled by Luciana Spracher. For a complete list of the references used to compile this table, see the note on tables in this chapter's endnotes on pages 219–20. The statistics for 1804 represent the period January 1, 1803, through September 30, 1804, a period of one and a half years, rather than one year. Rice exports were measured in tierces or casks—terms sometimes used interchangeably. A tierce equals a cask containing forty-two gallons. But casks came in different sizes. So the statistics provided in this table indicate specifically whether the rice exports were measured in tierces or casks.

Table 6. Export of lumber and timber from the Port of Savannah, 1800–1860 (board feet)

	Foreign	Coastwise	Total
1804	2,558,908	523,811	3,082,719
1841	—	—	14,295,200
1842	5,919,400	2,471,000	8,390,400
1843	5,532,750	1,986,000	7,518,750
1844	3,034,064	2,899,187	5,933,251
1845	3,333,646	4,936,936	8,270,582
1846	13,365,968	5,219,676	18,585,644
1847	4,886,425	5,197,024	10,083,449
1848	7,626,615	8,822,943	16,449,558
1850	9,405,281	8,326,383	17,731,664
1851	9,099,700	8,664,600	17,764,300
1852	15,804,500	9,704,000	25,508,500
1853	17,104,808	12,674,157	29,778,965
1854	27,353,600	22,502,100	49,855,700
1855	19,004,308	6,495,692	25,500,000
1856	21,500,000	13,387,500	34,887,500
1857	36,752,502	7,990,568	44,743,070
1858	19,611,391	8,754,265	28,365,656
1859	29,384,315	9,543,669	39,928,084
1860	25,175,046	11,478,952	36,653,998

Note: Compiled by Luciana Spracher. For a complete list of the references used to compile this table, see the note on tables in this chapter's endnotes on pages 219–20. The statistics for 1804 represent the period January 1, 1803, through September 30, 1804, a period of one and a half years, rather than one year.

Table 7. Total value of exports (foreign and coastwise) from the Port of Savannah, 1800–1860 ($)

1800	2,155,982
1801	3,008,508
1802	3,273,892
1803	3,877,652
1818	14,183,113
1821	6,032,862
1854	17,881,806
1855	20,129,230
1856	22,027,500
1857	22,500,000
1860	17,798,922 (foreign only)

Note: Compiled by Luciana Spracher. For a complete list of the references used to compile this table, see the note on tables in this chapter's endnotes on pages 219–20.

Enslaved Women in the Savannah Marketplace

The workforce at the bustling Savannah port transported and received cargo from all over the world. A large percentage of the vessels that anchored in the harbor were from West Africa, the Caribbean, and England. City merchants exported cash crops such as cotton and rice and imported enslaved people to sustain the production of these items. The involuntary African workers who arrived on these ships brought more than just their labor to Georgia; they also carried with them marketing customs that influenced how local trade was conducted.

Most of the petty traders on Savannah's city streets were women, and many of them were enslaved. Initially, certain bondwomen were granted special permission by their owners to sell surplus vegetables from their home plantations. Enslaved vendors soon became integral to supplying fresh food to the city. By 1775, these women had moved beyond just selling their masters' products and began trading on their own. Laws were regularly passed to restrict enslaved women's participation in the marketplace, but the statutes were either difficult to enforce or frequently ignored. Around the Savannah docks, enslaved female traders fashioned a market atmosphere that was more West African than European. They used their knowledge of traditional marketing techniques to establish connections with plantations and to collude on prices; further, they

employed shrewd business practices to earn cash for themselves and their families.

Under the task system in place in Georgia's coastal rice country, bonded laborers on large estates were encouraged to grow corn, yams, and gourds and to keep hogs, chickens, and cows. The arrangement allowed planters to minimize contributions to their bondpeople's food allotments. Slaveholders had mixed responses to the exchange of enslaved-grown foodstuffs for other items, including cash. The trade in goods created an informal economy that transcended racial lines and plantation boundaries, often contravening laws that limited the involvement of enslaved people, especially women, in the marketplace. In some years, city statutes forbade all bondpeople from participating in the market; in other years, participation was allowed with the proper license or ticket. Multiple restrictions were repeatedly imposed on female market sellers by state and local legislatures, but the mobile mass of women and the large quantity of provisions that they brought in from the surrounding plantations made enforcement of the changing laws nearly impossible for underpaid market clerks.

Enslaved women were not allowed to butcher meat, bake bread, or catch fish except shellfish, which they could sell alongside cooked meat, cakes, nuts, sweetgrass baskets, fresh produce from the plantations, and other snacks. Some rural slaveholders allowed their bonded workers to walk, ride, or canoe up to twenty miles one way on Sundays, an accustomed free day, to sell garden surpluses at marketplaces in Savannah. The proceeds provided plantation workers with the money necessary to supplement the meager clothing, blanket, and shoe allotments they received once a year.

In an adaptation of West African customs, female vendors met their suppliers along specific routes close to the city and purchased the plantation goods before they reached the market. Usually, buyers and sellers had done business previously, and their connections were often predicated on some form of kinship network. Bondwomen were able to use this strategy to appropriate particular goods, like yams or corn, in order to drive up the price in the marketplace. Because of the frequency of this practice, local laws against collusion became unenforceable. Besides providing material benefits, links between buyers and sellers allowed enslaved family members to visit or to pass information, even if only for a few moments during a marketing transaction.

Enslaved female vendors based in Savannah could maintain even more autonomy, developing business relationships with people other than their enslavers and even living outside their masters' realm. A large percentage of skilled enslaved urban workers, including carpenters, mechanics, stevedores, and market women, resided in their own shacks or rented rooms throughout the city. If these laborers paid their owners a stipulated sum each week, month, or year, they could pocket any other profits. With the cash they earned, bondwomen paid rent, bought food for their families, acquired fashionable dresses, and occasionally purchased freedom for themselves or their loved ones. In the marketplace, social status was ambiguous, and bondwomen who could buy cheap and sell high were as successful as their free counterparts. In this way, enslaved women in and around Savannah utilized customary African skills in the local market to gain a modicum of freedom and to establish themselves as an integral part of the urban economy.

ALISHA M. CROMWELL

rice planters, Charles Manigault, reserved a boat and boatmen for the express purpose of making weekly trips downriver from Argyll Island to fetch provisions from Savannah's grocers.[20]

The spread of cotton vastly expanded the geographic range of slaves' working lives, yet perhaps surprisingly, it was female domestic servants whose labor often carried them the farthest from home. To be sure, slaveholders had traveled with their cooks, nurses, and personal attendants in tow since the earliest days of American slavery. Thomas Jefferson, after all, had taken Sally Hemings and her brother with him to Paris.[21] As cotton dramatically expanded Savannah's sphere of influence, increasing numbers of slaveholders took to the road with their servants—for example, the manufacturer and planter Richard J. Arnold shuttled every year between his rice estate on Savannah's outskirts and Rhode Island, to tend his investments.[22] Others traveled to northern and foreign locations to visit resorts, shop for luxury goods, reconnect with relatives, or install children in college.[23] Slaveholders of means rarely made these journeys unaccompanied by one or more slaves, and according to one Savannah native, a white woman was especially unlikely to travel abroad "without her colored maid."[24] Personal attendants thus became, through their work, slavery's chief ambassadors to free-labor states.[25]

America's quest for cotton and the profits it promised meant that nearly all the nation's slaves came to live their lives in motion. This mobility often came at a high price. The domestic trade in slaves was well known to break apart slave families. This commerce preyed hard on young women and men (the age range prized most highly by planters), displacing nearly a million people between 1820 and 1860. It shattered marriages, splintered long-standing communities, and orphaned hundreds of thousands of black children, among them William Grimes, who, before arriving in Savannah, had been sold away from his mother as a ten-year-old.[26] But selling slaves away from their families was not the only way in which owners separated their laborers from loved ones. Slave hire was especially damaging to black people's social and domestic lives. By the late antebellum era, slaves were three to five (or more) times as likely to be hired away as to be sold away.[27] It was a practice that separated hundreds of thousands of husbands and wives, parents and children, friends and neighbors—sometimes for years at a time, sometimes for the rest of their lives. But even the simple act of transporting a housekeeper, dressmaker, or favorite valet to New York, Boston, Philadelphia, or even the California goldfields, where slaveholding forty-niners put their slaves to work panning for ore, could open up heartbreaking

M.S. Woodhull Master of the S. Ship called the Augusta of New York and The Owners or Shippers of the within specified Slaves, do solemnly swear, to the best of our knowledge and belief, that the Slaves herein described, were not imported or brought into the United States, from and after the first day of January, one thousand eight hundred and eight, and that under the laws of this State, they are held to service or labor.

Sworn to, this 28ᵗʰ day of July 186 0

Before

R S Arnold

G. W. M Commiss

H Knapp agt

Th. S. Wroahall

W. T Goodwin

Dep. COLLECTOR.

DISTRICT AND PORT OF SAVANNAH.

M S Woodhull Master of the S Ship Augusta having sworn as the law directs, to the within Manifest, consisting of Three Slaves

and delivered duplicates thereof, permission is hereby granted to the said S Ship to proceed to the port of New York in the State of New York

Given under our hands, at Savannah, the 28ᵗʰ day of July 186 0

W. T Goodwin

Dep. COLLECTOR.

B Hamilton

NAVAL OFFICER.

This manifest from the steamship Augusta lists Agnes, Nancy, and Ann as enslaved passengers on a voyage from Savannah, Georgia, to New York City. Slave manifest, S. Ship Augusta, M.S. Woodhull, Master, 28 July 1860, *File II—Subjects, Negroes*, RG 4-2-46, Georgia State Archives.

distances between enslaved laborers and those they loved best. One slaveholder inadvertently revealed the depth of that hurt in a postscript he scrawled at the bottom of a letter sent to his beloved and distant sister. "John sends howdy to all and wants some of them to write him," R. M. Dickson wrote of a slave he carried along to help him pan for gold on the western slope of the Sierra Nevada; "all the negros get letters from home but him."[28]

Yet despite the crushingly high social and emotional price that staple production and other forms of labor exacted of slaves, master-commanded movement provided slaves with some surprising advantages. Travel, after all, presents those in motion with myriad social and affective possibilities. Public roads and public spaces are not empty places. Caught up in a traffic that made a mockery of slaveholders' figurative, literal, and legislative attempts to quarantine slaves from outside influences, slaves on the move invariably came into contact with the rich diversity of American society. Not unlike the free people among whom they lived and labored, slaves traveled among what one observer described as a "heterogeneous comminglement" of all the people of the civilized world.[29] With the exception of the South's largest cities, few locations could match the polyglot and multicultural character of antebellum Savannah. A transportation hub fed by a growing network of roads and railroads, as well as an important Atlantic port, Savannah played host to people from around the globe. It was nothing out of the ordinary to see vessels from as far away as Glasgow, Hamburg, and Marseille tied up at the city's wharves.[30] As a consequence, antebellum Savannah's streets teemed with people of all classes, ages, races, and nations. So well known was the city's waterfront district for its multilingual and multicultural crowds that the more fastidious visitors and citizens knew to keep their distance. Emily Burke described Savannah's Bay Street as "always so thronged by sailors, slaves, and rowdies of all grades and color, that it is not safe for ladies to walk," whether they traveled in large groups or even in the company of men.[31]

Thus, in doing their owners' bidding—whether rolling over the roads in a wagon or guiding a boat along a southern river—Savannah's slaves found the means to restore what the cotton revolution had so badly disrupted. Strangers became friends; friends became families; families grew to include babies; and new communities grew up in place of those lost to slaveholders' machinations. These ongoing processes often took new forms for having emerged on new ground and under new sets of circumstances. In the wake of the cotton revolution, youthful families emerged, composed of the working-age young

Richard Richardson, the Owens-Thomas House, and the Slave Trade in Savannah

Ship manifest of the schooner Emigrant, *listing enslaved people sent by Richard Richardson from Savannah to Pensacola and New Orleans, probably for sale in those ports. National Archives and Records Administration—Southeast Region (Atlanta)* (NRCAA), *Morrow, Georgia; Coastwise Slave Manifests, 1801–1860; Record Group: 36, Records of the U.S. Customs Service;* ARC *Identifier: 1151775.*

Savannah began to prosper as Georgia's main industrial and trade center in the early nineteenth century, and many of its prominent citizens benefited financially from slave-produced goods and the interstate slave trade. The city was home to commission merchants, factors, agents, and other general businessmen who were the states' wealthiest slave owners and traders. Richard Richardson, the owner of the merchant firm Richard Richardson and Company and president of the Savannah branch of the Second Bank of the United States, became one of the city's wealthiest and most prominent citizens. In addition to marketing plantation staple crops, his firm sold slaves.

Richard Richardson was born on the island of Bermuda on November 5, 1785, and settled in Savannah as a young man. During the early nineteenth century, he began buying slaves for personal and domestic purposes. In 1811, he married Frances Lewis Bolton, and their marriage produced six children. In 1816, Richardson commissioned the English architect William Jay to construct a new residence for his family. The Richardson House (later renamed the Owens-Thomas House) was

59

completed in 1819; it represented one of the finest examples of English Regency architecture in the United States. Shortly after the construction of his house, Richardson's involvement in the domestic slave trade increased. From 1821 to 1834, his firm shipped slaves from Savannah to New Orleans, employing five principal ships: *Ariel, Orion, Robert Fulton, Susan*, and *Emigrant*.

Although Congress had abolished the slave trade from Africa on January 1, 1808, an active interstate slave trade remained. Richardson's firm became involved in this trade. Rapid expansion by settlers into Florida and the southwestern frontier of Louisiana, Mississippi, and Alabama created new markets for slavery. As a result, the coastal and waterway slave trade in the United States increased in the half decade following the War of 1812. Slave-trading vessels owned by Richardson's firm shipped slaves, along with cotton, rice, and other commodities, via both the coastal trade to southern ports along the Atlantic and the trade along the Gulf Coast and the Mississippi. For example, Richardson's firm sold slaves from Savannah directly to Pensacola and New Orleans—the largest slave-trading port in the South—during the 1820s, which represented the most active period for the firm. In 1821, the firm consigned 150 slaves from Savannah to New Orleans on the schooner *Emigrant*.

Although the 1820s were the most active period for Richardson's firm, a weakening economy during that decade led to severe financial losses. In addition, his wife, Frances, died in 1822. That year, Richardson liquidated many assets, including his house, which became the property of the Bank of the United States and was leased to Mary Maxwell from 1822 to 1830, who used it as a boardinghouse. Richardson's firm continued to trade in slaves and plantation staples; the profits allowed him a measure of economic comfort until his death in 1833.

KAREN COOK BELL

Torn Asunder

Savannah's "Weepin' Time" Slave Sale of 1859

On March 2 and 3, 1859, at the Ten Broeck race-course, two and a half miles west of Savannah, a Philadelphian named Pierce Mease Butler authorized the sale of 429 enslaved persons at the largest single slave sale recorded in American history, which became known as the "Weepin' Time." The slaves came from his 1,500-acre Butler Island rice plantation, near Darien, about fifty miles south of Savannah in McIntosh County; and his nearby 1,700-acre cotton plantation on St. Simons Island, Glynn County. Pierce Butler (1810–1867) and his brother John inherited the plantations from their maternal grandfather, Major Pierce Butler (1744–1822), a signatory to the U.S. Constitution who had started the plantations in the 1790s. John Butler died in 1847, and his widow, Gabriella, became co-owner, with Pierce, of the plantations and the enslaved people. Pierce gambled away his portion of the substantial monies left to the brothers by their grandfather, and lost more money in the stock market panic of 1857. In debt, he had the 919 Butler Island slaves appraised and divided between him and Gabriella. Pierce engaged the Savannah slave broker Joseph Bryan to sell the 443 slaves allotted to him.

Initially, Bryan advertised that the sale would occur at Savannah's Johnson Square, where he had his slave pens and brokerage business, but he ultimately decided that the enslaved would be inspected and sold at a larger venue, the Ten Broeck racecourse, which would be more likely to accommodate the expected crowd of slave purchasers. The racecourse, where the Savannah Jockey Club held races, had been in use since the 1790s, and early deeds termed it the Oglethorpe or Jencks track. It was later named for Richard Ten Broeck (1812–1892), of Albany, New York, a well-known horse-racing promoter. Ads for the slave sale ran daily, except Sundays, in the *Savannah Republican* and the *Savannah*

FOR SALE.
LONG COTTON AND RICE NEGROES.

A GANG OF 460 NEGROES, accustomed to the culture of Rice and Provisions; among whom are a number of good mechanics, and house servants. Will be sold on the 2d and 3d of March next, at Savannah, by JOSEPH BRYAN.

TERMS OF SALE.—One-third cash; remainder by bond, bearing interest from day of sale, payable in two equal annual instalments, to be secured by mortgage on the negroes, and approved personal security, or for approved city acceptance on Savannah or Charleston. Purchasers paying for papers.

The Negroes will be sold in families, and can be seen on the premises of JOSEPH BRYAN, in Savannah, three days prior to the day of sale, when catalogues will be furnished.

⁎ The Charleston Courier, (daily and tri-weekly;) Christian Index, Macon, Ga.; Albany Patriot, Augusta Constitutionalist, Mobile Register, New Orleans Picayune, Memphis Appeal, and Vicksburg Southron, will publish till day of sale and send bills to this office.

feb 8   td

Joseph Bryan's initial advertisement for Pierce Mease Butler's sale of slaves, Savannah Republican, February 8, 1859.

Morning News, from February 8 until the sale ended. The sale generated interest throughout the United States. In 1859, the country was polarized over slavery. The *New York Tribune* dispatched its star reporter, William Mortimer Thomson, alias "Doesticks," to Savannah to observe the sale. His eyewitness account, published in the newspaper's March 9 issue, is the most complete description of the sale.

Some slaves to be sold were brought to Savannah from McIntosh and Glynn Counties by steamboat, others by train. The last group arrived on Friday, February 25, five days before the sale. They were housed in the racecourse's stables, with no beds or tables, and ate and slept on the floor. From February 26 through Tuesday, March 1, the slaves were inspected by buyers, who poked, pinched, and fondled them, inspected their teeth, and searched for "ruptures" or defects on their bodies that might affect their productivity. Two hundred–odd "Negro speculators" came from Virginia, North and South Carolina, Georgia, Alabama, and Louisiana.

On March 2 and 3, the enslaved were taken to a room underneath the racecourse's grandstand, where the sale took place. For those two days, ominous, brooding clouds burst out in torrential rains. Though the heavens seemingly wept, Thomson states that few of the enslaved cried. The enslaved and their descendants called the event the "Weepin' Time" for the sorrow that, even if held in check, they

undoubtedly experienced. Thomson mentions that the faces of many of the enslaved expressed their anguish, though some were nonchalant, sales being a familiar part of the enslaved experience.

Four hundred and thirty-six persons were advertised in the sale catalogue, but only 429 ultimately were sold. Margaret, number 139 in the catalogue, gave birth on February 16, and she, Dr. George, and their four children, including the baby, though advertised, escaped being sold, likely because of illness. And the word "Withdrawn" appears adjacent to the name of nine-year-old Sally, number 358 in the catalogue, and thus she was not sold. The majority of those sold were rice and cotton fieldworkers; some were skilled coopers, carpenters, shoemakers, and blacksmiths. Buyers were required to bid on whole families, so prices were equalized among family members. The first family sold was that of George and Sue, with their sons, George and Harry, for a total of $2,480, or $620 each. The oldest person sold was Ned, fifty-six, a "Cotton hand," sold along with Sena, his fifty-year-old wife, "Cotton—cook," for $485 each. Many children were sold, including thirty babies—the youngest only fifteen days old. Although the enslaved were sold in nuclear families, parents were sold away from their adult children, and extended families were "torn asunder," according to Doesticks. Desperate lovers and betrothed couples implored their new owners to purchase their loved ones, to no avail, and went to different areas of the South, many never to see each other again.

Pierce Butler, present at the sale, shook hands with some of the people he was selling off, albeit condescendingly, with "his gloved hand." After the sale, which netted him $303,850, Butler gave each of the 429 persons sold a silver dollar. Bryan popped open bottles of champagne, and while he, Butler, and the buyers celebrated, the enslaved said farewells to one another with heavy hearts. These Africans and African Americans—multiple generations of whom had been forced to labor, unrecompensed, for the profit of multiple generations of the Butler family—had been callously sold at the caprice of Butler and Bryan. Significantly, however, the sale, publicized by the *Tribune* and other northern newspapers, further polarized North and South on the eve of the Civil War. Thus, the tragic "Weepin' Time" slave sale became, ironically, an important catalyst for the war that led to the emancipation of all the enslaved in the United States. The tears sown at Ten Broeck ultimately nourished a river of freedom for all Americans.

KWESI DEGRAFT-HANSON

adults that most antebellum Deep South slaveholders favored, as did differently configured families. These new domestic groups frequently included people not necessarily related to one another by blood or marriage, but brought together instead as a slaveholder's solution to a practical problem. Planters might, for example, designate proxy parents for orphaned slave children or assign newly arrived adults to already-occupied cabins, a practice that compelled strangers to negotiate safe and efficient ways to relate with one another in their new surroundings.[32] There was no way to predict the results of such forced cohabitation. On arriving in Savannah with his new owner, the Virginia-born William Grimes, for instance, found himself living in the company of an elderly female slave who, he was convinced, was a shape-changing witch. "I slept in the same room with her under the kitchen," Grimes later recounted. "My blankets were on the floor. She had a straw bed . . . about four paces from mine." Grimes had not been in Savannah long before the woman's evil presence began to interrupt his nights. Coming at him in the dark, she would "hag ride" her young roommate, sitting on the sleeping boy's chest, choking him, and rendering him speechless. When reporting these incidents to his new master gave Grimes no relief (the slaveholder thought the boy was making up stories), Grimes took to sleeping on a corner of the old woman's bed. "I thought she would not dare to ride me on her own bed," he later explained.[33] Not every slave experienced a similarly dysfunctional "family" life. But even voluntary unions between slaves could be influenced by market imperatives. Thus, when Richard Arnold's slave Amos sought permission to marry a woman named Mary, he urged Arnold to buy her, hoping to improve the odds that the couple could stay together. To increase the probability that Arnold would purchase Mary, Amos assured his master that he would not lose in the exchange. "She is a good house made and a very good seamstress," Amos explained of the woman he would go on to wed.[34]

Whether trapped in Grimes's surreal existence or embedded in a loving marriage of the sort that Amos and Mary evidentially made and sustained, slaves trying to reassemble their lives in the wake of cotton's revolution required a shared language and a shared inclination to talk. America's antebellum slaves had both, and talk they did as they moved in, around, and out of Savannah in the years leading up to the Civil War. Forming what is popularly known as the "grapevine telegraph," America's slaves were not at all bashful about talking to those they met—whether free or slave, stranger or acquaintance—as they bumped along on a wagon, floated downriver on a boat, or ran errands through the streets of Savannah. They shared information with each other about their pasts, where they had come from, where they were going, and any acquaintances they might have in common. Slaves used the opportunities presented by travel to expand their geo-social literacy: memorizing the lay of the land, its roads, its villages, and, above all, the people who inhabited it. "Hal knows every inch of the road," noted one slaveholder when requesting that the slave be ordered to make a 180-mile overland trip on foot and on his own.[35] The more important that Savannah became as a commercial hub, the more information that slaves had to convey. Ships, after all, included more than the goods stored in their holds. They carried news, a commodity often carried ashore by their crews. It was precisely by means of a sailor that John Brown, a slave in the middle part of Georgia, came to know about international trade, Demerara (in present-day Guyana), Liverpool, and Liverpool's population of young "lasses." Brown's confidant was a West Indian seafarer who, on docking at Savannah, had been snatched up and sold into slavery, an act that enabled him to share what he knew with those he met on his new master's plantation.[36]

A large part of what slaves learned about their world involved politics. Debates between free people had always been of interest to the enslaved, but as an accelerating staple economy put an even larger part of the South's bound workers in motion, and as sectional tensions intensified, the slaves' telegraph hummed with political news. Along open roads, under cover of darkness, at remote laborers' camps, on the decks of steamboats, in mill yards, on factory floors, and in the dank interiors of both public and private jails, America's slaves overheard, embellished on, and passed along all manner of knowledge that their owners would consider subversive.[37] In conversations that an enslaved teamster assured Frederick Law Olmsted were not all extraordinary ("dats all dey talk, master—dat's all, sir"), America's bound black workers schooled themselves on local and global affairs.[38] They spoke about Haiti, the only New World nation in which black people reigned. They spoke about the groundswell of antislavery activity in England, the rest of Europe, and New England. They talked about geography and about how a person might safely pass out of the slaveholding states. They talked about whom slaves could trust, and whom they ought not to. William Robinson's father, a boatman, learned about abolitionist activity in Canada while conveying travelers by water. Later, Robinson senior assumed the role of teacher and passed along to his son information about California, a state in which the father spent the late 1850s as an enslaved laborer on a surveying crew.[39] Slaves who could read—like the William Henry Harrison supporter whom Emily Burke encountered during her stay in Savannah—eagerly consumed every newspaper or pamphlet that came within their reach and then shared what they had learned with trusted family and friends.[40] Through such means, the slaves kept "well up on the politicks of those days the Democratice Partie the Whigg partie the no nothing partie the nulifires and the anteno nothing parties," one black Georgian later explained as he reeled off details with a confidence that eludes many Americans to this day.[41]

Slaves did not always stop at talk. When circumstances permitted, they were quick to use what they had heard or learned to redress some of slavery's wrongs. Savannah, with its growing population and commercial network, lent itself to enslaved people's efforts to deflect or escape slavery's brutal impositions. Runaways found the city especially inviting. The ships that visited Savannah's harbor sometimes opened portals to freedom, and the streets, with their teeming populations, offered near-instant anonymity to those who wanted to vanish from a slave owner's sight. Many of the slaves who sought refuge in Savannah came from nearby areas: down the river from upcountry estates or, like a slave named Rafe, from one of the surrounding plantation districts.[42] As seen in the advertisements published regularly by aggrieved owners in Savannah newspapers, it was not at all uncommon for fugitives to travel much longer distances. Take, for example, Ellen and William Craft of Macon, Georgia. Testifying to the breadth and depth of slaves'

William Craft.

knowledge—about slaveholders' habit of carrying personal servants along on their travels, about a thickening system of rail and steamboat transportation, and above all about the opportunities that beckoned from Georgia's largest seaport—the Crafts (who were husband and wife) disguised themselves as master and slave and boarded a train for Savannah on what turned out to be the first leg of their journey to freedom.[43]

As the slave Rafe discovered, not every fugitive who sought shelter in Savannah met with success. A fugitive from Liberty County, Rafe was captured in Savannah and sent back to stand trial for the murder of his owner. But even if recaptured and sent back into bondage, black women and men carried with them memories and experiences they could pass on to slaves deep in the southern interior. This process helps explain the uproar that erupted when, in December 1829, Savannah authorities seized sixty copies of *An Appeal to the Colored Citizens of the World*, by a black resident of Boston named David Walker. Considered one of the most radical political documents of the age, the pamphlet, which arrived in Savannah in the hands of a white sailor, galvanized white southerners, who moved swiftly to quarantine their slaves from Walker's call for rebellion. Within a matter of months, Georgia legislators passed a flurry of laws meant to curtail contact between slaves and their antislavery allies, to forbid the education of slaves, to limit the ability of slaves to congregate together without white supervision, and, in recognition of the key role Savannah played in slaves' lives, to quarantine all black sailors who entered the state's ports.[44]

Despite such draconian measures, slaveholders could not silence their slaves nor quiet their minds. Not only did Walker's vehement critique of slavery reverberate across the slaveholding South, but slaves continued to turn the contacts and conversations that came their way through work—as shipboard crew members, as teamsters, as ladies' maids, and as laborers on their way to new homes and new owners—into the means to deflect some of slavery's most egregious abuses. Along the path of one of the South's many new railways, enslaved laborers who had started their work as strangers but had eventually become acquaintances and perhaps even friends conspired to deceive their owners into thinking they had been misused by the contractor, in hopes of convincing their owners they would be better off working closer to home.[45] Before the oft-sold and well-traveled William Webb translated his hard-won knowledge into personal freedom, he and a party of slaves emphatically established what they saw as the boundary of slaveholders' power. As Webb later remarked of a plan that involved vines and a road known to be popular with the local patrol, a plan that, when put into effect, knocked horses to their knees and sent riders flying, he and his friends had helped adjust the local dynamics of power in black people's favor by convincing their owners that "it was bad policy to go riding about" in search of slaves after dark.[46]

Slaveholders were not oblivious of what slaves were doing. As antislavery forces at home and abroad attracted more followers, and as the circulation of slaves picked up speed, slaveholders grew increasingly uneasy about their ability to manage, channel, and control slaves' conversations. Mary Chesnut later only half-jestingly likened her husband's well-traveled enslaved valet of this period to a fictional international spy.[47] William Capers, an overseer working for Charles Manigault, was not jesting at all when in 1859 he angrily described his enslaved teamsters as the "Tackeys among us," an unsubtle reference to an eighteenth-century Jamaican slave rebel.[48] Chesnut and Capers were not alone in their misgivings. The growth of slaveholders' anxieties across the South could be measured by a debate in the late 1850s about reopening the transatlantic slave trade. Although slaveholders publicly touted the initiative as a way to secure slavery's future by making slaves more widely affordable, privately they saw the measure as a way to fend off domestic disaster. By bringing in quantities of "saltwater slaves," who did not speak the same language, never mind English, proponents of the measure hoped to diffuse an increasingly tense situation by diluting the South's increasingly restless, native-born, English-speaking laboring population. As one advocate waxed enthusiastically, newly arrived slaves such as the people who staggered ashore when the *Wanderer* disgorged its involuntary passengers on Jekyll Island in 1858 were so "good-humored & contented" that they made the use of chains obsolete.[49] On Savannah's hinterland plantations, slaveholders encouraged white clergymen to minister to slave communities, hoping to instill in their laborers an increased "affection and confidence."[50] Many more simply launched what Walter J. Fraser Jr. has described as a campaign of repression: reducing slaves' ability to maneuver by removing free people of color from the state, forming vigilance committees, goading patrols to greater activity, and restricting slaves' ability to hire themselves out.[51] The ultimate response came in the wake of Abraham Lincoln's election, when Deep South slaveholders came to the conclusion that the only way they could retain control over the laborers on whom their livelihoods rested was to quarantine their slaves in a separate nation.

As one of the main ports through which cotton flowed, and as the largest such port on the eastern seaboard, Savannah, along with the enslaved women and men who lived there, could not escape the changes wrought by cotton's rise. Enmeshed in a vast commercial and productive network that stretched from the deep interior of America to the manufacturing capitals of Europe, the city and its enslaved laborers were as much a part of an unfolding revolution as were planters, plantations, and plantation slaves. The fluidity of the system required the movement of people between urban and rural, making it impossible to draw a clear line between those who served Savannah's interests and those who served planters'. Families, friendships, work, and resistance all took shape within that system. Thus, to tell the story of cotton's rise is, in many respects, to tell the story of slavery in antebellum Savannah.

To "Venerate the Spot" of "Airy Visions"
Slavery and the Romantic Conception of Place in Mary Telfair's Savannah

Jeffrey Robert Young

In the summer of 1828, Mary Telfair experienced "a circumstance of a most unpleasant nature." Heading homeward by carriage through the streets of Savannah after a visit with friends, Telfair and her brother Alexander looked into the evening's "fine moonlight" and saw, to their horror, that their coachman was no longer in his seat. "In a state of intoxication," the aged slave had toppled out of the carriage, leaving the Telfairs helplessly trapped inside the moving vehicle. No one was holding the reins of the horses, and these elite slaveholders were careering out of control through the city streets. While Alexander ineffectually attempted to bring the horses to a halt through vocal commands, Mary—as she would later relate with discernible pride—"had (though dreadfully alarmed) presence of mind enough to order our footman to run & stop them." Imagining that she had only narrowly avoided being "dashed to pieces," she was upset enough to delay for a week her scheduled trip to the North. Reporting that she "knew nothing that could have depressed me so much but the death of an intimate acquaintance," Telfair revealed outraged disappointment at the coachman's conduct. The inebriated driver had been, according to Telfair, a particularly favored slave whom Alexander had purchased "to gratify" Mary and her sister Margaret. They placed "so much confidence in him that it was a terrible shock to find him unworthy of it." "Every indulgence was granted him," noted Mary, and yet, she concluded, "our best intentions often are productive of evil consequences." The moral of the story, which she told with literary flair, was simple: "if he had been kept constantly employed" with more taxing work, "he would not have had time enough to indulge" in his vices.[1]

In the early nineteenth century, Mary Telfair was one of an increasing number of slaveholders who believed that their mastery actively benefitted their slaves, who would be otherwise lost without concerned white guidance.[2] In Savannah and across the

slaveholding South, slaveholders were acutely aware that the modern world was beginning to look askance at slavery, so in response they developed a culture that allowed them to sidestep mounting charges that their ownership of slaves constituted a terrible crime. Although the American Revolution had raised unavoidable questions about a natural right to liberty, elite residents of Savannah hastened to rebuild the region's plantation economy following the war. Slavery played a defining role in these plans. As the prominent Savannah merchant Joseph Clay observed in 1785, "The Negroe business is a great object with us. . . . It is to the Trade of the Country, as the Soul [is] to the Body." Georgia politicians such as the Savannah lawyer James Jackson defended human bondage in the U.S. Congress against the antislavery movement, which he derisively dismissed as "the fashion of the day." In the face of accusations that they were "destitute of Humanity," Savannah slaveholders deflected moral criticism by claiming that their mastery benefitted their slaves. Though self-serving in the extreme, the proslavery rationale purported, with cruel irony, to celebrate a vision of the slaveholding household as one defined by lasting human connections rather than by short-term economic relationships between employers and wageworkers. Instead of exploiting their slaves, wealthy slaveholders claimed to regard them with paternalistic concern.[3]

Prominent Savannah slaveholders such as Mary Telfair did not simply justify slavery out of misplaced confidence in the sanctity and permanence of their own racist social order. Nor did they turn a blind eye toward the ways in which their city compared unfavorably to locales in the North on matters of health, economy, and landscape. In a weird ideological twist, slaveholders such as Mary Telfair drew upon assumptions established by the culture of romanticism to embrace rather than to deny the impermanence of all human endeavors. By acknowledging with morbid enthusiasm the inevitability of decay and ruin, powerful slaveholders such as the Telfairs counterintuitively constructed a coherent sense of purpose as self-appointed guardians of social virtue. Their defense of slavery was embedded in a heroic ideal defined by their assumption that only they were soldiering on as the world was falling to pieces around them. Of course, these cultural pretensions did not change the horrible reality of slavery for African Americans living in bondage. Instead, the slaves' suffering was subsumed into a larger white narrative about the beautiful, sublime sacrifice that enlightened whites nobly were making on behalf of American society as a whole, and of slaves in particular. The more that elite planters such

Frances Lewis Bolton Richardson

The first mistress of the Owens-Thomas House was Frances Richardson, who was, like Mary Telfair, a slave-owning woman of Savannah. Born in 1794, she was the daughter of the prominent Savannah businessman Robert Bolton, founder of the firm of Newell and Bolton, one of the state's first exporters of Sea Island cotton. Her mother, Sara McLean Bolton, was a descendant of one of Scotland's oldest clans of highland warriors. Frances's father died in 1802, when she was only eight years old. In his will, he bequeathed to her "the north half part of lot No. one with the improvements, and . . . I give the following Negroes: Jack, a blacksmith, Cudjoe, a boy, Ben, and George, a painter." In addition to the real estate and the enslaved "gifts," she received a large sum of money. Therefore, when her mother passed away four years later, leaving Frances orphaned at age thirteen, she was a wealthy heiress with excellent marriage prospects.

In 1811, Frances married her brothers' business partner, Richard Richardson. Because she entered matrimony with a substantial amount of money and human property, her brothers, Robert and John, persuaded Richardson to sign a marriage settlement, ensuring that some or all of the property that his wife brought into the union ultimately belonged to her. The settlement specified that should Richardson die first, the inheritance would revert to their children; to Richardson, if she had no children upon her death; and if Richardson died and they had no children, she could dispose of the property as she saw fit. Therefore, unless widowed and childless, Frances lacked substantive personal control over her own property.

In 1819, the Richardsons moved into their English Regency mansion on Oglethorpe Square, diagonally across from her childhood home, and Frances assumed her role as mistress of the house. In the first ten years of marriage, Frances bore six children. Only four, Frances, Richard, Robert, and James, survived to adulthood. The family experienced a series of troubles beginning in 1819, with the loss of their three-year-old son John. By late 1819, financial difficulties were plaguing the nation and the Richardsons. Richard resigned his presidency of the Bank of the United States. In 1822, two-year-old Rebecca Richardson died. On June 16, 1822, Frances died of "a fever" while her husband was away in New Orleans, arranging to relocate the family. She was buried in the Bolton family plot in Colonial Cemetery.

PAULETTE THOMPSON

as Mary Telfair claimed to be valiantly shouldering a burden as masters, the more that millions of African Americans labored and suffered in the confines of enslavement.

Born into one of Georgia's most prominent families in January 1791, Mary Telfair entered the world just as a revitalized national government sought to place the young nation on a more secure footing.[4] From the beginning of that political initiative, the institution of slavery cast an ominous shadow on the future of America. Although proslavery delegates to the Constitutional Convention from southern states had succeeded in obtaining powerful protection for the institution in the final document, the new federal government became a battleground over the morality of human bondage. Unlike their colonial predecessors, slaveholders who came of age following the American Revolution had to grapple with an antislavery movement that was gathering strength in the North. The strident accusations made against the moral character of southern masters stung, all the more so when a few southern families of high standing defected from the slaveholding ranks.

Mary Telfair's father, Georgia governor Edward Telfair, confronted this problem first-hand around 1800 when his close friend William Few turned against slavery. Few, a prominent participant in the Revolution and a delegate to the Constitutional Convention, resigned his position as a federal judge in Georgia and relocated to New York (where his wife's family lived). In 1804, Few audaciously challenged Telfair (whose principal wealth was tied up in the plantation economy) to acknowledge that slavery could have no secure place in the future republic. "Is there one person of understanding & reflection among you who will not admit that every confederation of justice, humanity, and safety, forbids that any more Negroes should be brought into your state," Few asked Telfair as he bemoaned Georgia merchants' eagerness to take part in the African slave trade. In Few's judgment, the "avarice" of Georgia "citizens, and the rage for acquiring that property has broke through all legal restrictions, and . . .they are carrying that diabolical and injurious traffic, and hastening those evils in their nature most dreadfull." Suggesting that slave importation not only was inhumane but also posed the risk of a wholesale slave insurrection that would be disastrous for the white population, Few warned that, notwithstanding the proslavery guarantees of the Constitution, southern slaveholders should not expect assistance from fellow citizens in the North in case of such an event: "Trust not on your Eastern friends for aid; if you do not enforce righteous measures for your own safety; they will laugh at your calamity and seek for profit by your misfortunes."[5]

The prospect that slavery might drive a wedge between these old friends must have been all the more galling because Few and his family had been chaperoning a rotating group of the Telfair children in New York since 1801, when Mary and her brother Alexander were sent north for their schooling. For Mary, the Few residence became a second home, and she forged intensely intimate relationships with the Few daughters, Mary (whom she called her "Siamese twin") and Frances.[6] These female friendships were by no means unusual by the standards of early American elite culture, and there is no evidence to suggest that the Telfair-Few relationships were sexual. The context for that intimacy, however, was clearly conceptualized for Telfair by the language of early nineteenth-century romantic literature. Telfair later repeatedly referred, with language steeped in romantic imagery, to her very powerful attachment to the northern landscape. Recalling the "banks of the Hudson where Natur sports in all the varieties of wild and cultivated beauty," Telfair rapturously vowed that she would never "forget the feelings inspired by a first contemplation of that noble river," which left her "lost in wonder and delight at the awful and sublime works of nature." Enthralled by the beauty of the northern countryside and waxing poetic about the depth of her attachment to the Few sisters, Telfair willingly conceded that life in the New York countryside was superior to that in Savannah. Although noting that "it would be a more difficult task to tear myself from Georgia for I find ties cling around my heart that nothing could sever," she acknowledged that "still I give your Country the preference in almost every respect, and think *its soil* more conducive to the growth of *Virtues* as well as the graces than ours."[7]

When Telfair described Savannah and its hinterlands as "our barren wastes," she was decrying the southern character as well as the landscape for its shortcomings. In a letter written in early June 1818, when wealthy Savannah residents evacuated the city to avoid summer outbreaks of disease, Telfair reported that *the Southrons* have already begun to flock to the North, to inhale your delicious breezes and gaze on your wild romantic scenery, as well as your cultivated Farms." She claimed that she found it "provoking . . . that you should have so greatly the advantage over us in every respect."[8] Five years later, she repeated this refrain, claiming that as another trip in the North wound down, she would be leaving for home "with *the deepest regret.*" "The deathlike stillness which reigns throughout our streets and the languid air & *silent tongues* of many of its inhabitants," she concluded, "affords a striking contrast to the animation & spirit left behind" in the

North.[9] Telfair believed that the South's "unhealthy climate creates great timidity of character & weakens our energies not a little," and her admiration for "Yankee enterprise" led her to "almost wish [she] was a Yankee."[10]

When Telfair made such unfavorable comparisons between her native region and healthier, thriving regions of the North, she was willing to concede that slavery posed a moral and economic problem for the South. She repeatedly expressed concerns about the possibility of insurrection by what she derisively referred to as "the *sable* tribe." During the War of 1812, she fretted over the "very alarming intelligence" that "the British have landed a large force consisting of two thousand Blacks on Cumberland Island," off the southeastern coast of Georgia. Anticipating that "Savannah the emporium of the State will not escape the inhuman" strategy of the English commanders, Telfair had "no doubt a number of slaves will flock" to the enemies. And amid the Seminole campaigns of the 1830s, a struggle in no small part motivated by the threat that runaway slaves were posing to the plantation economy of Georgia, Telfair fearfully predicted that "there will be an internal enemy to contend with too."[11]

Telfair sometimes sounded as if slave owning were more trouble than it was worth. If slaves were capable of directly opposing their owners' authority, they were also, in Telfair's estimation, less than ideal workers, even when they were secure as property. "You have often heard me deprecate *Plantations* and contrast them with fine looking Farms, and elegant country seats at the north," she wrote to Few. Southern slaveholders, according to Telfair, needed to battle against slaves' "regular system" of theft against their owners.[12] Telfair even related the story of a southern woman who inherited fourteen slaves, only to discover that they were "fourteen Plagues" destined to "annoy her incessantly." In the end, the South would always have to contend with "the sloth of the sable population," which, together with extreme heat, waged "war against improvements physical, moral and intellectual." This bias was communicated to her circle of friends sufficiently often that Mary and her sister Margaret were accused on at least one occasion of being "*too northern* in our taste & habits."[13]

Had Mary Telfair relocated permanently to the North, these attitudes might have pushed her into the antislavery ranks. Instead, she remained a southerner at heart and built for herself a romantic conception of time and place that allowed her to harbor a positive vision of slavery. In doing so, Telfair did not principally draw upon southern sources for the ideas that allowed her to make peace with her region's reliance upon slavery.

The Marquis de Lafayette in Savannah

Preston Russell, Lafayette at the Owens-Thomas House, 1825, 1992. *Courtesy of Preston Russell.*

In March 1825, Marie-Joseph-Paul-Yves-Roch-Gilbert du Motier, marquis de Lafayette, the Hero of Yorktown, arrived in Savannah for a three-day visit as part of his farewell tour of America in 1824–25. It was a moment when slavery and antislavery ideas came into conflict in the city. Lafayette stayed at Mary Maxwell's boardinghouse, later known as the Owens-Thomas House. Throughout the nation, men and women of all social ranks turned out to honor this hero of the American Revolution and the last surviving major general of the Continental army. Lafayette was feted by the finest and the humblest as he observed the new nation he had helped create through his wartime service.

Lafayette's tour through the South was accompanied by concern from white southerners that his well-known antislavery views would inspire unrest among the slave population. Many towns and cities in the South, including Savannah, prohibited enslaved or free blacks from attending any of the public ceremonies held in his honor. On March 14, 1825, days before Lafayette's arrival, Savannah mayor William Daniell published a letter in the *Savannah Georgian* asking the white citizens of Savannah "as much as possible . . . to confine to their own yards and houses, their servants and especially the children, whilst military honors are paying to General Lafayette." He continued, "The City Marshals and City Constables are required to take into custody all such negroes and persons of color as may be found at all tresspassing upon or attending the procession, parades, etc., during the stay of General Lafayette in this city."

But Savannah's white citizens were unable to completely segregate Lafayette from African Americans. A story in the *Savannah Georgian* dated March 24, 1825, noted that he received as a visitor "an old negro man, now entirely blind, who was his servant during his services in the Country, and now belongs to Mr. M'Queen near this city." Lafayette hosted the man "with that affability and kindness characteristic of the individual."

Lafayette's attention to the enslaved man in part reflected his beliefs as an early and consistent abolitionist. On February 5, 1783, Lafayette wrote George Washington to propose a plan that "might become greatly beneficial to the Black Part of Mankind." Washington and Lafayette should buy a plantation in America, free the enslaved blacks, and then hire them as tenants. Washington's name attached to the project "might render it a general practice." "If it be a wild scheme," Lafayette added, "I would rather be mad that way, than be thought wise on the other tack." When Washington, himself a slave owner, demurred, Lafayette and his wife bought a plantation in Cayenne (present-day French Guiana) and undertook the project there.

During his farewell tour, Lafayette communicated his abolitionist views — gradual emancipation and education — privately to his friends Thomas Jefferson and James Madison, but avoided public advocacy in deference to his being a "Guest of the Nation." Yet in small and symbolic ways, he demonstrated his interest in furthering the cause of African Americans, free or enslaved. In addition to receiving black guests in Savannah and other parts of the South, Lafayette visited the New York African Free School operated by the New York Manumission Society, which he had joined in the 1780s. While in Yorktown for the celebration of Surrender Day on October 19, 1824, he recognized James Armistead and publicly embraced him. While still enslaved, Armistead had worked as a spy for Lafayette during the American Revolution. In 1787, the Virginia legislature, prompted by a testimonial written in his behalf by Lafayette, had given Armistead his freedom. Upon his emancipation, the grateful Armistead took the name "James Armistead Lafayette." On April 18, 1825 in New Orleans, Lafayette greeted African American veterans of the War of 1812. According to the *Courier of New Orleans*, he thanked them for their services, commenting that he "had often during the War of Independence seen African blood shed with honor in our ranks for the cause of the United States," and shook hands with each of them.

Lafayette's tour through the South does not appear to have directly encouraged large numbers of southerners to consider emancipation. But after Lafayette's death in 1834, northern abolitionists embraced his words and example as part of their arsenal against slavery. In a letter published in 1846 in the *Liberator*

(William Lloyd Garrison's antislavery journal), the English abolitionist Thomas Clarkson wrote that his friend General Lafayette frequently told him: "I would never have drawn my sword in the cause of America if I could have conceived that thereby I was founding a land of slavery." (Clarkson had written this to the Massachusetts abolitionist Maria Weston Chapman on October 3, 1845.) Northern abolitionists, including Charles Sumner, William C. Nell—one of the first African American historians—and Wendell Phillips, frequently quoted this statement of the deceased hero of the American Revolution to further the cause.

ALAN R. HOFFMAN

Instead, the poems and novels that attracted her sustained attention were part of the emerging transatlantic canon of romantic literature. Like countless American readers during this era, both southern and northern, Telfair particularly revered the chivalric fantasies of Walter Scott (her "favorite author") and the brooding and brilliant verse of Lord Byron.[14]

In numerous letters, Telfair discussed "feasting" on books, sometimes sequestering herself to read entire works with minimal interruption, as she did when she and her friends "shut ourselves up half a dozen of us, in a snug little room for two rainy days" to have a "rich mental banquet" with Scott's *Ivanhoe*. His *Lady of the Lake*, which runs to 5,000 lines, she claimed to know "almost by heart."[15] Her reading was social in that she frequently discussed with the people around her what she was reading. Yet as the unmarried Telfair came to feel increasingly alienated from the Savannah social scene in subsequent years, her reading substituted for interaction with those people—and there were many of them—who failed to meet her standards for proper company.[16] In 1828, she told Mary Few, "I must return to Books as I derive my chief enjoyment from them at home." When her sense of social alienation reached a climax, in 1835, she noted that she was "living in the world without any interest in its concerns": "I have become so accustomed to solitude that I do not care for any society beyond my books and my own thoughts."[17] Oddly enough, for all that Telfair professed to be rejecting social convention by immersing herself in literary diversions, her emotional embrace of romantic literature was completely typical for well-educated women in her rank of plantation society.[18]

For Telfair, making sense of her books and her thoughts required her to negotiate between the living world and the literary scenes painted by her favorite authors. Books provided the prism through which she interpreted the people around her. When describing people encountered at gatherings, she routinely likened them to characters in books when rendering judgments about their perceived qualities.[19] Telfair at times seemed aware that she might be drawing too deeply upon literature to fashion her understanding of the world, reminding herself, "If I sometimes indulge in my admiration for these fictitious characters I shall forget that there are real ones in existence." In contrast to her low opinion of the many members of polite society who bored or repulsed her, she noted in herself the ability to empathize very deeply with the characters she encountered on the page, admitting at one point, "I wish I had all the tears back that I have shed over fictitious woes." Recognizing that this tendency was absurd when she saw it surfacing in others, Telfair attempted to police it in herself. She even claimed on one occasion that she had "become too old to enjoy *Fiction* in any form—Wholesome *Reality* is what I crave."[20] Such feelings, however, quickly gave way to the impulse to read voraciously. A series of commonplace books in which she (and sometimes her friends) copied out meaningful passages testifies to the depth of her literary interests.

From her reading, Mary Telfair developed a heightened sense of romantic nostalgia at a relatively young age. At twenty, for example, she reflected with morose self-consciousness on the "halcyon days" of her youth with the Few sisters. She waxed eloquently upon her "remembrance of the many happy days spent there, in the happiest period of my life," before noting that "these pleasures have long since past and now only to be re-enjoyed in memory where they appear fresh as the incidents of yesterday."[21] Poets such as Byron, William Cowper, and Edward Young provided Telfair with a vocabulary with which to express the sense that the best age had already passed, leaving behind splendid ruins that moldered away in a degraded world. Quoting Shakespeare, she noted the inefficacy of mortal intent in the face of such corrosive natural forces: "What are human resolutions, and human efforts? They are 'like the baseless fabric of a vision.'"[22] That she grounded her own melancholic commentary in direct quotation underscored her complicated dance between fiction and reality. Telfair understood each category dialectically with reference to the other, the permanently printed words evoking the ephemeral nature of a living world that was understood to be passing away even as it was being experienced. Hungering for childhood recollections from Mary Few (which she deemed her "favorite topic"),

Telfair remarked, quoting from the supposedly ancient and mystical epic *Fingal*, "'Lovely are the tales of other times' and to revert to them always produces a sad but pleasing melancholy."[23]

As a resident of Savannah in the early nineteenth century, Mary Telfair fashioned a morbid aesthetic that was, unfortunately for her, rooted as much in the unhealthful Low-country landscape as in the artful literary constructions of her favorite authors. Death haunted the Telfairs, as it did the rest of a coastal population regularly exposed to yellow fever, malaria, cholera, and dysentery (not to mention the threat of fire and the afore-mentioned specters of slave rebellion and attack by hostile Native American or European foes).[24] In one terrible stretch between 1816 and 1818, Mary Telfair lost to illness her brothers Josiah and Thomas, her brother-in-law George Haig, and two nephews (shortly after which, much of Savannah burned in a massive conflagration in 1820). In the wake of these losses, Telfair described herself as "doomed to wither and to die in this sultry clime" and, quoting the poet Samuel Rogers, stated that "all our enjoyments are transitory 'And such is Human Life so gliding on, It glimmers like a meteor and is gone.'" Her last surviv-ing brother, Alexander, with whom she and her sisters lived, passed away in 1832. In her deep despair, Telfair admitted to Mary Few, "All my former pursuits are tasteless, and I feel that there is no enjoyment left for me in this world."[25]

Haunted by the deaths of so many loved ones, Telfair reacted all the more strongly to verse that evoked her pain and recast inevitable human loss as the foundation for beau-tiful but aching artistic expression. Herein lay the appeal of Telfair's "much loved" Byron to an enormous early nineteenth-century audience whose admiration approached wor-ship. Explaining her attraction to his work, Telfair wrote that "he is at times beautifully pathetic & extremely melancholy." Comparing him to Scott, she noted that Byron's "Muse is of a different cast . . . dark, gloomy mysterious and often grandly sublime."[26] Telfair cer-tainly turned to him when trying to convey the impact of mourning on human character. For it was death, wrote Byron, "that stamps the wrinkle deeper on the brow, To view each lov'd one blotted from lifes page, And feel alone on Earth as I do now," a feeling that Tel-fair confessed she felt "in heart and mind."[27] Her reading exposed Telfair to a Romantic sensibility that simultaneously bemoaned and revered the inexorable power of nature to erode human achievement, leaving only ruins (in the idealized literary formulation) to mark the passage of what men and women had built.

Telfair obviously enjoyed ruins, taking great pains to see them. When she traveled to

To Lord Byron.

On reading Childe Harold's pilgrimage.—

By I H Nicholson Esq.

Thou man of gloom! I would not be
A cold, insensate thing like thee,
Nor bear that icy heart of thine
That worships not at woman's shrine,
That feels not woman's magic smile
Nor suffers beauty to beguile;
For all the wealth o'er Ocean glides,
And all the gems Golconda hides.

For me would Spring her incense breathe,
And youth's unfading roses blow,
Would Glory twine her laurel wreath,
Her richest garlands for my brow;
To sway the proud luxurious East
Or save my native freeborn West
From Tyrants minions round her prest,
And live by countless millions blest

Would all be lost, and worthless prove
Unreturn'd, unblest by woman's love.—

the site of her family's former home outside Augusta in 1833, she noted that "the hand of desolation had swept away every trace of former grandeur—the venerable grove where Druids might have worshipped, and the clustering grape vines under which we used to swing in the sunny days of childhood were all gone." She bemoaned that "the garden too where Nature & Art had lavished their choicest gifts" had been "converted into a meadow." The visit led her to insist that the word "*Perishable* is inscribed upon every object in this visible world."[28] In this vein, when Telfair traveled to Europe in 1841, she predictably discerned "a poetical beauty" in the ravished landscape of a "dreary moor" near Southampton, and characterized as "a Noble specimen of Gothic architecture" the ruins of Netley Abbey.[29] In her commonplace book, she rendered an illustration of the Scottish castle at Crookston, the haunting beauty of which must have struck Telfair with even greater poignancy after learning, while abroad, of yet more deaths in her family. The "*airy* visions" of ruin offered by the romantic perspective empowered Telfair to "*venerate* the spot" where her losses were most acutely felt. For to be the one "in twilight's pensive hour" watching "the moss-clad dome, the mould'ring Tower, in awful ruin stand" was to hold a place of narrative power—a power to shape that destruction into a beautiful marker of anguish in the face of adversity.[30]

Indeed, the myriad (and artistically expressed) refrains of ineluctable, haunting mortality running throughout Telfair's writings signify an empowering inversion. The more she conveyed to her friends the extent of suffering that she endured, the more she was able to cast herself into the role of a romantic heroine, bravely marching toward an inevitable fate from which others recoiled. Those people around her who sported cheerful outlooks earned Telfair's scorn. "Gay people are very annoying to me," she observed with characteristically sharp wit. "I always find them boisterous and usually devoid of delicacy & feelings." What was evocative about the Lowcountry landscape was the barely contained menace of its lush exoticism. This was the South that Telfair wished to show off to visitors. When her great friend Frances Few visited Savannah in 1820, Mary arranged for them to spend a day at the ruins of Wormsloe Plantation, the property of her uncle George Jones. The spooky beauty moved Few to recount the experience to a correspondent: "But nothing struck me more strongly than the venerable old trees which everywhere adorn this desolate spot." "They were covered with a species of moss," she continued, that "waves with every breeze." Few described the dream-like drama of approaching the crumbling

Mary Telfair, Castle of Crookstone. *"I've seen, in twilight's pensive hour, / The moss-clad dome, the mouldering Tower; / In awful ruin stand"* ("The Ruins," by Selleck Osborn). Telfair Family Papers 793, box 6, folder 58, item 256: Commonplace Book. Courtesy of the Georgia Historical Society.

tabby structure of the main house "thro' an avenue of live oak whose branches formed a complete arch where the moss waved in solemn grandeur."[31]

For southerners, the romantic aesthetic offered a trump card to play against the more rapidly developing society of their elite northern counterparts. Savannah might have been falling far behind bustling northern centers of commerce in the 1820s, even shrinking considerably in population. Yet that very retardation in the pace of its economic development was understood as potentially ennobling for its regional character. Notwithstanding Telfair's enormous wealth (which was derived from her family's slaveholding), she identified materialism as an ugly, corrosive force. Telfair blasted the desire "to *appear* rich," which she believed was the "acme of ambition" for the majority of the population. "The national character has been deeply injured by it," she maintained, likening capitalist ambition to the outbreak of disease: "There are times for Moral Epidemics as well as physical." Folding her critique of materialism into her romantic sensibility, Telfair bemoaned the destructive force of the growing modern American economy. "What a sad innovator is Time," she remarked, "for it transforms Forests into Cities." The price paid for material progress was the sacrifice of beautiful scenes remembered to have taken place in "an antique mansion" now "burst in awful state": "The active, bustling Citizen, who figures in the Great Drama of Wall Street, calls this *levelling* system, the march of improvement, while the contemplating lover of rural beauty considers it Natures requiem over the loss of her precious antiquities."[32]

In contrast to the ruthlessly expanding business culture epitomized by Wall Street, Telfair characterized plantation life by using pastoral imagery that de-emphasized the slaveholders' regard for profit.[33] Such rhetoric starkly contradicted the economic reality in which slaveholding entrepreneurs such as Telfair sought, like thoroughgoing capitalists, to maximize their profits. And these savvy businessmen and businesswomen never hesitated to interact with bankers, lawyers, or policy makers in order to enhance the profitability of their plantations. Precisely because they were so embedded in the world of financial transactions, paternalistic assumptions about the master-slave relationship were valuable to the planters: they enabled them to ignore the obvious economic motivation driving the exploitation of slave labor. According to white slaveholders, their mastery was wielded with a familial concern for the well-being of their bondservants. Denying that they bought, sold, and managed their human property in order to create wealth, elite Savannah residents such as Mary Telfair instead focused on assuredly isolated moments when they sacrificed on behalf of their slaves. Telfair, for example, told Mary Few one Christmas season that she had declined several social invitations because "it is a custom with us to cook a large dinner for our servants" to which "each has the privilege of inviting their friends." In Telfair's story about the master-slave relationship, the slaves enjoyed fully the holiday "festival and are made happy by it." By contrast, she claimed to be unable to recall "the joyous feelings of my youth," when holidays "gladdened my heart."[34]

Rather than contemplating the difficult and dangerous labor that she exacted from her slaves in her Savannah home and on her family's plantations, she instead dwelled on the paternalistic fantasy that they loved and appreciated her for her kind regard for their welfare. In 1842, Telfair reported the slaves' gushing response to her return to Savannah from a trip to the North. The slaves, she claimed, "seemed quite overcome by the sight of us." Catering to their owner's paternalistic identity, the slaves told her that, during her absence, "it seemed to them as if we had all passed away," and therefore "they could not bear to look at the house." In relating the episode to her friend, Telfair conveyed the deep satisfaction of having been made aware of the powerful attachment that her bond-servants felt toward their masters: "I never knew before how much they valued us."[35]

Telfair's perspective on her longtime relationship with her house slave, Juddy, reveals how slaveholder paternalism operated. Telfair took obvious pride in the attention that she paid to Juddy's feelings (while simultaneously demeaning her) as they traveled from Philadelphia to Savannah in 1838. Describing the scene when their carriage bumped its way over rough terrain, Telfair observed that "poor Juddy," fearing death in her assigned role as a comic figure in Telfair's tale, "screamed out 'we are over.'" Telfair reasoned that the slave "had not been accustomed to such buffetings," because *coach riding* [was] a novelty to her unsophisticated nature." Having reduced Juddy to an utterly dependent figure in her narrative, Telfair then added that Juddy "tells her *comrades* here that she was very much pleased with her northern summer—every body was kind to her." To herself, Telfair then assigned the role of benevolent master, claiming, "We never compel any of them to do what will make them unhappy." Hence, when viewed through the prism of these warped assumptions, slavery entailed the hard work of masters exerting themselves on behalf of their slaves' happiness. This perspective surfaced in 1840 as Telfair was preparing for a journey to Charleston. She described Juddy as "preparing her *toilette* for the last week while we have been toiling—she takes it very leisurely and says that she loves Home better than the *Norrard* [North] but is willing to go."[36] African Americans such as Juddy seldom had the luxury of confronting their masters about the self-serving distortions clearly at work in proslavery thought. The historical record, however, leaves no doubt that African Americans and other critics of slavery found this logic to be repulsive in its hypocrisy. Runaway slaves such as Frederick Douglass marshaled some of their harshest rhetoric in denouncing proslavery platitudes as language that comforted masters rather than rescuing slaves from the abuse and suffering.[37]

Telfair wanted to portray the master-slave relationship as somehow unconnected to her pursuit of profit, which she claimed to care nothing about. Paternalism was valuable to Telfair because it allowed her to finesse her way past the obvious truth that she owned human beings in order to exploit their labor. Paternalism's uses in this regard were apparent when she negotiated the possibility of hiring out Juddy and her other house slaves to her Savannah neighbor William Neyle Habersham during one of the Telfairs' European excursions. She suggested that a payment of six to eight dollars a month for each of the slaves in question would be a fair fee. To help close the deal, she described the slaves' fine qualities paternalistically: Juddy, for example, was "an excellent tempered woman" who was part of "an affectionate trio" of slaves. Summing up the entire commercial transaction in the rhetoric of warm concern for all parties, Telfair said, "We shall be very glad . . . to have them domesticated with you." Of course, Telfair could afford to be very glad about the proposed arrangement because each of the hired-out slaves was to receive just one dollar a month for their own use, giving Telfair a profit margin of some 85 percent on the transaction.[38]

Juddy Telfair Jackson, the Telfairs' cook and maid, with her granddaughter Lavinia, Mary Telfair's maid. This image, given to the Telfair Academy of Arts and Sciences in the twentieth century, identifies Juddy as Judy. Courtesy of the Georgia Historical Society, 793-05-56-254A.

Paternalism and romanticism blended together perfectly in the domestic ideal that Telfair championed in Savannah. With the grasping pursuit of profit increasingly associated in her mind with northern business culture, she imagined her mastery as a moral undertaking misunderstood by the modern world. While other Americans enthusiastically embraced the innovations of the burgeoning industrial age, Telfair fretted about the passing of tradition. "I am now an advocate for *old fashions*," she insisted. The modernizing economy, in her mind, signified the abandonment of the citizenry's sense of duty to a larger set of morals: "Self seems to be the predominating principle with most people . . . I have come to another conclusion that the high toned in character has passed away."[39] Abolitionism represented one of the worst examples of this decline, all the more so because antislavery activists justified their agenda with warped references to Christian principles. Telfair rejected out of hand the critique of southern slavery offered by the radical Unitarian minister William Ellery Channing. As the world outside Savannah seemed to be stumbling toward moral disorder, Telfair observed the efforts of refined planters to minister to the spiritual as well as physical needs of their slaves. The Christian mission to the slave population had roots extending back to the early colonial period, but it was in the nineteenth century that the master class firmly wedded its proslavery thought to Christian theology. The ministers whom Telfair most admired were the ones spearheading the campaign to defend slavery as a Christian enterprise.[40]

While this cultural initiative led wealthy southerners into philanthropic ventures designed to improve their society, Telfair's romanticism kept her from developing a progressive mindset about the prospects for improvement in the plantation South. Her paternalist sensibility allowed her to admire slaveholders who were attempting to educate their slaves in the teachings of the Gospels. Yet she was uncertain about the extent to which such a mission would actually improve the slaves. Telfair was willing at times to concede that in matters of faith, slaves were being awakened to a deeper understanding of Christianity, but her racism, coupled with her understanding of time as a corrosive force, did not allow her to envision a brighter future for the plantation system. Ultimately, the significance of the missions rested not in their potential for overcoming the inferiority of the African character but rather in their expression of white motives of benevolence.[41]

Telfair held out no real hope that American slaves could develop the same capabilities as the servant class in England, which she admired for its supposed efficiency. Ideally, she reasoned, Americans should aim for a simple domesticity that would allow them to avoid the challenges of managing large households, especially ones that required the labor of many slaves and therefore "enslaved" the mistress who had to supervise them. For Telfair, republican simplicity was the defining virtue of the generation of the American founders, who were already passing from the ranks of the living. To live simply was to resist the moral decline that was just one more product of the destructive passage of time, continually grinding away at precious human achievement.[42]

The Telfairs' magnificent Regency mansion revealed how Mary Telfair executed her domestic ideals. Designed by the Englishman William Jay III during his stay in Savannah (1818–22), the Telfair house was one of the earliest southern homes to benefit from the ideas of a formally trained architect. Jay (who also designed the Owens-Thomas House) brilliantly manipulated neoclassical elements to create a structure that was infused with drama and gravitas but also delivered a measure of comfort and intimacy to its residents.

In the Telfair mansion, Jay rewarded arriving visitors with the grandeur of a beautifully scaled Corinthian porch, accessed by symmetrical sets of stairs and opening onto an imposing central hall. The original design of the double drawing room, opening to the right of the hall, allowed for the room to be partitioned by a set of pocket doors in order to create a cozier scale for smaller gatherings. The Telfairs could therefore host large parties, yet also scale back their domestic aesthetic to communicate a lack of pretension when the virtue of restraint was called for in the name of comfort. Of course, while the Telfairs' guests were enjoying the hospitality of their hosts, Juddy and the other Telfair slaves would have been working furiously in the kitchen, located in the basement. The intimate social exchanges in the drawing room were staged to mediate the distance between domestic comfort and the domestic labor that made it possible.[43]

Classical motifs meshed neatly with the reverence for the ancient past expressed by the romantic authors so cherished by Mary Telfair. And Jay, like the romantic poets, playfully alluded to tradition without trying to seamlessly re-create an intact ancient aesthetic. The

Oak Room, Telfair Mansion. Telfair Museums, Savannah, Georgia. Photograph: Daniel L. Grantham Jr., Graphic Communication.

most compelling space in the house, an octagonal room that opened to the left of the front door, displayed the strange relationship between architectural mimicry and "authentic" references to meaningful tradition. Following, perhaps, the example of the English Regency architect John Soane, Jay directed that the plaster walls be painted to create a faux-bois effect of oak graining, giving the Oak Room the look of a wood-paneled space. The Telfairs gathered here with friends in scenes of cozy retirement that were remembered fondly by those welcomed into this inner sanctum of domesticity. Their friend Louisa Mae Albrite stated that she "would gladly find myself sitting by the fire in the dear Oak Room." In her mind's eye, she told the Telfairs, she could "see you all with [the house slave] Friday bringing in the tea tray and your little page," (probably Friday's brother George Gibbons), "in devoted attendance." Like the wood grain of the Oak Room's walls, the image of faithful slaves tending to the needs of caring masters was an illusion that allowed the Telfairs to reconcile their domestic needs with their notions of a moral tradition.[44]

Romantic literature fostered the belief that enlightened individuals could locate, through art, powerful currents of something essential in humanity, rushing from the wellspring of antiquity. When Telfair contemplated the foibles of human character, she

Salley and Her Children
Maria, Emma, and John Charles Gibbons

In the South in the late eighteenth and early nineteenth centuries, a small number of children born to enslaved women and white men gained economic and social advantages that would become increasingly unusual down to the onset of the Civil War. In Savannah, William Gibbons (1754–1803), Mary Telfair's uncle, entered into a sexual relationship with Salley, an enslaved woman he owned. Together, they had three children. We do not know anything of Salley's feelings about the relationship. But William Gibbons freed Salley in 1796, shortly before she gave birth to their first child. His action ensured her freedom and that of their children.

Neither the relationship between Salley and William Gibbons, nor their children, are recorded in the Gibbons family Bible, which is held in the Telfair Family Papers at the Georgia Historical Society in Savannah. Yet notations in Gibbons's account book, such as "Schooling for Maria," "one pair of earrings for Emma," and "a leather cap for John Charles," indicate his interest in the three children. And his legacies to his children show his concern for their future. Comparing their legacies to those Gibbons left to his white siblings, nieces, and nephews (whose names *were* inscribed in the family Bible) indicates the possibilities and limits of William Gibbons's relationship with his children of partial African descent.

Gibbons's bequests to his daughters and nieces indicate that he assumed their lives might run parallel in some ways. Just as he had left "one doz silver dessert spoons" to his niece Sarah Telfair (Mary Telfair's sister), Gibbons earmarked "6 large, plain silver tablespoons" and "6 silver teaspoons" for Maria. Embedded in the legacies of silver and in his commitment to Maria's education is the presumption of gentility. Emma too received a specific bequest of silver, but as the younger sister, she inherited only "6 large silver tablespoons." In addition to the individual bequests Gibbons made to his daughters, he designated a group of household furnishings for them to share, including a new mahogany breakfast table. Stylistically, the breakfast table was on a par with the sideboard he left to his sister Sarah Telfair (Mary's mother). Both pieces were crafted from top-of-the-line mahogany. But their forms embody a distinction. A sideboard was a centerpiece for entertaining guests, while a breakfast table was for family use. Here Gibbons tacitly acknowledged that his sister and her heirs would move in a wider circle than his daughters were likely to. To each he was providing what he deemed appropriate to her station.

A new maple field bedstead that Gibbons left to his daughters conveyed a similar meaning. Gibbons had purchased it from the renowned New York craftsman George Shipley in 1802. It was the best of its kind; yet in both material and form, it was a lesser object than the large mahogany bedstead he left to his sister. The material, maple, is an American wood, and the form of a field bed is lightweight and small. Nevertheless, few Savannahians could ever hope to own such an elegant and expensive item made by a New York craftsman. Here again, the higher-status object went to the higher-ranking person, yet the objects that his daughters inherited suggested their entitlement to a genteel lifestyle.

In addition to furniture, Gibbons left what might be considered trousseau items to Maria and Emma. They inherited a set of blue and white bed curtains that probably went with the field bed and undoubtedly were made from the "London Blue Chintz" that Gibbons bought in New York in 1802. Textiles were very expensive furnishings for the average householder, so Gibbons's bequest of damask tablecloths and fine linen sheets and pillowcases well equipped his daughters for housekeeping. Kitchen utensils and tableware besides the silver spoons were also included in their inheritance.

Gibbons made monetary bequests to Salley and their children as well as to his nieces and nephews. The legacies that Gibbons established for Salley, Maria, Emma, and John Charles were left in trust for the beneficiaries to his brother Barack Gibbons and his "kinsman" John Gibbons. It is clear that William Gibbons understood that his family would need white male legal surrogates to protect their interests, and from all appearances, his confidence was well placed in his kinsmen. After the deaths of Barack Gibbons and John Gibbons (in 1814 and 1816), Alexander Telfair, who was Gibbons's nephew, continued to administer the trust. By the time Telfair took over as trustee, Savannah required free persons of color to have "guardians," so Telfair served in that capacity as well as acting as trustee until his death in 1832.

Gibbons designed legacies for Salley and their children that would produce immediate and long-term income for them. He left real estate comprising town lots and farm acreage, as well as slaves, in trust for each of the children. As the first-born male, John Charles received a valuable interest in a lot and buildings on the Savannah River, and he would have the right to manage his own property when he turned twenty-one.

William Gibbons's legacies to Salley and their three children epitomize a brief moment in Savannah's history when a white planter hoped that class might trump race in determining a person's status. But hardening racial attitudes and restrictive legislation in the decades following Gibbons's death made it unlikely that his hopes for his children would be realized.

FEAY SHELLMAN COLEMAN

identified "subterfuge" as "the foundation of every thing that is odious in character." "How few," she bemoaned, "think it is a sin to appear through life in a fictitious character—always masquerading." Instead of recognizing the theatricality of her own self-depiction, Telfair mobilized her romantic assumptions to underscore the fierce sincerity by which she claimed to live her life. Witnessing all around her in Savannah the ephemeral nature of human achievement, Telfair imagined that she lived according to a higher standard of truth and beauty. Indeed, her desire that the Telfair name be associated with an artistic aesthetic was the catalyst for her decision to bequeath the Telfair home (and considerable other property) to the Georgia Historical Society for the purpose of establishing an academy of the arts.[45]

Fittingly, given her lifelong preoccupation with time's destructive march, Mary Telfair lived long enough to witness the sectional conflict over slavery escalate into Civil War. As the national political order came unglued during the 1850s, Telfair held fast to her proslavery assumptions. Visiting one of her plantations in 1852, she noted with satisfaction that the slaves appeared "well & happy and seemed disposed to *worship* me." She followed this paternalistic rhetoric with a romantic rumination on the painful passage of time. Telfair described how her cheerful slaves took notice of her own *"grave"* expression, which resulted from her feeling "sad in revisiting a spot where I had passed so many happy days & months, with those who were the lights of other years, and gave a charm to Earth & Earthly things that can never, never be renewed."[46] Instead of engendering feelings of helplessness or victimization, this appeal to romantic imagery empowered her feelings of righteous social conduct as a slaveholder. All those years earlier when she found herself racing through Savannah's streets in a runaway carriage, Telfair had spun the tale to convey her mastery of the situation. Decades later, the story she told about her own life continued to reveal the power of her literary imagination, her proslavery fantasies grounded in romantic verse and warped nostalgia.

Despite Telfair's self-professed sense of alienation from the world around her, her defense of slavery was typical of elite slaveholding women and men. Her privilege and wealth allowed her to immerse herself in the prevailing literary sentiments of her era—sentiments that she then twisted to serve and to justify the unequal society that made possible her own social standing. Like other mistresses and masters of the plantation system, Telfair ultimately sought to police it from the threats posed by the modern world. The great paradox of this proslavery stance was that it purported to reject avarice and to uphold instead a conservative reverence for moral and humane standards governing the relationships between all members of society. Hence, when Telfair did her best to maintain the rigid hierarchies of the antebellum plantation social order, she congratulated herself on nobly—even heroically—confronting the materialistic challenges posed by the selfish modern world. Her slaves, by contrast, understood that their terrible predicament resulted from white greed, however much it might have been justified through an eloquently expressed poetic sensibility wielded by Telfair and her elite counterparts.[47]

Slave Life in Savannah
Geographies of Autonomy and Control
Leslie M. Harris and Daina Ramey Berry

In February 1822, Freeman Walker of Augusta wrote to Alexander Telfair of Savannah on behalf of Dorothy Walton of Florida for information regarding "Sanders," a "negro man of hers" who had been living in Savannah. This was a communication among some of Georgia's wealthiest and most elite politicians and slave owners. Walker had served as a U.S. senator and congressman from Georgia and as mayor of Augusta, a post he took up again in 1823. Telfair was the youngest son of the prominent and wealthy Telfair family of Savannah. In 1818, following the deaths of his three older brothers, he became head of one of the richest families in Georgia, overseeing the family's urban mercantile businesses (including slave trading), rural plantation holdings, and numerous slaves. He commissioned William Jay to build the Telfair mansion, which was completed in 1819; Alexander lived there with his mother, Sarah Gibbons Telfair, and his sisters Mary Telfair, Sarah Telfair Haig, and Margaret Telfair (later Hodgson), until his death in 1832. Dorothy Walton was the widow of George Walton, who had been a signatory to the Declaration of Independence and a former governor of Georgia. The Waltons had retired to Augusta in the 1780s. Following her husband's death, Dorothy Walton had followed her son, George Walton II, to Florida, where he served as secretary of the territory.[1]

It was from her new home in Florida that Walton asked Walker to track down Sanders so that she might "receive his wages." Walker wrote to Telfair with the "understanding that this fellow . . . has a wife at your house or some where among your negroes," and asked him whether he had seen Sanders, "a boat hand," recently. "What is he employed about?" asked Walker. And did he appear "disposed to make wages for his mistress?" Walker had no instructions from Mrs. Walton to send Sanders to Florida; nor did he desire to supervise Sanders himself: "If Sanders prefers remaining in Savannah, I would certainly have no objection." Walker made a request of Telfair: "If you would be so obliging as to

5

receive his wages in behalf of his mistress or if there is any persons in whom you would have confidence who you would recommend as an agent for that purpose."[2]

Walker's request reveals the complicated nature of slaveholding in Savannah and in Georgia generally. The history of slavery in urban areas challenges simplistic notions of how slave owners exercised control over their human property. Understanding the nature of control and resistance in southern slavery entails examining the written laws of slavery, which limited black mobility and autonomy and denied freedom. But the actual practices of slaveholders and the enslaved defined the lived experience of whites and blacks in the South. In urban areas, slave systems were adaptable to the methods by which slave owners sought to ensure the fundamental purpose of the system: the accrual of wealth through the ownership of human beings as property. Southern society worked to maintain control over that human property by relegating African Americans to the lowest levels of society through laws, ideologies, and practices. These social norms reinforced a widespread belief among whites in the racial inferiority of people of African descent, which in turn justified their enslavement.[3] But maintenance of the institution did not always entail whips, chains, and restricting slaves to plantations. Indeed, slaveholders constantly negotiated the laws and practices of slavery in order to ensure the continuation of a system that was fundamental to the southern way of life, even as enslaved people worked to make the system as livable as possible for themselves.

The system of slavery encompassed areas of rural production—plantations—and urban markets. Both were central to the continuation of slavery. Indeed, elite whites such as Freeman Walker, Alexander Telfair, and Dorothy Walton, as well as the Owens family, often circulated between urban areas (such as Savannah and Augusta) and their numerous and extensive plantation holdings in nearby counties. In this way, rural and urban slaveholding practices crossed geographic boundaries via slaves and slaveholders. Urban life might necessitate means of controlling enslaved property different from those used on plantations; and urban settings provided opportunities for autonomy different from those available on plantations. But the system of slavery was secure, embedded in legal, social, and political frameworks that upheld slaveholder authority over any privileges given to enslaved people.

At the time of Walker's letter to Telfair, slavery had been legal in Georgia for just more than seventy years. Savannah, along with Baltimore, Richmond, Charleston, Mobile, and New Orleans, played a pivotal role in the southern economic system. These port cities were entrepôts of goods—slaves, cotton, rice, and other products of the slave regime. Thus, the control and management of labor within cities was an important element of the broader slave system. European immigrant laborers were largely unwilling to travel south until the late antebellum period because of competition from slave labor, so governmental and economic leaders had to ensure that slave labor completed the work of building and maintaining city infrastructures; managing waterways, particularly those that led to ocean-going ports; hauling goods traveling from plantations through urban markets and onto ships; and performing the domestic labor of urban households.

In Savannah and the rest of Georgia, the establishment and refinement of slave codes in the antebellum era followed legal trends in other places throughout the South and grew in response to regional and local events. The colony passed a limited set of slave codes in 1750 as it moved from restricting slavery to accepting the system as central to its economy. But in 1755 and 1765 the colony's assembly, influenced by practices in South Carolina, passed a more comprehensive set of codes, which did not change substantially before the Civil War. These slave codes limited the movement of enslaved blacks and outlawed their possession, except with their owners' permission, of weapons or items that might be used as weapons. Without white supervision, enslaved people could not assemble in Georgia except in limited numbers. Enslaved people were not allowed to rent property for themselves; to sell or barter goods; to hire themselves out to employers; to own property such as boats, livestock, and other goods; or to own real estate. It was illegal to teach enslaved people to write, but they could be taught to read: reading could be useful to the owners of some highly trained slaves, but writing could lead to forged passes and other sorts of trickery. Acts deemed rebellious or dangerous to the slave system or to white slave owners were deemed capital crimes: arson, murder, rebellion, inciting rebellion, and destroying crops and property.[4]

The enforcement of some laws appeared petty, and probably occurred only intermittently, such as laws against owning dogs, smoking in public, and drinking alcohol. Indeed, law enforcement might step in to prosecute blacks for such activities only if requested to do so by slaveholders; if slaveholders were excessively abusive or lax; or if activities such as drinking alcohol led to violence against whites or against the property of whites—including violence against other slaves. In the South, it was more important to maintain slave owners' control than to build up a strong law-enforcement infrastructure.[5] But such laws could be used also to rein in black populations at times of communal stress, such as threats or fears of a slave rebellion. Similarly, the autonomy of drinking and smoking could be taken away as part of the punishment for other infractions. Ultimately, such relatively petty laws reinforced lines of behavior and respect between enslaved blacks and whites—behaviors allowable to whites without penalty, such as smoking, drinking, and owning dogs, were legitimate for enslaved blacks only with whites' permission.[6]

But central to all slave codes was the control of labor. In Savannah, enslaved people who hired out their time, whether on their own initiative or at the command of their masters, were required to buy badges, which they had to display at all times. Although white workers from the late eighteenth century onward worried about competition from enslaved workers and sought to limit their access to skilled jobs, they were largely unsuccessful. Slaves were excluded from skilled occupations in the slave code of 1758, but that was overturned in 1785, after the American Revolution. In 1839, three jobs were briefly made off-limits to enslaved folk—masons, painters, and coopers—but by 1854 only masons were excluded.[7] Other limitations on slave employments were rarely obeyed. In 1815, a law was passed to restrict blacks from piloting on the Savannah River, but it was never enforced. Indeed, in one of the early skirmishes of the Civil War, white Confederates were unable to capitalize on the capture of a Union boat in the Savannah River because the enslaved black pilot, Moses Dallas, had been shot and killed. The boat was abandoned in the river.[8]

In addition to monitoring the work that enslaved people performed, slave codes limited the possibility of black freedom. After 1801, owners could manumit enslaved people only by permission of the state legislature. Owners who wished to free their slaves created a variety of legal documents to get around this law and provide them some measure of autonomy, even if not outright freedom. For example, Benoit Wall sold the slave Antonio on the condition that Antonio pay his new owner fifty cents a year, after which Antonio need not provide him any further labor. Antonio could "depart from Savannah, when he pleases . . . to enjoy his freedom and liberty." This unusual deed was enacted "to protect . . . Antonio until an act of the Legislature can be procured to sanction [his] freedom and manumission."[9] Such an agreement probably signaled an unusual relationship between owner and slave: perhaps the slave was the owner's child or had performed some exemplary service on behalf of the owner or the owner's family. Further, such agreements depended on the new owner's honesty and financial stability. But such special agreements were fairly rare and went against the impetus of the time, which was to retain blacks in bondage. Slave owners feared that the presence of large numbers of free blacks would create a restive slave population. This fear was further codified in a state law of 1818 that restricted manumissions to the point that they all but disappeared from the records. Instead, owners provided autonomy, but not freedom, to favored slaves.[10]

As the manumission laws reveal, free whites and free blacks as well as enslaved blacks were subject to legal control in the service of maintaining the system of slavery. Whites and free blacks were forbidden to sell certain goods, particularly alcohol, to slaves. Slaves could not sell to other slaves; and neither free nor enslaved blacks were to sell goods in shops unless under the supervision of whites. Slave vendors, particularly those traveling from rural to urban areas to sell agricultural products—poultry, fruit, vegetables—had to have a special ticket verifying the legitimacy of the goods. And whites could be charged with a capital crime for inciting a slave rebellion.[11]

Although these and other codes, as written, restricted the lives of everyone within slave societies, enforcement of the laws fluctuated throughout the antebellum period. Antebellum slavery in the South was shaped by opposing trends and tensions between slavery and freedom, hierarchy and equality, which were debated and negotiated down to the Civil War. The decision to keep enslaved labor as the bedrock of the southern economic system—a decision bolstered by the emergence of the nineteenth-century cotton economy and its centrality to the worldwide Industrial Revolution—meant that black labor needed to be controlled. Ensuring that the wealth flowed upward—to slave owners and to white society more generally—was the goal of the slave system.

In Savannah, Georgia's slave laws were adapted to the conditions of city life and the city's role in the southern slave economy. Laws limiting mobility, independent housing, and literacy were enforced only as needed, and enslaved people learned how far to push the boundaries of the acceptable. Although enslaved people were subject to curfews and had to wear their badges at all times, watchmen often got to know the enslaved people within the relatively small city. With an easy "get on home now," they encouraged blacks off streets rather than arresting them at every offense.

Although whites may have been concerned about the possibility that widespread knowledge of reading and writing among blacks could lead to mischief, such as forging passes or reading antislavery literature, in reality, having an enslaved person or two who could read could be quite useful in the business of the city. Despite laws passed in 1817 by the city and in 1829 by the state that prohibited teaching free or enslaved blacks to read, secret schools for the education of blacks, free and enslaved, flourished in the antebellum period, led by free blacks who taught in their homes. Catherine Deveaux and her daughter Jane were the most well-known black teachers in antebellum Savannah, a group that included Julien Fromatin, James Porter, Mary Woodhouse, and Mathilda Beasley. James Simms, a black teacher and later the historian of the First African Baptist Church, was whipped and fined for operating a school in the antebellum period. In some white households, white children taught black children to read, and owners could benefit from the knowledge possessed by particular slaves. A few whites ran schools for blacks. In July 1833, Mary Telfair visited a school for slaves run by a white teacher, Mrs. Edward Campbell, who instructed about forty-five black enslaved children in her washroom.[12]

Unwilling or unable to completely limit the literacy of blacks, whites censored the most inflammatory antislavery propaganda, especially after the fiery David Walker's *Appeal . . . to the Coloured Citizens of the World* turned up in the hands of blacks in Savannah and other areas throughout the South in 1829.[13]

But urban slave owners also knew that the constables and the city jail could be marshaled to assist in punishing wayward slaves. Rural slave owners used public whippings, confinements, and other forms of punishment by law enforcement as examples to the broader slave population; they were not averse to enforcing such punishments themselves either, although the wealthier among them might make overseers or slave drivers perform such tasks. Urban slave owners used the city jail to confine wayward slaves, and whippings occurred at the jail rather than in relatively cramped squares, where neighbors might witness their brutality. But such punishments were still public events, informing enslaved people of the limits within which they lived. The Owens family used the city jail to contain or to punish their bondpeople on several occasions. Emma, for example, was jailed for one night for "safekeeping," perhaps indicating an attempt to prevent her from doing something of which the family disapproved, such as visiting a family member outside Savannah. The Owenses paid $1.50 in jail fees to make sure she was there when they returned. Molly was punished with five nights in jail for running away. Tom was jailed for "improper conduct." Osburn, declared a "lunitic," endured the longest jail stint of the family slaves, thirty-four days, costing the Owenses $11.40 by the end of his term.[14]

The complicated dance between allowing enslaved people some autonomy while still controlling them had its greatest impact on the establishment of Savannah's black churches. Savannah's strong tradition of black Baptist churches was anomalous in the

antebellum South, particularly after Nat Turner's religion-inspired slave rebellion in Virginia led to the death of fifty-eight whites in 1831. The founding of the First African Baptist Church points to the ways that individual, often influential whites could help blacks circumvent laws. But such actions were not without penalty for those involved, particularly African Americans.

In 1782, Andrew Bryan and his wife, Hannah, along with two other enslaved women, Cate and Hagar, were baptized into a fledgling Baptist congregation led by George Liele, a recently freed African American and ordained minister. Several months later, after Liele had departed Savannah with the British army, Bryan began leading the small group and others in morning and evening prayer. In 1788, Abraham Marshall, a white minister, ordained Bryan, baptized forty-five slaves, and organized them into a church that Marshall named the Ethiopian Church of Jesus Christ at Savannah. Through the 1820s, the congregation was known as the "colored" Baptist church by the Sunbury Association (one of the governing bodies of the Baptist Church in Georgia) and subsequently was widely known as the First African Baptist Church.[15]

The organization of the church, and Andrew Bryan's leadership of it, were allowed and encouraged by his and his wife's owner, William Bryan of Brampton Plantation. But neither William Bryan's influence nor the support of other white plantation owners who allowed their slaves to be baptized in the new church was enough to prevent William Bryan, Andrew Bryan, and numerous congregants from being brought before the grand jury. William Bryan was named as the defendant, and the church was characterized as a "pretence of religion . . . a mere mockery . . . a cloak for every species of blasphemy, theft, and debauchery." William Bryan was charged with violating the patrol law for "permitting Negroes to assemble, in large bodies, at the plantation called Brampton." Individual congregants were captured by the patrol with increasing frequency until 1789 or 1790, when Andrew Bryan and his brother Sampson, who served as a deacon, along with as many as fifty members of the congregation, were subjected to public whippings administered by the slave patrol. The Bryan brothers' "backs were so lacerated that their blood ran down to the earth," and then all were placed in the city jail.[16]

But soon after, maybe even as a result of, this painful humiliation, Savannah-area whites began to see the church not as a potential hotbed of black radicalism intent on slave rebellion, but as an institution that could support the system of slavery. No doubt the continuing support and intercession of William Bryan and other white slave owners contributed to this détente. In addition, the lack of reprisal by blacks in the face of the continuing persecution eased the concerns of whites. Whites spying on Andrew Bryan in his home supposedly witnessed him praying for the whites who had abused him and his congregants.[17] Indeed, the First, Second and Third African Baptist Churches of Savannah form together one of the most intriguing areas of compliance and negotiation among black and white Christians entangled together in southern slavery. Savannah-area whites came to see the churches as more pro- than antislavery, though they were led by free black men, some of whom had gained freedom as a result of their time and experiences in the church. The example of economically successful free blacks leading congregations largely made up of enslaved people may have given urban slaves reason to hope, even if freedom was largely unattainable because of the limits placed on manumission after 1801.

Savannah's black Baptist churches survived the fear that swept the South in the aftermath of Denmark Vesey's conspiracy in Charleston in 1822 and Nat Turner's rebellion in Virginia in 1831. Both Vesey and Turner were associated with strong religious beliefs—Vesey with the brief life of the AME Church in the pre–Civil War South, and Turner with his own brand of slave preaching in the shadow of a large white Methodist congregation. In the wake of the Vesey conspiracy, the AME Church was swept out of Charleston and much of the South. After Turner's rebellion, enslaved ministers were, at best, restricted in the kinds of lessons they could preach; some could not preach safely at all unless hidden from view, leading to the rise of the "invisible institution," as the practice of slave religion has been termed by scholars.[18] Yet Savannah's blacks managed not only to maintain sizable congregations (in 1840, First African Baptist had more than two thousand congregants; Second African, more than thirteen hundred; and Third African, more than two hundred) but also to own land and erect church buildings rivaling similar structures in northern cities—property holdings that survive to this day.[19]

The First African Baptist Church became the center of one well-known and distinctive settlement, Yamacraw, in Oglethorpe Ward on the west side of Savannah, where enslaved and free blacks lived fairly independently in the city, renting their own homes and raising families. (See Sidebar, "Slavery and Freedom in Savannah's Industrial Corridor" (p. 45), for an account of Oglethorpe Ward.) Although it was against the law for slaves to live independently, settlements such as Yamacraw aligned with the needs of the urban slave system and the desires of urban slave owners. In some cases, urban slaves who hired out their own time returned set payments to their masters but paid for their own housing and meals. In return, they were able to live autonomously in family groupings. The housing available to blacks in these areas, though of poor quality, made independence possible. In addition to Yamacraw to the west, the Old Fort and Springhill neighborhoods on the eastern edges of the city were well known for similar settlements. But Yamacraw was the largest, containing more enslaved and free blacks throughout the antebellum era than any other part of the city.

Some critics complained that such autonomy undermined the institution of slavery. But the management of enslaved people in Savannah did not happen because whites were in physical proximity to the blacks they owned, but instead relied on a constellation of laws, law enforcement, and social understandings among whites, free blacks, and enslaved people, in which enslaved blacks were under the watchful eyes of whites and some

The First African Baptist Church of Savannah, Georgia, Front View, from Franklin Square, *frontispiece of E. K. Love,* History of the First African Baptist Church, from Its Organization, January 20th, 1788, to July 1st, 1888; Including the Centennial Celebration, Addresses, Sermons, etc. *(Savannah: Morning News Print, 1888). Courtesy of Documenting the American South, University of North Carolina at Chapel Hill Libraries.*

Andrew Cox Marshall

Andrew C. Marshall. In James M. Simms, The First Colored Baptist Church in North America, Constituted at Savannah, Georgia, January 20, A.D. 1788, with Biographical Sketches of the Pastors *(Philadelphia: Lippincott, 1888), 76. Courtesy of Documenting the American South, University of North Carolina at Chapel Hill Libraries.*

Andrew Cox Marshall was Savannah's most important African American in the pre–Civil War period. Born into slavery in the mid-eighteenth century, Marshall acquired his freedom and went on to become a successful businessman and an influential religious leader with far-reaching ties throughout Savannah's diverse free and enslaved African American community; he was also well known among Savannah's white elite. The lives of those who gained freedom before slavery ended were restricted by laws that limited their economic and social opportunities. Yet Marshall managed to navigate such constraints and achieve some level of success and autonomy.

Born in South Carolina around 1755 to an enslaved woman and an English overseer, Marshall wound up in Savannah as a result of two failed manumission promises and ownership by five prominent slaveholders, including John Houstoun, the governor of Georgia in 1778 and 1784, and Joseph Clay, a businessman and judge. Accounts of Marshall's life indicate he participated in activities that supported the United States in the American Revolution and the War of 1812. He purportedly received pay for his work in both wars and had the opportunity to meet General George Washington. Marshall later served as President Washington's personal servant on his visit to Savannah in 1791. Richard Richardson purchased Marshall in 1812, and Marshall purchased his freedom

at some point soon thereafter with funds lent to him by Richardson, who was a merchant, banker, slave trader, and the first owner of the Owens-Thomas House. Richardson became Marshall's first guardian, which the law required of free blacks. Marshall's wife, Rachel, and their three daughters—Rose, Amy, and Peggy—had previously gained their freedom through the efforts of Marshall's uncle, Andrew Bryan, the popular and influential pastor of the First African Baptist Church, as well as Richardson and other white elites in the community. As a free man, Marshall established a home with his family in Yamacraw on Savannah's west side. He set up a successful drayage (hauling) business that allowed him to accumulate sizable wealth. In 1824, the tax assessment of his real estate was valued at $8,400, and his will indicates that he had acquired shares in a state bank. At the time of his death, in 1856, he owned several buildings, including a brick house that he left to his immediate family. His fine clothes and silver watch he bequeathed to his enslaved cousin Andrew, showing the strong connections binding the enslaved and the free.

In addition to family, home, and business, Marshall focused his attentions on building up the congregations of black Baptists in Savannah. In 1815, at about the age of sixty, Marshall took over as pastor of the First African Baptist Church. He served in that position twice for a total of more than thirty years. During his leadership, Marshall baptized nearly 3,800 people, converted 4,000, and married 2,000. His widespread and diverse religious activities included traveling around the country to preach, taking a special interest in the poor and infirm, and beginning a Sunday school. He even addressed the Georgia legislature. Beginning in 1840, he directed that church funds be used for foreign missions to Liberia, the African country established by Americans for the resettlement of free blacks.

Marshall's prominent position did not keep him from suffering the indignities visited upon other free or enslaved blacks. He did not always agree with his peers or guardians and was sometimes called out or put in his place. Around 1820 he was sentenced to be publicly whipped for making an illegal purchase of bricks from slaves. His guardian and former master, Richard Richardson, and others spoke in his behalf to ensure the whipping did not "scratch his skin or draw blood." Nonetheless, the public spectacle was meant to make clear to Marshall and all the free and enslaved people of Savannah the limits of their power.

Within the Baptist association and his own church, Marshall suffered repercussions because of his support of the work of the controversial white minister Alexander Campbell of Virginia, a reformed clergyman who favored the emancipation of slaves. Marshall showed interest in Campbell's movement, known as the Disciples of Christ, and invited him to speak at First African Baptist. Marshall's association with Campbell resulted in a split within the church, with 155 members leaving First African Baptist to establish their own church, Third African Baptist. The Sunbury Baptist Association, the regional Baptist organization run by whites, sought to have Marshall dismissed from his post by the members of his church. When that didn't work, they removed First African Baptist from their association from 1832 to 1837. The First African Baptist Church was readmitted to the association only after Marshall recanted his support of Campbell and asked forgiveness for his errant ways. In addition, his apology helped ease tensions with the white elites in the community.

Andrew Cox Marshall lived an extraordinary life, not least for reaching the age of one hundred. He experienced slavery and freedom, witnessed and participated in key moments in American history, and spent much of his time helping his fellow men and women. He died in December 1856 after returning home from a preaching tour in Richmond, Virginia, meant in part to raise money to build a new church in Savannah. Hundreds of people attended his funeral. A newspaper account noted "an immense throng without respect to color or condition collected in the Church, the floor, aisles, galleries and even steps and windows of which were densely packed [and] hundreds [were] unable to gain admittance." He was buried in a family vault at Laurel Grove South Cemetery.

TANIA SAMMONS

free blacks, who were likely to be their employers, landlords, or neighborhood constables as well as their owners. By 1848, the practice of slaves living apart from their owners was so common in Savannah that Joseph Bancroft, a census taker, counted slaves at their residences rather than seeking them at their owners' homes.[20]

In addition to Yamacraw, Old Fort, and Springhill, enslaved blacks lived in every ward of the city. Most slaves lived with their owners. The wealthiest slave owners, such as the residents of the Owens-Thomas House, built relatively spacious slave quarters that reflected the grandeur of their own homes. Other slave owners housed slaves in kitchens, storerooms, basements, and carriage houses. Some scholars assume that urban slaves had better living conditions than their rural counterparts. But female cooks at the Marshall House, the largest hotel in the state, became the topic of concern when a northern visitor in 1853 noticed that they did not have any beds and slept on "the solid brick hearth." Male servants at the same facility were discovered sleeping "behind the bar-room door . . . on narrow boards placed on chairs." The hotel employed "fifty or more" slaves who worked in this "first-class establishment," which had opened in 1851.[21]

The enslaved population grew in Savannah throughout the antebellum period, in contrast to other southern cities, which saw steep declines in the numbers of slaves between 1840 and 1860. But Savannah by 1860 had a much smaller overall population (22,292) than Baltimore (212,418), New Orleans (168,675), Mobile (29,258), or Charleston (40,522). Only Norfolk, Virginia, had a smaller population among major southern cities (14,620). Slaves made up just over 30 percent of Savannah's population (7,712) on the eve of the Civil War, down from about 40 percent (3,075) in 1820. As in other urban areas, north and south, women outnumbered men in the slave and free black populations, while men outnumbered women in the white population.[22] This can be seen in Anson Ward, the area containing the Owens-Thomas House, where 176 enslaved women and 105 enslaved men lived in the late 1840s.

Savannah's urban slave population was inextricably linked to the rural areas surrounding it. Most of the bondpeople who worked in the Owens-Thomas House had begun their lives on rural estates in nearby counties. Slaveholding families connected to the Owens-Thomas House were some of the largest and most influential ones in the state. The Owens family had more than eight thousand acres of land on rural plantations spread across seven counties. In April 1856, at the time of his death, George Welshman Owens owned 340 slaves. Four years later, his estate inventory included 327 slaves, of which

Left: Slave quarters, west façade,
Owens-Thomas House.
Telfair Museums, Savannah.
Photograph: Olivia Alison.

Below: J.D. Perry, Hermitage Plantation—
Slave Quarters. *Courtesy of the Georgia
Historical Society, 1361PH-01-15-0136B.*

Above: Unknown artist, George Welshman Owens (1786–1856). Telfair Museums, Savannah, Georgia. Bequest of Margaret Gray Thomas, OT1951.84.

Right: Listing of 53 of George W. Owens's 193 Slaves in Chatham County. U.S. Census, 1850, Slave Schedule. Courtesy of the Georgia Historical Society.

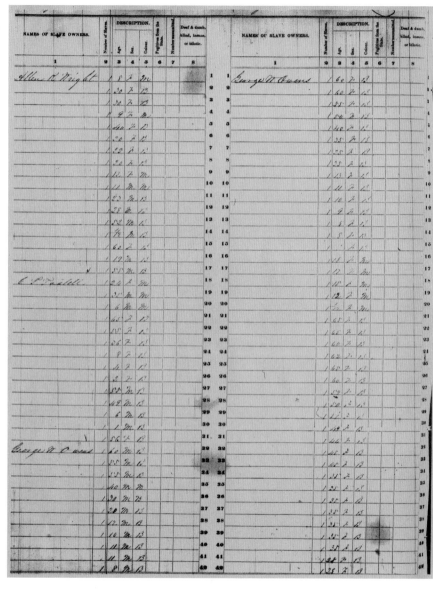

256 resided in rural Camden County, about a hundred miles south of Savannah; and 71 in Chatham County, of which Savannah was the county seat.[23] The Owens bondpeople lived amid sixteen urban dwellings in Chatham County and thirty rural dwellings in Camden County.[24] No doubt the urban dwellings were located in the Yamacraw, Old Fort, and Springhill neighborhoods of Savannah.

At times, the connections between enslaved and free blacks disturbed slave owners' sense of control over them. Enslaved people could suffer dire consequences for putting family and community loyalties ahead of their owners' needs. This was experienced by enslaved workers at the Owens-Thomas House, such as John, Jane, Denbingh, Tom and others. John frequently traveled twenty-five miles outside Savannah to see his wife. He was whipped repeatedly for leaving without permission, but still kept visiting her.[25] When the Owens family hired out Jane to work for the Bowens family, the enslaved woman took the liberty of moving about the greater Savannah community as she pleased, "visiting some of her friends after bell-ring . . . without a ticket." Upon her arrest in 1857, she "swore no white man should carry her to the Guard House." George S. Owens decided to let her "stay in the caboose all night, with the bed bugs," as punishment.[26] Denbingh, one the Owens family's most trusted servants, did not want to live in Savannah, preferring to stay at Ossabaw Island, where he had served George W. Owens's father, Owen Owens, since birth.[27]

In other instances, family ties could inspire allegiance, thus stabilizing labor regimes and white ownership of human property. And of course the birth of children both ensured the continuance of the slave population and added to the wealth of slave owners. The autonomy that Dorothy Walton granted to her slave Sanders was perhaps due to the existence of his wife and, possibly, children. Those family ties may have assured Walton that Sanders would not leave the region. In addition, Sanders had remained with the family through the tumultuous Revolutionary War years, when many enslaved blacks chose to leave plantations and slave owners behind, either striking out for other parts of the United States or departing with the British in search of freedom. As the South settled into its commitment to slavery in the late eighteenth and early nineteenth centuries, the Waltons knew that it would become increasingly difficult for a family (husband, wife, and children) to flee slavery in the Deep South.

Although perhaps 100,000 African Americans did escape from southern slavery and into the North over the course of the antebellum era, that figure represented only

Owens Family Plantations

The Owens family is perhaps best known for owning their stately Savannah mansion at 124 Abercorn Street, but throughout the eighteenth and nineteenth centuries the family owned plantations and estates in several Georgia counties in addition to numerous Savannah properties. The rural landholdings, which specialized in rice, cotton, timber, and a diversity of food crops, provided the family members with considerable wealth, power, and prestige, besides giving them a stake in Georgia's booming slave economy and serving as a basis for land speculation. What follows is a description of the major Owens plantations.

COLERAIN PLANTATION
(*sometimes referred to as Tweedside*)
Owen Owens, the father of George Welshman Owens, purchased some six hundred acres of land along the Savannah River from the British government following the Revolutionary War. Once the site of an extensive indigo and rice plantation, Colerain had fallen into disarray and suffered great damage after being pillaged throughout the war. The British government confiscated the land from its former owner, Alexander Wylly, a Savannah mercantilist and lawyer, and put it in the hands of local loyalists, including Owens. Hoping to use the land for speculation purposes, Owens and two other men of means purchased Colerain

for £122 in June 1784. Because of his sizable landholdings near Savannah, Owens decided to remain in the city after the British evacuation, and he officially became an active and loyal citizen of Georgia that same year. In 1785, Owens and his partners sold Colerain to Dr. James Houstoun, a surgeon in the Continental army, earning an impressive profit of £478. Houstoun improved the estate, purchased many slaves, and prospered as one of Savannah's wealthiest men. Colerain was expanded throughout the eighteenth and nineteenth centuries and endured industrial improvements up through the 1930s.

MONTEITH PLANTATION
(*or possibly, Moutwith Plantation*)
In March 1791, Owen Owens made another large land purchase, Monteith Plantation, a 6,000-acre estate in Effingham and Chatham Counties. Few details survive about the plantation, but estate records reveal that George W. Owens later inherited the property from his father, Owen Owens. It is difficult to determine how many slaves worked at Monteith. Two advertisements in 1797 for runaway slaves place a bondman named William and a young boy named Caddy on Monteith Plantation. Today, Monteith is the name of a town in Effingham County north of Savannah.

ST. CATHERINES ISLAND PLANTATION

This Liberty County property sat south of Savannah and off the coast of the Sunbury River. When Owen Owens died in 1814, he willed to his son, George W. Owens, the bulk of his personal items and property, which included a plantation on the south half of St. Catherines Island. According to Owen Owens's will, the property was valued at $20,215 and included some eighty-seven slaves, all listed by name in a property inventory. It is unknown how long the property remained in the Owens family.

OSSABAW ISLAND PLANTATION

In 1814, George Welshman Owens acquired five hundred acres and an adjoining marsh on the eastern division of the north end of Ossabaw Island. At least part of the land was inherited from his father, Owen Owens; George may also have purchased additional acreage. It is likely that a large slave force grew Sea Island cotton, rice, indigo, and timber on the plantation. In 1833, Bryan M. Morel sold George Owens three hundred acres; within two years, Owens transferred all of his rights to that parcel back to Morel. The Morels, who had owned large tracts of land on the island since the colonial period, were central to the island's early forays into Sea Island cotton cultivation.

SILK HOPE PLANTATION

Located on Salt Creek in Chatham County, Silk Hope was a legendary Savannah River plantation. First owned by James Habersham, one of the largest and wealthiest rice planters in Georgia, the property consisted of five hundred acres granted by King George II in 1756. The king hoped that the plantation would produce some of the world's finest silk, but that dream was dashed when rice became the most lucrative crop on the estate. George W. Owens purchased the property in 1827 for $5,000 at a tax sale. Their Silk Hope plantation grew to seven thousand acres on the Ogeechee River and Beverly Road, producing mostly rice, cotton, and pine. In 1840, Owens sold the plantation's main house and four slave cabins to Dr. Richard D. Arnold of Savannah, who served as mayor of the city from time to time throughout the late nineteenth century and cofounded the Georgia Historical Society.

OAKLAND PROPERTY

In 1834, George W. Owens paid $22,000 for a thousand acres of land and 150 Negroes in Chatham County. The estate, with its large enslaved workforce, underscored George W. Owens's status as one of Savannah's most productive planters.

GUINAS/QUINAS PLANTATION

This property of more than a thousand acres was in Habersham County, near present-day Clarksville. George W. Owens purchased the property for $5,000 and spent an additional $3,000 to improve it. From the 1830s through the 1850s, the plantation served as a summer retreat for the Owens family. The family may have named the property in honor of "Gwynas," which was "the old family place in Wales." The family kept a small slave force on site to tend to their needs. According to the 1840 Census, five slaves resided at Guinas. These bondpeople ranged in age from twelve to fifty. In 1856, George W. Owens deeded the property to his wife, Sarah, upon his death.

SPRING HILL PLANTATION
(*or Egypt Plantation*)
Between 1835 and 1843, George W. Owens owned this Bryan County property, which had been purchased for $1,000. The plantation was located in both Bryan and Effingham Counties. Little is known about the enslaved persons who lived there or about the agricultural output of the property.

IVANHOE PLANTATION
This Camden County property was located on the north side of the Satilla River and covered more than 4,600 acres. By the 1850s, it had become the Owens family's second home away from Savannah, replacing Guinas as the favored summer destination. Ivanhoe contained lucrative timber reserves, a sawmill, and rice fields, which by 1860 were producing some 2.4 million pounds of rice. The 1850 Census indicates that there were 182 slaves either living on the property or owned by George W. Owens in the county. By 1860, that figure had increased to 256. Undoubtedly, Ivanhoe remained a bountiful source of income for the Owens family for years. In fact, it stayed in the family for three generations. In 1902, George W. Owens II sold both Ivanhoe and Roseneath Plantations, thus ending the family's storied history in Georgia's thriving rice economy.

ROSENEATH PLANTATION
Little is known about Roseneath Plantation other than its location in Jefferson County. Most likely, the Owens family owned this property briefly before selling it.

SATILLA PROPERTY
In 1815, George W. Owens purchased this property, located some seventy-five miles south of Savannah, for $18,000 from the Elliott family. It came with a sawmill, which cost $20,000, and a threshing mill, valued at $6,000. To work the plantation, Owens purchased "three gangs of Negroes worth $37,000." Besides grain and lumber, the slaves almost certainly grew cotton and rice. The family owned the plantation through 1832.

JERMAINE THIBODEAUX

Ossabaw Island and the Atlantic World

Located sixteen miles south of Savannah, Ossabaw Island, the third-largest barrier island off the coast of Georgia, contains 26,000 acres of salt marsh and maritime upland forest. The many economic and demographic ties between Savannah and Ossabaw included ownership of island property by prominent white families in Savannah; the movement of slaves between plantations on the island and the mainland; and the production of indigo, Sea Island cotton, beef, and lumber on Ossabaw for shipping through the Port of Savannah. Native Americans inhabited the island before the 1700s, followed by African Americans during the eighteenth and nineteenth centuries, and a small number of wealthy northern families in the twentieth century.

Rich archaeological deposits of shell mounds indicate that Native Americans exploited the island's resources for about thirty-five hundred years, up until the sixteenth century, although only a small group of them remained at the time the Spanish created missions along the Georgia coast in the late 1500s. In a treaty to establish the colony of Georgia in 1733, native Creek ceded to the British government control of a narrow strip of coastal land between the Savannah and Altamaha Rivers, with the exception of three barrier islands—Ossabaw, St. Catherines, and Sapelo. Mary Musgrove Bosomworth, who was part Creek and part English, later claimed the islands in an attempt to recover expenses she incurred while acting as broker between Natives and the English. To resolve the dispute, Georgia magistrates auctioned the island for £1,350, giving her the proceeds and ownership of neighboring St. Catherines.

In 1760, John Morel, the son of French Swiss emigrants, and his father-in-law bought Ossabaw from a land speculator. For the next hundred years, the island participated fully in the economic and social life of the Atlantic world through the Port of Savannah. As a part-time partner with the Savannah-based slave traders Edward and William Telfair, Morel brought thirty-odd enslaved Africans onto the island. They herded cattle, killed feral hogs, and packed barrels of beef and pork for the Savannah and West Indian markets. They made the plantation into one of the largest producers of indigo in Georgia, a crop that was well known to many West Africans. They felled live oak trees for sale, mainly for use in boat construction, and built at least one vessel destined for the transatlantic trade. They were skilled in carpentry and blacksmithing, and many were adept sailors. Nine of them managed to escape in a yawl and make it all the way to St. Augustine and the relative safety of the British during the Revolution.

On Morel's death in 1776, the island was

divided among his surviving sons. John Morel Jr. inherited what became South End Plantation; Peter Henry Morel, Middle Place Plantation; and Bryan Morel, North End Plantation. A fourth plantation, called Buckhead, was later carved from South End. By the early 1790s, Sea Island cotton had supplanted indigo as a primary crop, and as many as 174 Africans and African Americans worked at cultivating the silky, long-fiber cotton that commanded a premium on the Liverpool market. By the start of the Civil War, the four plantations held approximately 225 African Americans, who worked as field hands, carpenters, boatmen, wagoners, gardeners, nurses, cooks, and "cow-minders." On North End Plantation in 1850, there were 36 men (average age 19.7 years) and 27 women (average age 20.6 years). The succession of owners on the island during the antebellum period included George Welshman Owens, who exemplified the instrumental role played by prominent Savannah families in the development of the coastal islands.

After emancipation, former slaves who had been carried off the island by their owners returned to claim land. They learned that black Union troops had already received warrants under General Sherman's Special Field Order No. 15, a measure for confiscating coastal lands in behalf of African Americans. The frustrated freedmen and freedwomen became tenant farmers or day laborers under the Freedmen's Bureau supervisor, John W. Magill, who was setting up his own cotton plantation. A three-way rivalry ensued as two sets of African Americans contended against each other and a white supervisor exploited the situation.

Within weeks of their return, the freedpeople created the Hinder-Me-Not Baptist Church, which became the center of black cultural life for the next twenty-five years. After the return of the land to pre–Civil War owners, the former Union troops left the island and the remaining freedmen became tenant farmers. When the white landlords refused to sell any of their property, the 150 African Americans on Ossabaw migrated to the mainland during the 1880s, where many helped found a new community, Pin Point, built around crabbing and oystering. With its tight-knit families, Pin Point became a place where the cultural and social life of the island was replicated. The Hinder-Me-Not Church served as a foundation for two mainland churches, Sweetfield-of-Eden Baptist Church and First Beulah Baptist.

As happened on many of the Georgia barrier islands in the twentieth century, a succession of northern families purchased Ossabaw for hunting and other recreational purposes. In 1924, the Torrey family of Grosse Pointe, Michigan, acquired the island, built a Spanish-style house, and came for five months each year to escape the winter weather. They employed people from Pin Point and elsewhere to work as servants, hunt managers, and ranch hands. Many of these workers lived in the three tabby cabins that had been built in the 1840s and were continuously occupied until the 1980s. In 1960, Eleanor Torrey West, together with her brother's family, inherited the island. They invited artists, writers, and intellectuals to renew their creative energies on the island as guests of the family, and allowed Ossabaw to return to a natural state. In 1978, the Torrey family sold the island to the State of Georgia on the condition that it be used only for study, research, and education. Today, students, teachers, artists, writers, naturalists, and others participate in programs that explore life and labor on North End Plantation during the eighteenth and nineteenth centuries, incorporate art and writing workshops, investigate the ecosystems of the island, and use of a network of monitors and web cameras to transmit environmental data wirelessly.

PAUL PRESSLY

2.5 percent of the 3.9 million enslaved people on the eve of the Civil War. It was often thought that slaves would find it easier to leave the South in a city rather than the countryside, but running away from either setting was incredibly difficult. Those enslaved people who seemingly had the greatest opportunity to run away—members of urban communities who, like Sanders, appeared to be under relatively loose control; those who traveled with masters to the free North; those who were literate or had other special skills—also learned just how difficult escape could be. No doubt they learned of the limits of northern support for black freedom. The abolitionists were considered a fanatical fringe group until late in the antebellum period, and even the spread of political antislavery sentiment in the 1850s did not always translate to a desire among whites for black freedom or for providing assistance to African Americans. Life in northern states became more, not less, difficult for free blacks as the Civil War approached.

In Savannah and the surrounding area, efforts by the enslaved to retain their humanity while part of an inhumane system were evident throughout the pre–Civil War period. If slave owners sometimes tried to classify enslaved people with their livestock, those attempts were often made ridiculous. More often, enslaved people and slave owners balanced competing needs and desires, creating an equilibrium that did not completely efface the long-term unease evident on both sides. Enslaved people learned to resist slavery pragmatically, in small ways and large, at certain times and not others. Sometimes in concert with free blacks, they challenged the boundaries and limits of enslavement on behalf of family, religion, culture, and self.

But enslaved people could also go for broke when pushed beyond endurance. At least twice—once in Savannah and once in the countryside—enslaved people rose up and murdered masters. Other slave owners took note, even when accounts of the events did not appear in the newspapers for fear of inflaming northern abolitionist sentiment. In 1852, George S. Owens wrote his father of the fate of James Houstoun Jr. of Marengo Plantation in McIntosh County (about sixty miles south of Savannah), who was murdered "by his negroes." According to Owens, Houstoun was "a drunk and very violent in his cups." When Houstoun "commit[ted] some outrage on one of the women, she aroused the gang, who fell upon him when asleep, tied & whipped him, and then knocked him in the head, after which they burnt his clothes carried the body off & buried it." Houstoun was the son of a well-known and wealthy family. His father, James Houstoun, died in 1819, the year he was born. That same year, his mother, Mary Ann Williams Houstoun, married Major Jonathan Thomas, whom Houstoun probably considered his father. Four enslaved men and one enslaved woman were eventually arrested and taken to the Darien jail for their part in the murder, although, as George S. informed his father, "Randolph Spalding has been proposing *to hang them at once*." Randolph Spalding was the scion of another planter family in McIntosh County; he and Houstoun likely had been friends. The fate of the five enslaved people was decided by an extralegal "citizens' court" consisting of all those who wished to participate and presided over by a "prominent citizen" of McIntosh County, despite the orders of a superior court judge and the solicitor general that the "court" should not continue. The five were sentenced to death by hanging.[28]

The outcome of the Houstoun murder reveals the limits of laws to prevent whites from taking the legal process into their own hands when enslaved people were involved. White actions were controlled by slave laws, but enforcement of those laws was far more limited. Whites were not to sell alcohol to enslaved people. Slave owners could be punished for murdering the second enslaved person he or she killed, but not the first, and only if the crime was deemed premeditated. But overall, the need to uphold the power of slave owners prevented the prosecution of most whites for actions against slaves. Further, in the Houstoun case, no doubt the desire to keep out of public view Houstoun's abuse of the enslaved woman (actions that may have been common knowledge among his white friends) led to the white citizens' swift retribution.[29]

An incident in 1858 involving enslaved laborers at William B. Giles and Company's lumberyard went all the way to the Georgia Supreme Court. On July 24, forty-one slaves who had been accused of murder arrived in the Chatham County jail. They were held for one to eight days while investigators tried to gather the facts of the case. When authorities determined that "Willis" was the alleged culprit, all the others were released to William B. Giles, their owner. Giles paid $75 in jail fees for all of the bondmen except "Willis," whom authorities believed should stand trial for the murder. Although we do not know the identity or fate of the victim, we know that Giles sued the state to recover the jail fees charged for the uncharged bondmen. In January 1859, Judge Fleming of the Georgia Supreme Court determined that earlier legislation (the Act of 1811) allowed the fees to be collected.[30] But Judge Stephens reversed the decision on appeal, stating, "It is an abuse of the direction given" by the Act of 1811 "to award costs against an accused person in a case . . . when there is *no evidence* against him."[31]

This was not the first time the Giles slaves became part of public record. In 1854, they were scrutinized for their use of guns. Someone "complained that groups of Negroes, 'blacks of elegant leisure—the snobs of our colored population,' met regularly to test their marksmanship with pistols." It was further reported that "during the same month, some two-dozen Negroes were arrested when a ball they were holding at Giles and Bradley's sawmill ended in a riot." Giles apparently "had approved the dance."[32] These incidents suggest that the Giles slaves, like other enslaved laborers in and around Savannah, had an ambiguous relationship with the law.

We do not know the disposition of the bodies of the five slave rebels who slew James Houstoun or the outcome of Willis's fate. Perhaps their relatives and friends were allowed to claim their bodies following their executions, but it is just as likely that the bodies were retained by whites to impress on enslaved people the limits of black power. Many enslaved and free blacks who had not earned white disfavor were allowed to be celebrated in death in community-centered funerals. In Savannah, the death of Andrew Marshall, the pastor of Savannah's largest black Baptist church for over forty years, occasioned an interracial funeral service at the First African Baptist Church, followed by a mile-long procession of almost sixty carriages to the black section of Laurel Grove Cemetery.[33] Less public were the interments of numerous other enslaved blacks in Laurel Grove South.

Early in the morning of February 3, 1856, Maria Wallace was laid to rest in the Laurel Grove South Cemetery. She had spent all of her sixty-six years enslaved, first by the

Laurel Grove South Cemetery

Early in 1851, the City of Savannah purchased Springfield, a former rice plantation just outside the western edge of the city, with the intention of converting it into a cemetery. The city's primary burial ground, located on the corner of present-day Abercorn and Oglethorpe Streets, was full. On November 10, 1852, the city dedicated Laurel Grove Cemetery and officially opened plots to Savannah residents. In 1854, the city treasury began advertising lots; opening bids were $10, with $1 going to the clerk for title. All proceeds were held in a separate account from the treasury and were used solely for the preservation of the cemetery. The keeper of the cemetery, Alfred F. Torlay, collected a $1.50 fee for white burials, a "like sum" for digging a "colored grave," and $0.50 for supervising the digging of the latter. According to the cemetery's by-laws, Savannah's aldermen had "to provide a suitable place for the interment of deceased free persons of color and slaves." As a result, fifteen acres on the southern end of the property were set aside for African Americans. The rest of the property was open to white citizens and later became the final resting place for more than 1,500 Confederate soldiers. Today, Laurel Grove South is a historic resting place for Savannah's black citizens, the famous ones and those less renowned.

Once both sides of Laurel Grove opened, the city closed all cemeteries within the city limits to burials. Understanding that residents wanted to be buried near their relatives, city officials encouraged citizens to move their loved ones from the older burial grounds throughout the city to Laurel Grove, at the city's expense. The offer was extended to the white and the black communities, and many blacks took advantage of it. Some of the first bodies moved were those of Andrew Bryan and Henry Cunningham, two of the black community's most revered religious leaders. Bryan was one of the founding members and first ministers of the First African Baptist Church; Cunningham served as the first minister of the Second African Baptist Church. The Reverend Andrew C. Marshall, another former pastor at First African Baptist, joined these two prestigious men three years later, in 1856. (For an account of Marshall's life, see the first sidebar in this chapter.)

The cemetery contains the burials of many of the city's slaves. Their plots are largely unmarked, but some contain handsome headstones. The gravestone of "Sarah," for example, a bondwoman who died on the *Pulaski*, was purchased by her owner, who may have felt a particular attachment to her. Many other plots were purchased by family members, who no doubt had to work long hours on top of their other labors to afford a handsomely carved stone or wooden marker.

Although the ordinances establishing Laurel Grove set aside city funds for its upkeep, the southern half soon showed signs of neglect. In 1856, just three years after the cemetery opened, Frederick Law Olmsted, the famed landscape architect, visited the site. He described it as "dilapidated" and complained in his diary that many of the gravestones were covered by weeds and sand, making them impossible to read. A year after Olmsted's visit, complaints about the state of Laurel Grove South led the city council to determine that the cemetery was too big for the caretaker, Alfred Torlay, and a second one was installed to assist him.

Both the city and the caretakers, however, were powerless to stop the desecration of the cemetery during the Civil War. The war took a terrible toll on both halves of Laurel Grove. First, Confederate troops set up fortifications that ran through the cemetery, displacing both gravestones and plantings. When Union forces took control of the city in 1864, troops camped near Laurel Grove and used many of the remaining trees for firewood. After the war, most of Savannah's white families abandoned the cemetery and began to bury their dead in Bonaventure Cemetery. But since the city cemeteries were still segregated, Laurel Grove South remained the only option for Savannah's black community. During the postwar years, such notable figures as James M. Simms, one of the first black men to hold a seat in Georgia's state assembly, and John Deveaux, who rose to the rank of colonel in the state militia and then started the *Savannah Tribune*, the city's first black newspaper, found their final resting places in Laurel Grove South.

By 1931, many prominent African Americans had become fed up with the neglected state of the cemetery, and they pressured the city to clean it up. Although officials agreed that the cemetery needed work, it was twenty-eight years before the city took action. In 1959, Mayor Lee Mingledorff Jr. pledged to clean up the cemetery. The city spent nearly $3,000 on the project, and the Savannah Sugar Refinery donated a set of iron gates for Laurel Grove South. Despite the interest the project generated, in the 1960s the cemetery was threatened by the proposed path of the Interstate-16 connector, which was slated to run right through the middle of the cemetery. In 1966, the city determined that the 37th Street connector to I-16 would pass through an unused portion of the cemetery, permanently segregating the north and south portions. Although the cemetery was saved from I-16, no sustained efforts were made toward maintaining it until the famed civil rights advocate W. W. Law set out to identify the graves of

Wallace family and then by the Owens family. George Welshman Owens acquired her through his marriage to Sarah Wallace Owens, the daughter of John Wallace (a wealthy British merchant) and Mary Anderson. That Maria had a surname suggests her importance to the slaveholding family, since few enslaved people at this time were listed in records with last names. In fact, she is one of the few bondpeople in the Owens papers so designated. Although the historical record does not reveal whether she had a funeral, we do know that she died of "inflammatory bowels," a quite common condition during the nineteenth century and one that often led to an uncomfortable death.

The Owens family purchased the plot and arranged for Maria's body to be transported to the grave site. It is likely that her grave was dug by two enslaved men. The cemetery keeper, Alfred F. Torlay, often supervised interments to make sure the burial complied with Savannah city ordinances.[34] If other bondpeople were present, the makeshift service would have included an enslaved preacher quoting scripture, the singing of hymns, and then the lowering of the body in a pine coffin to its final resting place. In addition to Maria Wallace, at least eleven other slaves from the Owens family were buried at Laurel Grove South. Before their deaths, many had been treated by local physicians such as Richard Arnold, Harvey Bird, William N. King, and John D. Fish.

The level of infant mortality was high among enslaved and free people during this period. An unnamed infant from the Owens household, listed as "stillborn," was laid to rest at Laurel Grove South on May 2, 1855. Another infant died after a day or two of life.[35] A three-month-old boy named Jacob died from inflammatory bowel syndrome in July

Sarah Wallace Owens

Sarah Wallace Owens, born in 1789, was the daughter of John Wallace, a loyalist, successful merchant trader, and the British vice-consul for the State of Georgia. Her mother, Mary Anderson, was the daughter of George Anderson, who served as captain of the *Georgia Packet*, a pioneer ship in the direct trade between Savannah and London.

On June 12, 1815, Sarah Wallace married George Welshman Owens, a member of the South's most elite class of planters. At the time of his death, in 1856, he owned thousands of acres of prime real estate (including eight plantations), multiple urban dwellings, and more than 350 slaves. Sarah possessed her own wealth, including slaves. In the early years of their marriage, the couple lived in the house that her husband had inherited in Trustees Garden. In 1817, George Owens returned from a business trip to London and Paris, and shortly thereafter they bought their second house, located at the southeastern corner of Price and Broughton Streets in Green Ward. In 1830, George Owens purchased, for $10,000, the property—Lot X, Anson Ward—on which the Owens-Thomas House stands.

George's business affairs and political ambitions required him to travel abroad and domestically, leading to extensive periods of separation for the couple. During his long absences, Sarah handled many aspects of her husband's business affairs, as their correspondence suggests. He wrote to her on August 3, 1818: "If you should see Judge Berrien inform him that the business is in a fair way," and reminded her, "There is $1000 due Mr. Maxwell when he deliver possession you will pay him the amount." She was closely involved with matters concerning the family's slaves. Writing from Paris on September 23, 1818, George coached her in how to handle a possible transaction: "I am engaged in the speculation for the purchase of Johnston's Negroes, but fear shall not succeed . . . if they are sold, you will buy Smart's wife and Sampson's to comply with a promise I have made them . . . if there is any other prime Negro man also with any wife purchase for him also. If you have not money enough you can obtain it at Bank."

George and Sarah were often absent from Savannah. The family left the city during the "fever season" to take up summer residence at an inland plantation. This meant trusting a number of slaves to manage the Savannah properties. In winter, George awaited his wife's arrival in Washington, D.C. In 1836, he wrote to her requesting that she make "all and every preparation to leave Savannah . . . for Washington with all our children (with the exception of Richard) and with Peter, Dick and Kate." At nineteen years old, the eldest son took over the property management in his mother's absence.

On June 17, 1865, Sarah Wallace Owens died intestate. In accordance with her husband's will (he had died nine years earlier), the estate was not to be settled until three years after her death, which allowed the three unmarried daughters, Sarah Jane, Mary Bedford, and Margaret Wallace Owens, to stay in the house on Oglethorpe Square for the remainder of their lives. In August 1903, George W. Owens, W. W. Owens, and T. Lloyd Owens (all sons of George S. Owens) petitioned to be able to sell the house, including the furnishings, along with the plantation known as Guinas and the rest of the property jointly owned by the estate, now in the hands of Margaret Wallace Owens Thomas, George W. Owens's youngest daughter. Her sisters had deeded her their interest in the propery in their wills, and she wished to retain ownership. After hearing the case, the Georgia supreme court ruled that Margaret Thomas would retain ownership of the house. Her daughter Margaret Thomas bequeathed the house to the Telfair Academy of Arts and Sciences in 1951.

PAULETTE THOMPSON

1860. Records suggest that some of the women who lived on the Owens family's Savannah properties were pregnant. It is plausible that they were country slaves brought into the city for better medical care, as George W. Owens's letters indicate that he sometimes preferred that his domestic servants receive medical care from white physicians rather than from black midwives and healers. This indicates the degree to which he felt invested in the lives of the enslaved men and women who served him.

The inconsistency of racist claims that African Americans were unable to take care of their own affairs was perhaps most clearly evident in the South's towns and cities. White southerners, seeing the autonomy and mobility that enslaved people enjoyed in urban areas, worried that these places were weak spots in their control over blacks. But despite the mobility and autonomy of blacks in urban areas, their labor still served to produce wealth for their owners. In antebellum Savannah and other southern cities, slavery was perhaps not as stringently overseen as on rural plantations, but it was nonetheless part of a system that displayed stability and resiliency until the Union army occupation of the South during the Civil War.

The *Wanderer*

On the afternoon of November 13, 1859, a crowd gathered at the U.S. Custom House on Savannah's Bay Street. Those who arrived first climbed the stairs and seated themselves in the courtroom on the second floor. Others stood on the street under the trees or packed into Bay Lane, the alley behind the courtroom. The attorney for the defense, John Wallace Owens, arrived, as did the prosecutor, Joseph Ganahl. Shortly thereafter, the defendants were led to the prisoner's dock, and then the jury filed in. Finally, Justice James Wayne of the U.S. Supreme Court, a former mayor of Savannah, entered the courtroom. All rose, and silence settled upon the proceedings.

Thus began one of the most significant trials in Savannah's history. Although the proceedings are now nearly forgotten, in 1859 they rocked the nation. The issue at stake was great: whether a southern jury would condemn a group of fellow southerners on federal charges of illegally transporting African slaves to America.

The story begins with a sailing ship called the *Wanderer*. Built on Long Island, New York, in 1857, the 114-foot ultraluxurious yacht was meant for speed. Her owner, a Louisiana sugar baron with a summerhouse in New York, spent more than a year plying the waters of the Northeast with her, delighting crowds. He belonged to the New York Yacht Club, America's most exclusive millionaire's club; and so, atop her mast, the *Wanderer* flew the club's famous NYYC pennant. After little more than a year, the *Wanderer* was sold to William C. Corrie, a Charlestonian. He brought the *Wanderer* back to Charleston, where he met with Charles Lamar, one of Savannah's most prominent businessmen. Together they put into play one of the most audacious schemes of the Civil War era: within a few days, Lamar and Corrie transformed the elegant *Wanderer* into a slave ship. And despite the fact that Congress had outlawed the African slave trade in 1808, on July 4, 1858, they sent the ship to Africa on a quest for human cargo.

Arriving at the Congo River, the *Wanderer* took on some four hundred African slaves; then, with sails taut, it outran British patrol boats policing the coast of Africa in an attempt to halt the illegal slave trade, and headed back across the Atlantic. Forty days later the ship arrived at Jekyll Island, Georgia. The slaves were unloaded and dispersed, most of them sent by steamboat up the coast to the Savannah River and finally to the South Carolina plantation where most of them were sold.

Reports of hundreds of Africans—chained, speaking in strange tongues, faces etched with tattoos, teeth filed to points—could

Cover and interior pages of the logbook for the
Wanderer on its journey to the coast of Africa,
1858. Courtesy of the Manuscript, Archives and
Rare Book Library, Emory University, Atlanta.

not be suppressed, and within days the illicit adventures of the *Wanderer* had hit the front pages of newspapers nationwide. The country was stunned. The audacious and illegal act not only aggravated the sectional tensions between North and South, but also challenged the federal government to step into the southern courtrooms and prosecute those responsible for it.

For Savannah's Charles Lamar, the scheme succeeded beyond his wildest dreams. Lamar was a "fire-eater"—one of a small knot of southern radicals who demanded disunion and wanted to expand the Confederacy into a slaveholding republic that would include Mexico, Central America, and Cuba. Though the federal government had captured three of the *Wanderer*'s crewmen (who were awaiting trial), Lamar was certain that he, Corrie, and the other principals would not be implicated. Lamar's confidence rested to a great extent on the abilities of his attorney, John Owens. Son of the former Savannah mayor George Welshman Owens, a director of the Central of Georgia Railroad, and past president of the Savannah Jockey Club, Owens happened to be the town's best criminal lawyer as well. His law firm, Lloyd & Owens, was at 199 Bay Street, a few blocks from the U.S. Custom House.

As the trial progressed, Owens proved himself a skillful cross-examiner, tying the prosecution's witnesses in knots and leading them to conclusions that supported the defense. In the end, Owens succeeded. To cheers from the crowd within and surrounding the customhouse, the jury declared the three *Wanderer* defendants not guilty. In the short term, Charles Lamar and William Corrie got what they wanted: the *Wanderer* case worsened relations between the North and South. The incident, along with other inflammatory acts, including John Brown's raid and subsequent hanging, helped push the nation into civil war. The fire-eaters' dream of forming a slaveholding republic seemed to be coming true. Their elation was short-lived, however. Owens was committed to an asylum in Georgia, where he died in 1862. On April 16, 1865, several days after Lee's surrender, Lamar was killed during a skirmish with Union troops in Georgia. Corrie died of alcoholism in a Charleston hotel shortly after the war. Even the *Wanderer* reached an inglorious end: reduced to carrying fruit in the Caribbean, it sank off the coast of Cuba in January 1871. What is left standing of the *Wanderer* incident is the U.S. Custom House on Bay Street—and a historical marker on the corner of Bay and Bull Streets, partly obscured by bushes, a reminder that the *Wanderer* trial once played upon history's stage here, many years ago.

ERIK CALONIUS

Free Black Life in Savannah

Janice L. Sumler-Edmond

A notice in the *Daily Georgian* of December 6, 1819, provides important clues about the nature of free black life in Savannah: "Lewis [Louis] Mirault subscriber will be absent from the State for a few months. Alexander Hunter will act as his attorney during his absence. Messrs. Gaudry and Dufaure are authorized to receive his debts." The unusual nature of this notice was not in its message, but in the person of the subscriber. Louis Mirault was not the typical white tradesman taking a business trip. He was a free black man, living and practicing his tailoring trade in a society where blacks were considered outcasts. Although Mirault and other members of the free black community maintained cooperative and even familial relationships with some whites, other sectors of Savannah's majority population persisted in their commitment to white supremacy and the institution of slavery.

Throughout the antebellum period, interracial relationships in Savannah, as in other southern locales, ran along a broad and complicated spectrum. Interactions between free blacks and whites ranged from familial connections, guardianships, business ties, and religious affiliations as well as instances of racial bigotry. The lack of certainty surrounding such interactions tended to make life challenging and unpredictable for free blacks. Legal and social conventions of the time forced them to secure approval or assistance from whites before taking action concerning their lives. Before embarking on his business trip, for example, Louis Mirault was legally obligated by the state's guardianship law of 1808 to seek permission or advice from his white guardian, Alexander Hunter.[1]

Still, by nineteenth-century standards, Louis Mirault lived a good life in his adopted city of Savannah. He came to be well known in Savannah as a skilled artisan, family man, and one of a small handful of pioneering free black community leaders in the city. Mirault even owned slaves.[2] But collectively, the antiblack state laws, city ordinances, and

Charles Parsons, Image of Savannah circa 1855. *Lithograph after a painting by John William Hill.* I. N. Phelps Stokes Collection of American Historical Prints, 1856. Print Collection, Miriam and Ira D. Wallach Division of Art, Prints and Photographs, The New York Public Library, Astor, Lenox and Tilden Foundations.

customs thwarted black economic progress and generally made life difficult for free black people in Savannah. Indeed, the "free" label obscures the reality of their limited mobility and rights. Although free blacks served no slave masters, racial and, in some instances, familial affiliations linked them to the enslaved population. Free blacks suffered from a lack of personal liberty.[3] Many in the white community refused to acknowledge that slavery was not the black man's natural state. Whites feared that if free blacks were left to their own devices, unrestricted in their movements and activities, they would give enslaved blacks hope of achieving their own freedom. As a result, the white slaveholding class and its supporters restricted free blacks in order to lessen the alleged threat they posed. In addition, since the State of Georgia did not recognize them as persons possessing full citizenship rights, free people of color had little recourse when it came to protecting their property or the limited freedoms they did possess.[4]

It is doubtful whether Louis Mirault and other Saint-Domingue émigrés had any knowledge of the hostile legislative environment they would encounter in Savannah. Sometime around the year 1800, Mirault, his mother, and probably a few other relatives joined a large wave of black and white émigrés who left the West Indies in the 1790s, seeking refuge in North America from the turmoil of the Haitian Revolution. Race determined the kind of reception each émigré group received. For the most part, white émigrés received a sympathetic and cordial welcome to the United States, but those of partial or full African ancestry did not. Many whites went so far as to pressure elected officials to halt black immigration. Throughout the South, lawmakers were inundated with antiblack petitions. On at least one occasion, whites in Savannah took a more direct approach by diverting a ship from the West Indies from their harbor.[5]

Hostility toward black immigration was fueled by at least three objectives. First, many whites were determined to place the institution of black slavery on a solid footing in Georgia and other parts of the nation. Second, there was the apprehension that black people from Saint-Domingue would incite Georgia slaves to wage their own bloody revolt. Third, there was the widely held belief that blacks were inferior and undesirable as free residents of Georgia.[6]

Establishing white control over the enslaved population became a major concern in the years before the American Revolution. A statute of 1770 decreed corporal punishment for any slave and a hefty fine for any free black who "shall harbor, conceal, or entertain any slave that shall runaway or shall be charged or accused of any crime"; in 1835, corporal punishment was added to the penalty for free black offenders. In 1811, a special tribunal for prosecuting slaves and free blacks was established in the state. Local and state governments went on to design a host of laws to discourage the growth of the free black population. The Georgia legislature passed a law in 1835 that prohibited any black persons except slaves and court-registered free blacks from remaining in the state. Violators faced arrest and a trial; a conviction carried a $100 fine.[7] Two decades later, Savannah's board of aldermen enacted an ordinance requiring a $100 fee from all newly arrived free blacks intending to reside in the city. By order of the mayor or city marshall, those who failed to pay the residence tax within thirty days could be put to work until the debt had been paid. In addition, free blacks were taxed more heavily than their white counterparts. Louis Mirault and his fellow free blacks in Savannah were subject to an annual county poll tax as well as a city-generated business license tax.[8]

In spite of the groundswell of antiblack activism, several hundred free black émigrés, consisting of family units and individuals, settled in North American cities and towns, including Savannah. West Indian émigrés formed the largest portion of Savannah's free black community in the early nineteenth century, which also included natives of Africa and North America. For nearly a generation, they remained a clannish subgroup within Savannah's black population. Initially preferring to marry among themselves, over time they widened their circle to embrace other unions. Within a generation, the émigrés had blended into the mainstream of Savannah's free black community. A few of their members, like Louis Mirault, had sufficient prestige and clout to secure a position of respect and leadership within the larger black community.[9]

The Mirault family members were mulattos, and their family connections with whites in Saint-Domingue likely explained their free status. On arrival in Savannah, these free black émigrés set about making a life for themselves, and they assumed many of the responsibilities associated with their new place of residence, including paying their annual Chatham County taxes. As his tailoring business prospered and he accumulated a steady clientele, Louis Mirault decided to take a bride, Theresa, a fellow émigré. After Theresa's untimely death, probably around 1812 or 1813, Louis remarried. His second wife was Nicole, also a free black from Saint-Domingue. Louis and Nicole Mirault became the parents of two children, Josephine and Simon, the latter born in 1815.[10]

Judging from the frequency with which his name and signature appear in a Catholic church registry as a sponsor of baptisms, a witness at weddings, and an attendant at funerals, Louis Mirault assumed a key leadership role in Savannah's fledgling free black community. As a practicing Catholic, he attended St. John the Baptist Catholic Church, along with many other blacks, both enslaved and free. Of the nearly forty free blacks whose names appear on the local tax rolls from 1810 through 1812, thirteen of them attended St. John's. Over the decades, Louis lived to see his children grow up and start families of their own.[11] His direct descendants, extending to at least four generations, carved out respectable lives in Savannah throughout the nineteenth century.

Individuals and families who migrated to Savannah from other states and regions of the United States made up another source of free black people in the city. Josiah H. Grant, his wife, Mary, and their children returned to Savannah from New York during the 1850s, probably to reconnect with landowning relatives. Josiah had ties to agriculture and its products; he spent his post–Civil War years working as a cotton sampler and shipper. Josiah and Mary had been born free in Savannah; their daughters, Justine and Eliza Ann, were born in New York City and Darien, Georgia.

Other free black migrants from within the Unites States included Anne Oliver and her younger brother James, who settled in Savannah after leaving their home state of

Virginia. Anne became the owner of several parcels of land during the antebellum period, which James inherited upon her death, in either late 1819 or early 1820.[12]

Unlike the Grant and Oliver families, some members of the free black community in Savannah acquired their freedom after spending a portion of their lives enslaved. They gained freedom through either self-purchase arrangements or voluntary manumissions by their owners. There were also instances in which slaves were purchased by relatives. Andrew Bryan was born a slave in South Carolina in 1716. Years later, he purchased his freedom and that of his wife and daughter while establishing the First African Baptist Church.[13] Like Andrew Bryan, the Dolly family of Savannah gained their freedom through purchase agreements. Quamino Dolly, the family patriarch, purchased his freedom with, in part, the reward money he earned from assisting the British during the American Revolution.[14] Quamino's reward did not translate immediately into freedom. Instead, the reward probably became seed money for the family, whose members pooled together their meager resources. In 1786, after the war, the Dollys began purchasing their freedom. They continued making purchases until five members of the family, Quamino and Qua, who were probably brothers, as well as Qua's three children, Eve, Quash, and London, all enjoyed the status of free persons. The Dollys continued to live in Savannah over several generations and prospered as free black tradesmen and slave owners.[15]

It was not uncommon for free black men to marry enslaved women in Savannah, and free husbands often tried to buy their wives' freedom, which would ensure the freedom of their offspring also. Doing so was not always possible. After purchasing his freedom, Quash Dolly married an enslaved woman, Lucretia Gibbons, in 1803, likely with the intention of emancipating her and their offspring at the first opportunity. On July 17 of that year, Quash sponsored a baptism celebration for his infant daughter. The parish registry for St. John's Church indicated that Quash's wife was then still the slave property of John Gibbons of Savannah, which meant that the child was the property of Gibbons as well. A later ceremony at the same church united another free man and his enslaved bride. On February 27, 1829, Peter Cruvellier, a free man of color, married Betsey Redding, an enslaved woman. On his wedding day, the groom received the good wishes of his wife's owner as well as those of his sisters, Justine and Aspasia, two free black women.[16] Because he was a successful tailor, Peter may have already possessed sufficient finances to purchase his wife from her owner. Records list a Betsey Cruvellier along with other free black Cruvelliers, who were probably Peter and Betsey's children. They lived in Savannah throughout the antebellum decades.

Peter Cruvellier and Quash Dolly married enslaved women with the intention of transferring ownership of their spouses to themselves, meaning that, technically, they would have been slaveholders of their loved ones. This was a common practice among free blacks in southern areas where it was extremely difficult or even illegal to grant freedom to enslaved blacks. Antebellum southern legislators were often determined to diminish or eliminate slaveholders' power to emancipate bondpeople. During the legislative session of 1801, Georgia's elected representatives joined those of other southern states in requiring slaveholders to submit manumission requests for legislative review and approval. Slave owners who failed to comply were fined. In 1819, lawmakers stiffened the penalty for noncompliance: "Sound policy [and] the exercise of humanity towards the slave population . . . imperiously require that the number of free persons of color within this state should not be increased by manumission, or by the admission of such persons from other states to reside therein."[17] Although Andrew Bryan and other enterprising men and women managed to emancipate fully their family members, many others were not able to do so and thus had to hold their loved ones in legal slavery.

One historian has labeled the majority of free black slaveholders benevolent despots.[18] Evidence suggests that for many, the primary rationale for holding blacks in slavery was emotional and altruistic, unrelated to economic gain. Most free black slaveholders owned family members or friends in order to prevent their enslavement by strangers or their sale to out-of-state owners.[19] At the same time, slaveholding was undoubtedly a source of wealth, and some of Savannah's free blacks invested in slave property for its economic advantages, using enslaved laborers in their businesses. Contrasting attitudes toward enslaved people could exist among members of the same family. In 1816, Francis Cruvellier owned two enslaved workers, who labored in his Savannah tailor shop. On the other hand, Peter Cruvellier, Francis's younger brother, was never listed as a Savannah slaveholder, and in fact married an enslaved woman. After his move from Virginia to Savannah, James Oliver became a well-to-do free black property owner, employing his enslaved workers in his successful dray business during the early 1830s. After James's death, his widow, Rosella, continued her work as a Savannah street vendor with the help of the one enslaved person she owned, an elderly woman named Hetty. Louis Mirault's family, including Louis, his mother, and his wife, held as many as six persons in bondage. Mirault used their labor in his tailor shop and in other businesses around Savannah.[20]

Savannah's free black population remained small in the antebellum years. The 1790 census listed 112 free black men, women, and children in the city. Their numbers had increased to 530 by 1810, 632 by 1840, and 705 by the eve of the Civil War. As in most southern cities, enslaved blacks greatly outnumbered free blacks. In 1860, there were 7,712 enslaved blacks and 13,875 white residents of Savannah. Of the southern coastal port cities (including New Orleans, Charleston, Mobile, Richmond, and Baltimore), Savannah was the smallest in overall population and in the number of enslaved and free blacks. There appears to have been no rigid scheme designed for segregating the city's black population. Although a city census of 1848 revealed a sizable concentration of blacks residing in Savannah's Oglethorpe Ward, the remaining free and enslaved blacks were evenly distributed among the city's other twenty-three districts.[21]

Even though the size of the free black community was relatively small, Savannah officials felt threatened when any blacks, enslaved or free, congregated without white supervision or approval. A city ordinance of 1839 limited black gatherings to Sunday worship services or funerals: "No Negroes or persons of color, being more in number than seven, shall at any time (except when attending funerals or public worship on Sunday between the rising and setting of the sun, or any other occasions provided for by this or other Ordinances of the City) assemble or meet together, either in any house, building, or lot within the City, unless some white person is present or stays on the premises."[22] In addition, free and enslaved blacks were prohibited from holding any gathering for "dancing or other merriment" except with written permission from the mayor or two aldermen. Violations of these ordinances subjected the accused to incarceration in the city jail and fines of fifty dollars.

Confronted by such restrictions on their personal liberties, free and enslaved blacks in Savannah increasingly came to rely on churches as the most important institutions for sustaining their community. For whites in Savannah, the religious message of peace and conciliation between the races that was espoused by many of the formerly enslaved black leaders of these churches convinced them that these institutions posed no threat to white supremacy. But the black community viewed their churches very differently. Black congregations provided a strong institutional and ideological foundation from which the black community could sustain itself and grow. Besides allowing free and enslaved blacks to worship together, black churches offered congregants the opportunity to socialize, to reinforce their spiritual and cultural identities, and to affirm their individual and collective self-worth.[23] Church buildings became multipurpose black community centers as well as places for Sunday worship.

Congregations functioned under the leadership of savvy black ministers, many of whom had begun their lives in slavery but had managed to purchase freedom for themselves and their families. In doing so, they demonstrated antislavery activism under the cover of accommodation. Besides Andrew Bryan, another noted black Baptist minister of the time was Henry Cunningham, who likewise had been born into slavery. After Cunningham acquired his freedom and moved to Savannah, Andrew Bryan selected him and several other promising young black men for ordination. In 1802, Cunningham and a group of free black tradesmen, artisans, and house slaves founded the Second African Baptist Church.[24] A third Baptist minister and free black community leader was Andrew Marshall, a former slave. (For an account of Marshall's life, see p. 102.) Marshall was Andrew Bryan's nephew, and he succeeded his uncle as pastor of the First African Baptist Church. William Harden, a white Savannah resident during the antebellum period, praised the Reverend Marshall, calling him venerable and highly esteemed.[25] These free black religious leaders and others showed their parishioners how to tread the precarious lines between slavery, autonomy and freedom. Their examples of self-emancipation and the positive psychological reinforcement they offered likely lifted morale while encouraging community charity and unity. By maintaining relatively independent churches during the pre–Civil War period, these leaders and their descendants reaped the rewards of prudence after the war by using their congregations to support, politically and economically, the fully emancipated black community.

By the mid-1820s, the First, Second, and Third African Baptist Churches together had attracted more than three thousand members.[26] Although the Baptist denomination attracted the largest numbers of enslaved and free blacks, Catholicism remained strong in the free black community through its West Indian heritage. From the late eighteenth century, free and enslaved blacks were an integral part of St. John the Baptist Catholic Church in Savannah. The white priests of St. John's performed countless baptisms, weddings, and funerals for black parishioners. Blacks eventually formed an independent Catholic congregation after the Civil War.

The surviving St. John's registry, which provides details about the religious life of the black Catholic faithful, reveals how black Catholics created independent spaces for themselves within the church. In 1832, Bishop John England of St. John's described blacks in his congregation as "fond of entering little sodalities of devotion, and assembling in the afternoon in the church for prayer and singing; they also have great charity in assisting each other in time of sickness or distress, not only with temporal aid, if it be required, but by spiritual reading, prayer, and consolation."[27] Besides the charitable works observed by Bishop England, it is likely that the caring and service that Savannah's black Catholics extended to one another went beyond the church boundaries and into the homes and workplaces of those in need within the black community. No doubt these activities helped prepare the congregants to establish a black congregation in the post–Civil War years.

Throughout the antebellum era, free blacks contributed to the city's economy, and some managed to create comfortable lives for themselves. Free blacks owned real estate; others opened businesses; still others became community leaders. Skilled black men worked as tailors, carpenters, barbers, coopers, butchers, shoemakers, blacksmiths, and draymen, among other jobs. Free black tailors, including Louis Mirault, Francis and Peter Cruvellier, Andrew Morel, Jean Baptist, Ben Wall, and others competed for customers among Savannah's well-dressed and well-to-do residents. Mirault had a long list of paying customers. When he died, the administration of his estate listed more than fifty customers who together owed the deceased man about three hundred dollars for tailoring services.[28] Draying could be a profitable trade for free black men in Savannah. These workers were the nineteenth-century version of teamsters. Draymen such as James Oliver hauled agricultural goods from ships in the harbor to warehouses and retail establishments throughout the city.[29]

The labor of free black women helped support their families. James Oliver's wife, Rosella, was one of many black women who worked as hucksters, selling small wares and a variety of foodstuffs from market stalls or along the city streets. Aspasia Cruvellier Mirault formed a partnership with her sister Justine to open a bakery at Broughton and Bull Streets in Savannah during the 1840s, where they also sold ice cream. Black women worked also as seamstresses, nurses, and washerwomen. Hagar Cruvellier maintained a shop in the Reynolds Ward section of Savannah, and Louisa McIntosh worked as a seamstress. Nancy Cox was a washerwoman.[30]

Still other black women and some men served their community as teachers. Unlike other business owners and tradespeople, black teachers practiced their profession at a risk to themselves.[31] In their attempts to educate black children, they also violated state law. Section 14 of Savannah's Ordinance 173 mirrored similar laws throughout Georgia and other southern states by expressly prohibiting black education; white violators would be fined for educating black children, but blacks might be both fined and "whipped not exceeding thirty-nine lashes."[32] Fortunately for the free black children of Savannah, the ordinance was not strictly enforced. City officials seemed to look the other way as schools for blacks remained open year after year. There were few reports of black schools being shut down, and only one black teacher was chastised with a public whipping. Nevertheless, black parents and teachers took precautions to safeguard their children's educational opportunities. Parents instructed their children to be discreet and cautious on their way to and from school. Children kept their schoolbooks hidden under their clothing and took circuitous routes to class. Because of such secrecy and caution, coupled with lax enforcement of the city ordinance, many black children received an education in Savannah. Julien Fromatin, Mary Woodhouse, Jane Deveaux, and James Porter, all free blacks, were a few of the educators who maintained successful schools for black youth in the city. While the majority of the schools taught a primary curriculum, Porter's school may have included advanced subjects and studies because of his breadth of knowledge and musical talent.[33]

Even though Savannah officials largely ignored the antiblack education ordinance, they strictly enforced other state laws and city ordinances, and swiftly punished violators. In some instances, lawmakers treated free blacks as if they were enslaved. Under the Georgia legal code, one set of laws and procedures governed criminal trials for both free and enslaved blacks. Whites accused of crimes were tried and punished under a separate code. Typically, the penalties suffered by convicted blacks were harsher than those meted out to whites. During the 1817 legislative session, Georgia lawmakers enacted a statute that listed the capital crimes for black offenders: inciting a slave insurrection, raping a white woman, poisoning a white person, arson, or burglary.[34]

The law that most closely aligned free blacks' status with that of enslaved people was the Georgia Guardianship Statute of 1808, which mandated white control and oversight of free blacks. The law required blacks to affiliate themselves with a white person, whose approval was needed before blacks could transact most business and legal affairs. Although intended to circumscribe the liberties of free blacks, the guardianship relationship occasionally resulted in unexpected advantages for blacks. Guardians sometimes

Jane Deveaux and Her Secret School

During Georgia's early colonial period, no laws prohibited the education of slaves, so some Georgia slaveholders openly taught their bondpeople to read and write. Colonial Georgia issued its first laws against slave literacy in 1770, imposing a $20 fine on those caught teaching the enslaved. In 1829, the State of Georgia implemented a slave code that continued to ban the educating of slaves; a $500 fine and a possible public whipping served as punishment. The City of Savannah in 1833 called for a fine of $100 for anyone providing instruction to slaves; if the educator was of African descent, thirty-nine lashes were to be administered. Some African Americans and whites nonetheless continued to instruct slaves in secret or clandestine schools. One of the most well known was Jane Deveaux, a free African American woman who educated slaves and free blacks by operating a secret school for thirty years.

Jane Deveaux was born in approximately 1810 in Savannah to John Benjamin Deveaux, a former slave from Savannah, and Catherine Deveaux, a free woman of African descent from Antigua, both deeply religious people. Her father served Savannah's Second African Baptist Church as choir director. His efforts and dedication led him to a deaconate and, eventually, the pulpit. J. B. Deveaux's religious work culminated in his appointment as pastor of Savannah's Third African Baptist Church in 1841. Jane's mother operated a school for enslaved and free blacks; Jane grew up assisting her mother in the school. Jane's religious upbringing and her mother's work as an educator combined to encourage an interest in teaching the scriptures in her own school, one affiliated with the Second African Baptist Church.

Deveaux's secret school started in the 1830s. Like the schools of her contemporaries, including James Porter, Mary Woodhouse, and Mathilda Taylor (later Beasley), it offered instruction in reading, writing, and ciphering (mathematics). Many enslaved African Americans believed that education offered the potential for political and economic freedom. Deveaux taught free blacks and slaves, necessarily in secret. Elaborately conceived plans ensured that whites did not detect her activities. Some slaves, for example, carried their schoolwork in buckets, giving the impression that they were running errands for their owners. Others wrapped their books in newspaper or brown wrapping paper. However they transported school materials, her pupils took care to vary their daily paths to school. Sometimes when whites suspected instruction was going on, they assumed that students were learning a trade and allowed the education to continue.

During the Civil War, enslaved African Americans and free blacks increasingly defied Savannah's rigid laws. Even James M. Simms's public whipping for educating blacks did not deter Deveaux's efforts. When Deveaux was asked her occupation for city record-keeping purposes in the early 1860s, she reported being a pastry cook. Although compelled to assist in making uniforms for the Confederate army, she persisted in operating her clandestine school. When the Reverend John Alvord, the Freedmen's Bureau superintendent of education, evaluated the needs of Savannah's black community in 1868, he noted Deveaux's impressive record of antebellum educational activities over the previous thirty years; most schools for freedmen had been open for only a few months. Alvord concluded that Deveaux's school led to the "general elevation" of freedmen.

After the war, Deveaux continued to educate area blacks. Despite the creation of the all-black Savannah Education Association in 1865 to provide educational opportunities for Savannah's African American population, Deveaux's excellent reputation and prior educational experience led students to continue to enroll in her school. Its sessions ran from 9:00 a.m. until 2:00 p.m. daily, except on Saturday. Despite the fees charged and the frequency of class meetings, the school had an average attendance of thirty-five pupils.

Little is known of Jane Deveaux's personal life. Some historical works have indicated that she married an Isaac Deveaux and that the two were the parents of John Deveaux, who in 1875 cofounded Savannah's *Colored Tribune*, a newspaper dedicated to helping African Americans exercise citizenship rights. The newspaper was renamed the *Savannah Tribune* in 1876. Ultimately, the relationship of Isaac Deveaux to Jane Deveaux remains unclear; most likely Jane Deveaux was John Deveaux's aunt.

Jane Deveaux died in 1885 from acute diarrhea and was laid to rest in Laurel Grove Cemetery South. Currently, the home that Jane Deveaux used as her clandestine school proudly stands on display along Savannah's Negro Heritage Trail.

DAWN HERD-CLARK

assisted their black wards in establishing and furthering business interests, securing property, or maintaining credit. Some whites were especially liberal in their patronage of black people. Farish Carter, a Georgia planter, reportedly served as the guardian for about one hundred free blacks and offered assistance to many of them. Simon Mirault, Louis's son, maintained close ties with Jean Gaudry, his white guardian. The two men were lay leaders in their church and shared a common devotion to the Catholic faith. John Elliott Ward, a one-term mayor of Savannah in the 1850s, served as the guardian for the businesswoman Aspasia Mirault and also served as the godfather of her grandson.[35]

Although many free blacks benefited from supportive relationships with their white guardians under the Georgia Guardianship Statute, other antebellum laws severely limited their personal liberties. Section V of the Georgia Code of Laws for 1818, for example, mandated the annual registration of all free blacks. This registration included essential identifying information: name, age, guardian, nativity, and occupation. The registry was printed in the local newspaper, allowing white citizens to challenge the free status of any black person listed. During the same legislative session, lawmakers passed a statute requiring all free blacks between the ages of fifteen and sixty to perform thirty days of uncompensated public work assigned by county officials. In 1820, a group of free blacks was ordered to serve as nurses for victims of a yellow fever epidemic that had struck large portions of Chatham County, including Savannah. No concern was given to the health risks imposed on the conscripted black nurses. Several years later, black men satisfied their mandatory work requirement by doing heavy construction on a fort located on Farm Street in Savannah.[36]

Pursuant to a separate Savannah ordinance, free black men were exempted from paying an annual poll tax of ten dollars if they satisfied their unpaid-labor duty by working with the city's fire department, responding promptly and working diligently when a fire alarm sounded. Black firemen were more numerous than their white counterparts in the city's fire brigades during the antebellum period. White firemen served the city in all-white fire companies; free blacks served in uniformed units or companies commanded by white fire captains. Since they lacked horse-drawn equipment, free black firemen pulled the hose carriages and the engine trucks; they also were allowed to handle axes while fighting fires. Enslaved blacks, loaned to the fire department by their slaveholders, worked alongside them.[37]

Black fireman in Savannah.
Fragile Pictures Collection,
Manuscript, Archives, and
Rare Book Library, Emory
University, Atlanta.

One of the most egregious pieces of the 1818 antiblack legislation was Section VIII of the Georgia Code of Laws, which prohibited blacks from purchasing real estate or slaves. Blacks who owned such property were to forfeit their holdings to the state. The following year, likely realizing that they had overreached, lawmakers amended the statute by repealing the prohibition against the purchase of land in most of the state. But it remained in force in Savannah, Augusta, and Darien, as did the prohibition against new purchases of slaves by free blacks. They could keep all property acquired before the 1818 law went into effect; and black slaveholders were allowed to bequeath slave property to their descendants.[38] During the 1850s, Hannah Cohen, a free black seamstress and one of the few black congregants of Christ Episcopal Church in Savannah, inherited several slaves from her mother, Maria Cohen. Maria, a free woman originally from Florida, had earlier inherited seven slaves from her husband, Richard Cohen. Besides the two slaves she bequeathed to Hannah, Maria left a slave to her white guardian, Richard D. Arnold, a Savannah physician.[39]

In their desire to acquire real estate, free blacks in Savannah tried to circumvent the law against land purchases. Typically, blacks gave the purchase price to a trusted white person, who bought land in his name. The parties secretly agreed that the white person would hold the land in trust for the black. In 1842, Aspasia Mirault contracted a land purchase and secret trust agreement with a white friend, George Cally. The transaction was successful, and Aspasia built a house on the property and moved her business there. In 1878, twenty-one years after Aspasia's death, her heirs filed a lawsuit when Cally denied her ownership of the property and claimed the lot as his own. Although Mirault's heirs won in the lower court, they lost at the Georgia Supreme Court, which declared the trust agreement null and void because it violated the 1818 law prohibiting black landownership.[40]

From 1819 to 1860, free blacks in Savannah employed multiple strategies to buy real estate in contravention of the legal prohibition against doing so. Would-be free black slaveholders, on the other hand, found it difficult to purchase enslaved property after the 1818 law went into effect. Free blacks had to identify white slave traders willing to violate the law and accept their business, but most white Georgians thought that only whites should be slaveholders. As a result, the number of black slaveholders in Savannah decreased nearly every decade between 1810 and 1860. Tax collectors counted sixteen black slaveholders, along with their thirty-two slaves, in 1810. Although the number of slaveholders (nineteen) and slaves (fifty-three) had increased a decade later, the numbers in both categories diminished thereafter. In addition, free black slaveholders had to contend with hard economic times that resulted in a decline in slave values. By 1860, only nine free black slaveholders resided in Savannah.[41]

During the antebellum decades, free blacks were the targets of several Savannah ordinances that, in tandem with restrictive state laws, limited their economic progress. An ordinance passed in 1839 required "any free negro, mulatto or mestizoe" who sold small wares to purchase a badge for eight dollars or else be fined twenty-five dollars. A year later, capitalizing on that potentially lucrative revenue stream, Savannah officials expanded the badge requirement to include practically all black workers, free and enslaved. The ordinance included an elaborate fee schedule that imposed varying amounts depending on the worker's occupation, gender, and residence within or outside the city limits. Badges for free black butchers and bakers cost ten dollars; those for pilots, boatmen, and fishermen were eight dollars. A related city ordinance passed around the same time proscribed black employment in retail establishments, especially those selling "spirituous liquors," unless a white person over the age of sixteen closely supervised the black person. A shopkeeper who violated the ordinance was fined fifty dollars for each offense.[42]

Slave Tag. *Robert L. Heriot records,* MS 1371-1988-01, *Georgia Historical Society.*

Savannah also regulated the shore leave of black seamen, many of whom were free. An earlier law confining black seamen to a "quarantine of forty days" while their ships were docked was amended to make shipowners responsible for keeping track of their black crews. The owners were required to obtain passports—essentially, documentary permits—for black seamen before they could enter the city. Passports cost five dollars; the penalty for failing to follow the law resulted in a fine of one thousand dollars.[43]

In spite of the numerous legal obstacles facing them, many free blacks worked hard and managed to live good and even prosperous lives in Savannah. Andrew Bryan and his nephew Andrew Marshall began life as enslaved persons with few prospects. In time, each man earned his community's respect as a well-to-do free black minister and landowner. In Marshall's case, his entrepreneurial skills allowed him to pass on a successful dray business to his son. The drayman James Oliver used the profits from his business to improve his Savannah real estate. Similarly, the Cruvellier brothers, Francis and Peter, supported their households for more than a decade by the profits from their tailor shop on Jekyll Street.[44]

The Miraults were another of Savannah's successful free black families. They operated several thriving businesses, paid taxes, attended church, and provided community service and leadership, all while complying with onerous, race-specific restrictions. Like other free blacks, the Miraults cultivated interracial friendships and frequently extended assistance to their enslaved brethren. The institutional and economic strength of the antebellum free black community was central to the establishment of a strong post-emancipation black community in Savannah.

Wartime Workers, Moneymakers
Black Labor in Civil War–Era Savannah
Jacqueline Jones

By the summer of 1863, the city of Savannah was showing the devastating effects of a seemingly endless war, the gracious port of antebellum years having been transformed into a congested, weed-choked, dilapidated military entrepôt. Among white men and women, initial, wild enthusiasm for secession had gradually given way to distress over a number of frightening developments. Local newspapers replaced advertisements for runaway slaves with ads for runaway soldiers, deserters from the Confederate army. In a grim new twist to the city's fondness for parades, residents could now watch some of these army deserters dragged through the streets in chains on their way to jail or to public execution. The domain of wealthy cotton and rice factors, Savannah had become the site of bitter contention among powerful people as city authorities and army commanders jockeyed for influence. Meanwhile, white workers plying their regular trades were few and far between. In this rough-edged armed camp, the only white males not in uniform were boys, the elderly, and a favored few who had won exemptions from military service.[1]

For young recruits from the interior and the surrounding countryside, the romance of army life quickly faded. Bored, restless, and coated in grime, they subsisted on pitiable rations and contended with the sweltering heat and the irritating fleas, mosquitoes, and sand flies of the Lowcountry.[2] Surely these young men must have watched with resentment and envy as a vigorous twenty-eight-year-old butcher named Jackson B. Sheftall daily called his dog, mounted his horse, and rode a few blocks from his home in the northwestern part of the city, just east of Laurel Grove Cemetery, to the Central of Georgia Railroad depot. From there, he drove herds of cattle to a nearby slaughtering pen.

Commissioned by General W. H. Davis to supply the Confederate army with meat, Sheftall ran a bustling enterprise with as many as forty black men, enslaved and free, laboring under him. Davis did not pay Sheftall for his services, but he did allow the butcher to

R. H. Howell, Savannah Rally, 8 November 1860. *Lithograph after a drawing by Henry Cleenewerk. American Cartoon Prints Collection, Prints and Photographs Division, Library of Congress,* LC-DIG-PPMSCA-19610.

keep all the hides and offal (livers and tongues) of the cattle he slaughtered—by-products that he sold for a tidy profit to civilians, providing a comfortable living for himself, his wife, and young daughter. Certainly Sheftall's immense stockpiles of tallow, lard, and hay; his stores of corn, rice, flour, beef, and pork; and his barnyard menagerie of cows and poultry distinguished him from almost all other Savannahians at the time. With his four fine horses, four wagons, new buggy, extensive set of butchering tools, and three houses, Sheftall might have qualified as a war profiteer in the eyes of the weary, ragged soldiers who watched his daily perambulations through the streets, for he was prospering to the extent that the city suffered a scarcity of fresh food. And the fact that his name connected him with one of the oldest and most distinguished Jewish families in Savannah might have spurred some onlookers to participate in the wartime rise of anti-Semitism.[3]

Yet Jackson Sheftall was neither white nor Jewish—rather, though he appeared to be white, he identified with the city's African American community. The son of a white public official, Benjamin Sheftall Jr., and one of his enslaved workers, a woman whose name is not known, Jackson had been freed at birth; though he never spelled it out, his middle name was probably Benjamin. As a youth, he followed the trade of his uncle (whether black or white is unknown), and by 1853, at age eighteen, he was operating his own butchering business. Three years later he married an enslaved woman named Elizabeth; but it was not until February 1862 that he was able to buy her freedom and the freedom of their daughter—for $2,600.[4]

Sheftall would have been the first to admit that his success and his circumstances made him unique among Savannah blacks at the time. Later he stated, "There were very few free colored people like me. . . . I had been doing business here a long time, and was generally thought a great deal of among the whites here. Because I kept myself to myself." In other words, he literally minded his own business. City authorities required that all free blacks, regardless of skill or trade, have a white "guardian." Jackson Sheftall's guardian was his white half brother Mordecai, a county constable and inspector of customs. In fact, the white and black Sheftalls remained closely intertwined; several of the men worked as butchers, and together the men and women shared names, with Abraham, Emanuel, Isaac, Benjamin, Rebecca, Eve, and Susan predominating in both lines. A modern genealogist would have difficulty disentangling white from black kin.[5]

In 1860, Savannah was home to about twenty-two thousand people, almost half of them enslaved, and about a thousand of them free blacks. In certain significant respects, Jackson B. Sheftall was representative of Savannah's black population at the time. Possessed of a strong entrepreneurial streak, he had operated a butcher's stall in the central Savannah public market before the war and responded to the chaos ensuing after 1861 by profiting accordingly. One disapproving white man noted later that the wartime butchering business had yielded a handsome income, and "for that [Sheftall] went in zealously."[6]

At the same time, Sheftall's business mirrored some of the more modest marketing activities pursued by many of the seventy-five thousand Lowcountry black men and women. Up and down the coast, enslaved workers labored under the task system, which allowed them to organize their productive energies according to their own priorities for at least part of the day. Many engaged in petty commodity production and trade: they kept pigs, cattle and chickens; tended vegetable gardens and beehives; and made baskets, canoes, and moss-stuffed mattresses. Describing his contract with General Davis, Sheftall used the terms of the task system: "After I got through with [Davis's] work, he allowed me all the balance of the time to do my own."[7]

Not all black people were able to turn the war to material advantage. Some cooks and servants remained hostage to their owners, white men and women grown mournful over the loss of their soldiering kinfolk, and fearful and angry over the prospect of defeat. Before the Union occupation of the city, thousands of enslaved workers from Savannah and the interior of Georgia were forced at gunpoint to construct the city's Confederate defenses and riverfront batteries, labor as nurses in army hospitals, and excavate railroad beds; they remained susceptible to heat stroke, exhaustion, malnutrition, and disease. Though a free man, Sheftall himself was drafted to work on the Confederate fortifications at Tybee Island, eighteen miles downriver, where the Savannah River meets the sea.[8]

Fighting to preserve their own power, city elites had not anticipated that war would give rise to a concerted African American struggle for freedom. That struggle was personified and promoted not only by fugitives from plantations, and by spies, scouts, and uniformed soldiers in the service of the Union army, but also by people like Jackson Sheftall, men and women determined to carve out freedom and a sense of well-being.

For black men and women, the Savannah labor market on the eve of the war foreshadowed both the promise and peril embedded in the impending conflict. In the interest of maintaining trade and commercial prosperity, city authorities grudgingly tolerated challenges to the slave-free, white-black, and rich-poor binaries that underlay the power of white supremacists. The in-migration of several hundred immigrant dockworkers from New York each fall created a laboring class of blacks and whites who worked together during the day and ate, drank, and fought with one another at night. Together, poor people created an underground economy that facilitated the illicit exchange of goods such as alcohol and services such as prostitution and gambling.[9]

Even before Fort Sumter fell to the Confederates, Savannah registered the effects of a political crisis that had been provoked by South Carolina secessionists four months before. In early 1861, the city council sent immigrant workers back to New York: shippers feared the effects of the crisis, and trade with the North dried up. Vigilante groups instigated what one alarmed observer called a "reign of terror" as they prowled the city on the lookout for disloyal whites and recalcitrant blacks, in the process usurping the authority of judges and masters alike. The resulting "anarchical spirit introduced into the community," in the words of a prominent lawyer, threatened to undermine the very foundations of a city built on multiple forms of authority.[10]

Although accustomed to giving orders and being obeyed, planters and politicians could do little to halt the inexorable forces of social upheaval that accompanied a massive military buildup during the first year of the war. As many as nine thousand soldiers were stationed at one point in Savannah. Almost everyone believed that an invasion by Union forces would come from the east, and in fact federal gunboats were patrolling coastal waters unimpeded in late 1861.[11] Throughout the war, city officials, echoing debates among other Confederates, pondered the appropriate use of black workers while trying to balance security concerns with the labor shortage caused by the enlistment and conscription of soldiers. Confederate military officers early adopted a middle position, impressing slaves to toil as fatigue workers for the army—using them, for example, to dig trenches and cut down trees—while at the same time trying to maintain standards of plantation discipline. The so-called Twenty Slave Law of 1862 exempted one white man on a plantation from military service for every twenty slaves on that place. Yet impressment efforts ran into stiff resistance from owners, whose sense of southern nationalism did not extend to yielding up their human property to save the Confederate cause.[12]

During the war, Savannah faced unprecedented demands for new and traditional services. Local newspapers put out calls for a variety of skilled and unskilled workers: engineers, field hands, plantation drivers, carpenters; wheelwrights, machinists, molders, and pattern makers for ironworks; and laborers to load and unload ammunition and supplies. Some of these advertisements stipulated "Negroes wanted" or "colored engineer is preferred," but most made no mention of skin color at all. On December 19, 1861, the city council set the tone for the next few years when it rebuffed the petition from a group of white butchers to repeal the ordinance allowing black men to work as butchers. In the mobilization for war, the demands of white special-interest groups could not be allowed to limit the available number of workers. Instead, the council remained flexible, relying on a variety of strategies, some based on physical force, others on incentives, to best use the reserve of black labor. Complementing official policies were the impulses among blacks themselves to extract cold cash for their work from desperate Confederates. The resulting hybrid system of public mandates and private enterprise signaled the breakdown of slave discipline.[13]

A *New York Times* reporter found in early 1861 that many blacks understood the wider purpose of the war, describing them as "familiar with current events as the whites themselves," and noting that they expected "to be made free by the incoming administration." Black men and women bided their time and remained vigilant throughout the early part of the conflict. In June 1861, fifty-five black men volunteered to work on the fortifications of the city, a gesture that reassured authorities, who were always prone to self-delusion when it came to the "loyalty" of the city's people of color. A local newspaper editor congratulated "Our Colored Population": "It is gratifying to witness the public spirit that rules among this class of our community. Not content to be idle spectators of the military operations, they have nobly come forward and offered their services." Among the volunteers were George Jones, a tailor; the free bricklayer Simon Mirault; and carpenters' and engineers' apprentices. Around the same time, thirty-five black women began making uniforms for one hundred Confederate soldiers; these seamstresses included Jane Deveaux, longtime teacher at an illegal, clandestine school for black children; Georgiana Guard Kelley, a nurse; and Elizabeth Mirault, the wife of Simon.[14]

Overall, though, the city's larger efforts to harness black labor proved problematic. Authorities acknowledged that the onset of hostilities had prompted blacks to become "impertinent and insubordinate," their resentment taking the form not only of verbal assertiveness but also of stealing, refusing to work, and running away. Along the coast, black pilots, scouts, and spies played a critical role in guiding Union gunboats through the maze of rivers, creeks, and marshes. Lowcountry planters were at a loss for ways to stem the flood of fugitives headed for the barrier islands. One group of Liberty County slave owners wrote to General Hugh Mercer and requested that he summarily execute any black runaways, "intelligent beings" willing and able to pass along "information well calculated to aid the enemy." Ultimately, Mercer demurred, noting that he had no authority to destroy the private property of slave owners.[15]

As early as the summer of 1862, at least 417 Georgia black men, most of them young, joined the Union navy. Of the 220 who identified a hometown or county, nearly half (47 percent) reported that they hailed from Savannah or Chatham County. Of the 56 who listed an occupation, waiters and cooks constituted the largest category, with a total of 24, followed by laborers (10) and smaller numbers of carpenters, butchers, stevedores, engineers, and firemen. Many of these black Union seamen reenlisted multiple times during the war, indicating that they found work on gunboats appealing for whatever reason—pride in fighting for their freedom, the wages they earned, a sense of adventure, the

An Old Stairway on the Levée at Savannah. *In Edward King,* The Great South *(1875). Courtesy of Documenting the American South, University of North Carolina at Chapel Hill Libraries.*

camaraderie they embraced in the company of like-minded brothers and cousins. For example, Isaac Parlin, a twenty-five-year-old laborer, and Robert Parlin, a twenty-nine-year-old carpenter, joined the crew of the gunboat *Brandywine* at the end of June 1862.[16]

Savannah civilian and military authorities were not unaware of the initiative shown by black men and women, enslaved and free, before the war, and they aimed to exploit that initiative. A wartime census of free people of color found them thoroughly integrated into the city's economy; the men were working (in order of numerical significance) as carpenters, wagoners, bricklayers, laborers, coopers, butchers, and masons. Smaller numbers found jobs as machinists, barbers, blacksmiths, plasterers, engineers, and cabinetmakers. The women labored mostly as domestic servants, laundresses, nurses, and seamstresses. Yet the jobs blacks reported to census takers did not tell the whole story: James Porter registered himself as a tailor while he was conducting a clandestine school. Similarly, Jane Deveaux reported her occupation as pastry cook, though she continued to teach school.[17]

Confederate officers and engineers understood that some form of incentive would go a long way toward securing the compliance, even if not the wholehearted cooperation, of black workers. In early March 1861, slave owners in the Savannah area voluntarily sent seventeen black men to shore up Fort Pulaski; together, those workers completed 245 days' worth of labor. Payment went not to the owners but directly to the enslaved men—a total of $122.50, which amounted to $0.50 a day for each. In July of that year, the city council resolved that if Confederate officials refused to pay free people of color for their labor on the batteries outside the city, then the city should pick up the monthly tab of $11 per worker. In October, three free black men successfully petitioned the council to have the city pay their state and county taxes in compensation for their service at Tybee Island and Fort Pulaski.[18]

The plight of enslaved military laborers, most of them field hands impressed from plantations in Georgia's interior, contrasted with the more settled wartime existence of free black Savannahians. Forcibly transported from around the state, fatigue workers endured separation from their families and communities, often for months at a time. Military authorities in Savannah, the site of the state's most extensive defensive construction projects employing blacks, put enslaved people to work in a variety of jobs through the Quartermaster, Commissary, and Medical Departments, and through the Arsenal and Ordnance and Engineer Bureaus. These male and female laborers lived in drafty, poorly heated wooden barracks and subsisted on meager rations of bacon and cornmeal. Measles and other epidemics killed or laid low hundreds of workers at a time, and others died or became incapacitated as a result of industrial accidents involving drowning, wounding from the use of unfamiliar tools or falling off cliffs or half-finished walls.[19]

At the same time, some blacks offered their services to individual Confederate officers, working as cooks or nurses in hospitals, driving government drays or military wagons, cutting poles or chopping firewood, or digging trenches around forts; these laborers pressed for concessions that included either cash wages or time off after their tasks, or both. Civilian officials and military officers who wanted black women to cook their food or wash their clothes in some cases contracted with the women involved and paid them directly. Military employers often honored the conventions of the task system. The Engineer Bureau employed slaves to excavate and grade railroad beds, each with an assigned task of digging out twelve to fifteen cubic yards of dirt a day. Over and above that amount of work, each man would receive fifteen cents for each additional cubic yard he finished. Observers noted the way the men incorporated customs associated with fieldwork into this new setting. Led by a "headman" who sang a work song, they were able to finish their tasks by noon and then devote the afternoon to making money for themselves. In the case of more specialized workers, some military authorities dispensed with the task system altogether and simply paid enslaved men cash wages.[20]

In his annual report for 1863, Savannah mayor Thomas Holcombe noted that a spirit of speculation, combined with food shortages, had led to "fabulous rates" for "every article of consumption." Behind this statement was a story of widespread suffering. Only gradually did Georgia's planters heed calls from Milledgeville (the state capital) and the Confederate capital in Richmond to plow under their cotton and plant vegetables instead. In Savannah, the large number of troops, especially before the summer of 1862, created a high demand for food.[21]

Experienced in keeping dairy cows, raising chickens, and growing fruits and vegetables for their own consumption and for sale at market, black men and women in Savannah and the surrounding area were uniquely positioned to provision the city. Free before the war, Sarah Ann Black worked as a seamstress; by 1860 the twenty-six-year-old

mother of four small children had accumulated $2,000 worth of real estate and $550 in her personal estate (perhaps technically the property of her common-law husband, a white cotton trader who did not live in the city). Once the conflict started, she "kept a kind of milk depot" that provided her with a stable income—in her words, "Parties would bring their milk to me and I would sell it for them and get so much selling it." Clara Boisfeillet likewise drew on her antebellum resourcefulness. She had bought her freedom in 1860 and then during the war tended a two-acre garden of cabbage, white turnips, rutabaga, beets, and onions, among other vegetables. Her husband sold them in the Savannah market. She considered theirs a partnership, noting, "He and I are one."[22]

Because many gardeners owned (or at least controlled) wagons, they could offer draying services at a time when transporting food and military materiel formed an integral part of the wartime economy. Toby Adams combined "the business of selling milk" and "planting a piece of about 12 acres" with "hauling goods in a dray." David Moses plied his trade before and during the war with the use of a "common street wagon" and a "regular common dray," carts drawn by the horses and mules he owned. Charles Verene's drayage business was temporarily interrupted by a military officer who arrested him and pressed him into service on the batteries south of the city; but the black man managed to obtain a doctor's certificate stating that he was disabled, and he quickly returned to his own business.[23]

Some black men and women in Savannah were quick to seize other economic opportunities. By the time war broke out, Rachel Brownfield owned a large house on Bryan Street (probably a gift from her white father, a northerner); she responded to the city's chronic wartime housing shortage by renting out rooms to boarders. Many men and women became increasingly impervious to the demands of their masters, whose oversight became increasingly lax. Recalled Stephen Geldersleeve, "I hired my time and worked where I pleased." By late 1864, the brutal control that was the hallmark of slavery had largely disintegrated in the city and surrounding county. As James Custard recalled of life on his master's plantation then, "I was working for myself[,] for everybody was gone off the place."[24]

In November 1864, Sherman's sixty-three thousand troops set out on a southwest trek from Atlanta to the coast, and within a month they literally took Savannah by surprise. On his march, Sherman adopted a policy of living off the land, sending out parties of foragers to seize food and livestock from friend as well as foe, in the countryside and in the cities. For enslaved and free people of color in Chatham and Liberty Counties, Sherman's arrival proved a mixed blessing. Many would later recall, "I was a slave until Sherman came." At the same time, famished Union soldiers plundered local plantations and homesteads for food. The victims of their raids lost all or much of what they had accumulated over years of hard work. The timing—early winter—brought a harvest's worth of bounty to the soldiers. In Savannah, troops looted vegetables from provisioners, and horses, mules, and heavy wooden carts from teamsters. Soldiers dismantled modest dwellings belonging to blacks and used the wood to construct their own temporary barracks in the city's parks. Many Savannah blacks paid for their own liberation with virtually everything they owned—not only food, goods, and livestock, but also clothing, bedding, and kitchenware that the conquerors seized from them.[25]

Black households reacted with shock and anger when Union soldiers seized what they considered their due after a hard slog through the Georgia swamps. Jackson Sheftall

Experiencing Emancipation in Savannah and Its Environs

How and when did enslaved men and women in Savannah and Georgia's Lowcountry become free? President Lincoln announced the Emancipation Proclamation on January 1, 1863, declaring that enslaved blacks in places under Confederate control were free; the proclamation applied to many Georgia blacks in bondage, though the order itself had little practical effect at the time. On December 18, 1865, ratification of the Thirteenth Amendment to the Constitution abolished slavery in the United States. Yet enslaved and free blacks in and around Savannah did not wait for these federal-government initiatives and instead exploited wartime conditions in the search for full freedom and equality for themselves and their loved ones.

In fact, emancipation was not a sudden or singular event in the lives of the enslaved, nor was it a gift bestowed upon them by the president or Congress. For many Savannah and Lowcountry blacks, emancipation was a process that was shaped by black men and women themselves over time. As early as January 1861, while Georgia was seceding from the Union and preparing for armed conflict, some slaves in the city and the countryside responded to disruptions in the region's political and economic life by running away from their masters. Others bided their time, watching and waiting for opportunities to seize control over their own productive energies. Many blacks in Savannah and its environs, enslaved and free, took advantage of breakdowns in workplace discipline when employers, masters, and overseers joined the army. In the kitchens of the city's elegant hotels, in the parlors of gracious mansions, and on rice plantations along the coast, both enslaved and free black laborers shirked doing work for masters and instead toiled for themselves and their families. Whether free or still technically in bondage, some blacks engaged in entrepreneurial activities — providing food, fuel, and transportation services for civilians and military personnel alike — that enabled them to support themselves and their families. The free black butcher Jackson Sheftall used the money he earned by selling goods to Confederate forces to buy his wife and daughter their freedom during the war years.

The gradual crumbling of the institution of slavery affected free people of color as well as slaves in profound ways. Regardless of their legal status, blacks could not vote or participate in the body politic. In Savannah, free blacks were not allowed to own property (admittedly, a law only loosely enforced) and were barred from learning to read and write and from pursuing certain occupations. Moreover, all free blacks had to have a guardian, a white person who was legally responsible for them. These measures heightened the vulnerability of free blacks. During the war, as all blacks sought to resist the demands of whites, free people of color as well as enslaved laborers sought to make themselves truly free.

The advance of northern forces had a dramatic effect upon black people's quest for freedom. In 1862, free and enslaved blacks from Savannah and the surrounding area began to abscond to the Georgia coast and volunteer to serve on the federal gunboats stationed in the waters there. And in April of that year the efforts of the Union general David Hunter to organize a black fighting force galvanized men from all over the region. Although President Lincoln quickly quashed Hunter's initiative, issuance of the Emancipation Proclamation the following January opened the floodgates, and black men rushed to fight for their own freedom by joining the ranks of Union seamen and soldiers.

The formation of small independent colonies on the coastal islands revealed the eagerness of fugitives to make new lives for themselves apart from whites, feelings surely shared by other blacks in the city and the countryside. In the summer of 1862, members of Susie King Taylor's family came together from Savannah and coastal plantations and fled to St. Simons Island, where they fished and planted crops in a bid for self-sufficiency. They also sold foodstuffs and provided services such as laundry to the Union naval forces stationed on ships in the surrounding waters. Within a few months, military officers had forced them to abandon the colony; yet refugees continued to stream to the coast and the islands, coming in some instances from the far interior of the state. Because they lived in areas under Union control, the refugees who settled on some of Georgia's Sea Islands were not legally freed by Lincoln's Proclamation; yet by their own courage and physical exertion, they had managed to win a measure of freedom for themselves.

On the march from Atlanta to Savannah in late 1864, General William T. Sherman's army attracted thousands of enslaved people along the way, men, women, and children seeking safety and self-liberation. Sherman was no principled abolitionist—he refused to accept black men as soldiers—but at the same time he did not actively return slaves to their masters. Later, many Georgia blacks would recall, "I was a slave until Sherman came." Sherman's Special Field Order No. 15 of January 1865, establishing a "reservation" for black refugees on a swath of coastal territory, gave hope to blacks in Savannah and its environs that they could achieve true freedom even before the cessation of military hostilities. Certainly, the ecumenical group of black leaders who founded the Savannah Education Association that month, and the domestics and field hands who abandoned their workplaces for good then, began to live and act as free persons even before the end of the war or the formal abolition of slavery.

Taken as a whole, the wartime era revealed a process of emancipation that for black Savannahians often came in stages: resisting the demands of a master or employer, running away, seeking out long-lost loved ones, establishing a household apart from whites, forming religious and educational associations, and eventually (if only briefly) participating as full citizens of the United States. In this context, freedom was a relative, not absolute, state of being. White prejudice continued to limit black people's opportunities to live unthreatened by the demands of white landlords, politicians, and lynch mobs. After the war, many freedpeople lived in a state of "neoslavery," trapped by the exploitative labor systems of sharecropping and debt peonage. Even so, the war years demonstrated numerous ways that blacks, individually and collectively, acted in the interest of self-emancipation and freedom for themselves, their families, and their communities. Although freedom came to Savannah and the Georgia Lowcountry slowly and in stages, it was helped along at every step of the way by the emancipatory actions of black people themselves.

JACQUELINE JONES

was a prime target for the raiders; his house on the corner of Gwinnett and Roberts Streets stood on the outskirts of the city's northwest corner, in the path of the army as it advanced into the city. His cows, poultry, hogs, rice, and flour would provide sustenance for the troops. His wagons, buggies, and horses, together with saddles, bridles, and harnesses, would prove useful for ongoing military operations. The raiders destroyed his six-room, one-and-a-half-story house and its outbuildings, including a stable and two shops, presumably for firewood or construction materials for batteries. (Sheftall considered the house his own, though it sat on land owned by one of his white relatives, Emanuel Sheftall.) One witness, Joseph M. Snead, later recalled, "The Soldiers came through acted like Bull dogs. Commenced knocking down cattle and hogs helping themselves to anything they could get hold of." The white men seized the family's kitchen utensils, bedding, and bedclothes; yet Jackson's wife, Elizabeth, considered it the last straw only when they grabbed one of the horses. As she tried to stop them, they struck her.[26]

Views in and Around Savannah, Georgia— From Sketches by J. H. Peck, Theodore R. Davis, and William Waud, *Civil War edition of* Harper's Weekly, *January 21, 1865. Image Research: www .sonofthesouth.net.*

At the same time, for some Savannah blacks, the Union military occupation afforded new or renewed opportunities for moneymaking. Diana Cummings worked as a cook for the soldiers. April Walford gathered oysters on Whitemarsh Island and sold them in the city. Anthony Owens issued rations from the commissary department and unloaded boats with supplies for the occupying army. While some residents eagerly sought chances for wage earning, others found themselves laboring under orders from Sherman, who had his men round up all able-bodied black men. As early as January 4, 1865, army officers put out a call for "all unemployed negroes" to report to the post quartermaster for deployment as woodcutters and gatherers.[27]

Within two weeks of the Union occupation, the black community had come together to form the Savannah Education Association, an effort overseen by the city's black preachers. The association hired fifteen black teachers and paid them with funds pledged by local subscribers. By January 10, 1865, a thousand black children had been assigned to seven new schools, one of them the former Bryan Slave Mart near Ellis Square. Nevertheless, Sherman discouraged black initiative. By insisting on a "public order" that preserved the antebellum social division of labor, and by leaving the city government intact and fully operational, the general ensured the persistence and power of neo-Confederate municipal authorities. Under such conditions, white politicians, judges, and police officers thwarted black residents' drive for full citizenship for another hundred years.[28]

By 1870, a number of enterprising men and women had managed to regain some semblance of financial security for themselves and their families. Toby Adams, by then a cattle dealer, boasted $2,000 in real estate and $600 in personal estate. This literate man, a husband, father of three children, and member of the First African Baptist Church, was able to open an account in the Savannah branch of the Freedman's Savings Bank in 1867. Sarah Ann Black, the seamstress mentioned earlier, continued to support herself and five children on her own; they lived in a snug dwelling worth the not inconsiderable sum of $1,800. Celia Boisfeillet and her husband Mitchel, a cotton sampler, possessed both real and personal estate. Rachel Brownfield had held on to her boardinghouse, where eight men and women were lodging in 1870; she also worked as a seamstress and a laundress.[29]

Several people emerged as leaders of the dense network of religious and mutual-aid associations that crisscrossed the black community after the war. The drayman Thomas Garrett, a home owner, had become a Methodist preacher. The butcher Sandy Small had property worth $1,000 and served as president of the Butcher Benevolent Association. Charles Verene was a leader of the Daughters of Eastville, an organization led by both men and women. The widow Georgiana Kelley was a member of First African Baptist and at times an officer in the Poor and Needy Institution, the Ladies Committee of 35, and the Ladies Union. After the war, Jackson Sheftall served as captain of the Savannah Harbors Association. He resumed his butchering business and in 1868 ran unsuccessfully on the Radical (that is, Republican) ticket for Chatham justice of the peace.[30]

In March 1871, Congress established the Southern Claims Commission (scc) to compensate southerners loyal to the Union for losses suffered at the hands of northern troops; such losses had to relate directly to the military effort. Hence, claims for confiscated food

Daughter of Savannah
Susie Baker King Taylor, 1848–1912

Susie Baker King Taylor, born a slave, is one of Savannah's greatest heroines of the Civil War era. As a young girl, she left her home in the countryside to live with her grandmother in the city, and so was in position to become one of the first African Americans to emancipate herself by joining with Union forces when they poured into the Savannah area. Although a woman lacking any formalized tie to the Union army, she participated in the first all-black Union army regiment formed to fight in the war. During the war, she was the founder and sole instructor of the first school openly established for those recently freed, and in the immediate postwar period she founded several Savannah schools for emancipated blacks. Her role as educator of the newly freed placed her in line with predecessors such as Jane Deveaux, who opened a secret school for slaves in the 1830s. She was the only African American woman to publish a memoir of her direct experiences of the Civil War: *Reminiscences of My Life in Camp with the 33rd United States Colored Troops, Late 1st S.C. Volunteers* (Boston, 1902).

Susie was born to Hagar and Raymond Baker on August 6, 1848. The enslaved family lived on Grest Farm, a plantation located on the Isle of Wight in Liberty County, about thirty-five miles south of Savannah. In the

Susie King Taylor, 1902. In Susie King Taylor, Reminiscences of My Life in Camp with the 33rd United States Colored Troops, Late 1st S. C. Volunteers. Courtesy of the Rare Book Collection, J. Y. Joyner Library, East Carolina University, Greenville, North Carolina.

mid-1850s, Susie Baker and two of her siblings moved to Savannah to live with their freed grandmother, Dolly Reed, who made her living through trade and by renting rooms to boarders. Her grandmother saw to it that Susie received an education—despite having to do so surreptitiously. She was educated by free black women who taught black children to read and write in their homes under the pretense of teaching them trade skills. For two years, she received instruction from Mrs. Woodhouse, a widow who lived on Bay Lane between Habersham and Price Streets, and was then sent for advanced study to a woman whom Taylor refers to as Mary Beasley but who was most likely Mathilda Beasley. Susie received instruction from sympathetic white friends as well, including a white playmate named Katie O'Connor and James Blouis, the son of Dolly Reed's landlord.

The desire for freedom among African Americans in Savannah became infused with a new sense of urgency in the spring of 1862 as Union soldiers moved ever closer to the city. But on April 1, as Union forces began to shell Fort Pulaski, Dolly Reed sent Susie and her siblings back to their mother in the countryside. Susie believed that her grandmother did this either to protect them from the hostilities or to prevent them from fleeing to the Union army. Seeing that army as the best way to gain her freedom, Susie moved, along with an uncle and several cousins, back toward the city and boarded a gunboat bound for the Union army encampment on St. Simons Island. There, the value of her literacy and the skills imparted by her grandmother and other black women in Savannah, including sewing, cooking, and nursing, immediately became evident to Union

officers. After she passed a brief literacy test, a white officer put her in charge of organizing a school for the freedmen and their children on the island. That school was the first one in the South established by army officers specifically to educate the recently freed.

While en route to St. Simons Island, Susie Baker met Edward King, whom she later married. King became a noncommissioned officer in Company E of the 1st South Carolina Volunteers (later known as the 33rd U.S. Colored Infantry Regiment), the first black volunteer regiment composed of freedmen. After several months on St. Simons, Susie took charge of the laundry and the small nursing corps that accompanied King's regiment on its way to Old Fort (renamed Camp Saxton) on the mainland. By the end of 1862, at age fourteen, Susie Baker had left enslavement behind her forever, met the man she would marry, established a school for free persons, started a nursing corps, and set out for war with a regiment of troops.

Susie spent the rest of the war traveling with and serving the 33rd U.S. Colored Infantry Regiment as a nurse, teacher, cook, laundress, and weapons inspector. She was stationed for some time at Camp Shaw, South Carolina, and helped nurse wounded soldiers at the hospital in nearby Beaufort alongside the famed Clara Barton, founder of the Red Cross.

After the war, Susie and Edward King returned to Savannah, where, in 1866, she opened a school for recently freed people at their home on South Broad Street (now Oglethorpe Avenue). Her twenty students each paid a dollar a month, but competition from free schools receiving federal funding, such as the Beach Institute, chipped away at her enrollment. Edward, though trained as a carpenter, opened a business that hired men to unload vessels docked in Savannah's harbor. Within a few months of settling in to married life, Edward died on September 16, 1866, leaving Susie widowed and with an infant son to care for. In 1867, Susie King left her school in the charge of a woman named Susie Carrier and moved for a short time back to Liberty County, where she again established a school for freed blacks. Dissatisfied with "country life," Susie returned to Savannah less than a year later and found that her school had lost all its pupils to the Beach Institute. She reopened her home as an evening school for adults, but when the Beach Institute established a free night school, she was forced to close. All told, Susie King established three schools for freed people after the war, in addition to the first school on St. Simons Island and her continual tutoring of black soldiers during the war. King never received assistance from the Freedmen's Bureau or other aid societies to support her various educational ventures. Nor did she receive pay or a pension for her own service to the nation, although in 1872 she received a $100 payment for her husband's service, some

of which she deposited in a Freedman's Savings Bank.

Unable to continue her work as an educator, King worked as a maid, laundress, or cook in the homes of a number of wealthy white women in Savannah. By the late 1870s, she had moved north to Boston, which provided new personal and professional opportunities—indeed, she spent the remainder of her life there. There, she met and married her second husband, Russell L. Taylor, in 1879. In Boston, Susie King Taylor made the needs of Civil War veterans, especially black veterans, central to her clubwoman activities, organizing and serving as president of Corps 67, the Boston chapter of the Woman's Relief Corps—an auxiliary of the Grand Army of the Republic, a Union veteran's association.

Taylor returned to Savannah in 1888 to visit her aging grandmother. Ten years later, she escorted her severely ill son from Shreveport, Louisiana, to Boston for treatment. But the railroad denied him a sleeper berth because of the New South's statutory racial segregation in public accommodations, a system recently upheld as constitutional by the Supreme Court ruling in *Plessy v. Ferguson*. In the final chapter of her memoir Taylor writes with bitterness of her son's death and bemoans the Jim Crow atmosphere of disrespect and racial malevolence she found rife throughout the southern states in the late 1890s.

Taylor's decision to publish a memoir arose in part from her dismay at the level of contemporary racial injustice and in part from a desire to remind her readers of the war's true meaning—the liberation of her race from southern slavery. She wanted also to show appreciation for the black and white veterans of the Union army. But she sought specific public recognition for black women who had contributed to the war effort, helped secure black freedom, and engaged in community activism, education, and racial uplift following the war: "There are many people who do not know what some of the colored women did during the war. . . . These things should be kept in history before the people. There has never been a greater war in the United States than the one of 1861, where so many lives were lost,—not men alone but noble women as well."

Susie King Taylor died on October 6, 1912, and was buried next to her second husband in an unmarked grave in Mount Hope Cemetery, Roslindale, Massachusetts.

TRACEY JEAN BOISSEAU

and wagons were acceptable, while those for household goods and clothing were not. Many members of the scc, white Republicans all, expressed profound skepticism about the nature and extent of claims presented by freedpeople, calling into question lists of items recalled from memory, "on account of their [the claimants'] ignorance and the liveliness of their imagination." The commissioners were particularly "doubtful and suspicious" of claims that listed horses. Toby Adams claimed reimbursement for three dray horses and two colts, which he had used for the three wagons he operated in the city; his filing prompted the comment, "Some doubt whether the claimant (a colored man) owned the amount of property here charged as directed."[31]

Virtually no claimants received the full amount of money they applied for. Yet the accounts offered by those who received compensation suggest that some applicants devised a promising formula: persuading prominent whites to testify on their behalf. Georgiana Kelley, who had worked as a nurse for her guardian, the physician and former mayor Richard Arnold, benefited from the enthusiastic endorsement of Arnold's grown daughter Ellen. Many claimants answered in the affirmative when commissioners asked whether they had materially aided the Union cause. But one witness, asked whether he had been loyal to the Union, answered honestly, and with some exasperation, "I was a Union man— I had to work all the time—there wasn't any Union in dem days—with an overseer behind me with a whip in his hand—that was all the Union there was before the war."[32]

Asked whether they owed anything to their former masters and mistresses, many black men and women reacted indignantly. Referring to his former mistress, April Walford declared, "I don't owe her anything. She owes me for money she took out of a savings bank that belonged to me." Harriet Dallas maintained that her deceased husband "did not owe his master anyone or anybody else a dollar." In speaking of his former master, Madison Smith stressed that, to the contrary, "he owes me." The teamster William Harris told an interviewer, "I do not owe him anything now. I think by rights, *he owes me* for all the money [I] *paid him*." Similarly, Peter Miller noted, "I don't owe my old master anything. I think that he owes me a great deal. He was a very hard man."[33]

One question in particular proved a stumbling block to a number of claimants who had made money in wartime Savannah: "Did you ever do anything for the Confederate cause, or render any aid or comfort to the rebellion?" In July 1871, Jackson Sheftall filed a claim for the exceptionally large sum of $3,886. Like John Laurence and Sandy Small, other black butchers who had worked for the Confederacy, Sheftall pointed out that he had had little choice in the matter. Nevertheless, his inquisitors found in his wartime activities evidence of what they considered disloyalty to the Union.[34]

Describing Sheftall as "a colored man nearly white," the commissioners concluded that the butcher had "carried on the business during the war, a portion of the time in the employ of the Confederate army." More damningly, Sheftall had worked as "a partner with the [Confederate] post commissary." They decided he was "not loyal," since "he made money by his service and rendered as much aid and comfort to the Confederacy as a white man under similar circumstances."[35]

In May 1873, Sheftall appealed the scc's denial of his claim and reiterated his defense: "They forced me. Well, if you was a butcher you had to butcher for the Government, and if you were a cook you had to cook for them." Five years later, Sheftall was still pressing his case, now with the aid of a (presumably white) law firm, Gilmore and Company, which made this statement on his behalf: "It seems rather far-fetched to *infer* that he was a *Rebel* because he did the best he could in his trade. Prudence required him to keep his mouth shut among white people. It seems to us that fair dealing required some proof of disloyal feelings and preferences before pronouncing him a rebel." Just because he secured a contract with Confederate military authorities did not mean that "he desired to aid the Rebel cause and preferred its success." In response, one of the commissioners wrote, "There was no compulsion about the butchering business, but there was large profit in it, and for that the claimant went in zealously." The commissioners' original finding stood.[36]

One of the witnesses appearing on behalf of Jackson Sheftall was Andrew McDowell, the former slave of a prominent Savannah banker. In his testimony, McDowell recounted a conversation he had had with Sheftall the night before the army came roaring through: "I saw how comfortable he was fixed and said to him he had got well fixed he said yes." McDowell continued, "The claimant is a free man smart industrious smart man. I have no doubt but what the property all belonged to him he always made money was a money making man."[37]

And indeed he was. Sheftall rebounded after the war and continued his moneymaking ways. Within a few years, he was operating a thriving business as a greengrocer and a butcher at West Broad and Anderson Streets. He was, by all accounts, a man of wealth and standing in the postwar Savannah black community.[38]

During the war, white Savannahians unexpectedly found themselves dependent on black labor for basic necessities, from food to firewood, circumstances that provided many enslaved workers and free people of color with unprecedented opportunities for moneymaking. Long accustomed to the task system of labor, black men and women took advantage of those opportunities to turn a profit in the midst of a long and bloody conflict. Ultimately, of course, the war led to the destruction of slavery and opened a new chapter in the black freedom struggle. In his resourcefulness and resilience, Jackson B. Sheftall represented a critical link between Georgia's antebellum past and its postslavery future.

"We Defy You!"
Politics and Violence in Reconstruction Savannah
Jonathan M. Bryant

During the night of December 31, 1864, the schooner *Rebecca Hertz* stole through the labyrinth of creeks winding through the islands near the city of Savannah. Whether by skill or by luck, she avoided Union warships and the guns of Fort Pulaski, finally dropping anchor opposite the city gasworks sometime before dawn on January 1. The crew, convinced it had safely run the Union blockade, was stunned when the rising sun revealed the Stars and Stripes of the United States flying over the city. Trapped and amazed by this turn of events, the crew surrendered to the triumphant federal army occupying the city.[1]

The crew members of the *Rebecca Hertz* were not alone in their amazement. During a brief campaign in December 1864, William Tecumseh Sherman's troops had stormed Fort McAllister, Confederate general William Hardee's troops had fled the city, and Savannah had fallen with what some thought unseemly ease into Union hands. Thus, in January 1865, General Sherman ruled Savannah as its conqueror. Even after those triumphs, however, Sherman found himself under attack. The attacks came not from the small Confederate bands that prowled the outskirts of the city, but from within the federal government itself.[2]

In letters and public statements made before his March to the Sea, Sherman had expressed little sympathy for the enslaved people of the South. A few in the northern press even suggested Sherman did not support the government's policy of emancipation. During the march, Sherman's forces often treated the slaves encountered along the route as a military impediment, and failed to protect from Confederate reprisals the thousands of freedpeople following the Union army. Several northern newspapers reported one incident in particular as characterizing Sherman's attitude toward the emancipated slaves. At flooded Ebenezer Creek northwest of Savannah, Sherman's forces took up a pontoon bridge immediately after crossing, stranding on the far side hundreds of black refugees

Samuel A. Cooley, Gen. Sherman's Troops Removing Ammunition from Fort McAllister, 1864, December 1864. Courtesy of the Civil War Glass Negatives and Related Prints Collection, Prints and Photographs Division, Library of Congress, LC-DIG-CWPB-03159.

who were following the army in hope of freedom. Fearing they would be set upon by Confederate cavalry and then murdered or reenslaved, the mass of freedpeople panicked. In the confusion that followed, an unknown number drowned while trying to cross the wide flood, and others were trampled in the crush. This tragedy greatly embarrassed the Lincoln administration. Thus, early on January 11, 1865, the secretary of war, Edwin Stanton, arrived in Savannah aboard a revenue cutter to investigate Sherman's activities and, if necessary, to disavow his actions.[3]

In taking the city, Sherman's forces had captured thousands of bales of cotton worth millions of dollars. Secretary Stanton made certain that this cotton was turned over to the Treasury Department agent who arrived with him. He insisted that all marks of

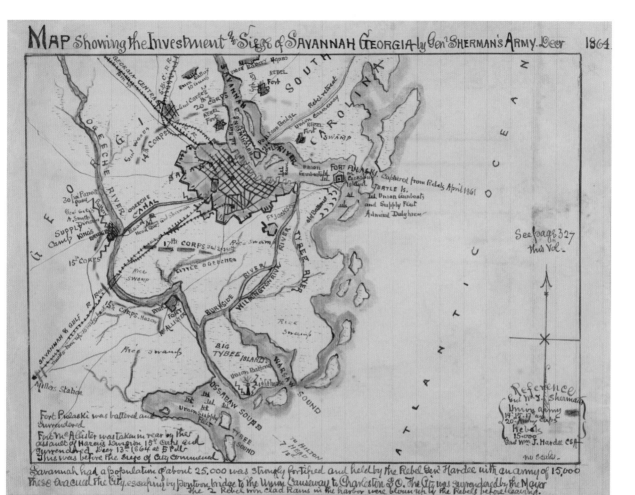

Robert Knox Sneden, Map Showing the Investment and Siege of Savannah, Georgia, 1864. *Courtesy of the Virginia Historical Society, 1994.80.378.*

REBEL PRISON AT SAVANNAH. GEORGIA. 5000 PRISONERS OF WAR. sketched Octr. 1864.

Occupied by Union Prisoners of War from Septr 19th to Octr 15th 1864.
Lt S.R Davis C.S.A had Command of the Prison — The Stockade was
torn down before Sherman's Army reached Savannah —

Robert Knox Sneden,
Rebel Prison at Savannah,
Georgia, 1864. *Virginia*
Historical Society,
Mss5:1 SN237:1 v.6 p. 18.

identification be removed from the bales, presumably to make federal confiscation more certain. Then Sherman and Stanton walked through the captured city together, admiring the squares and the ingenious housing created by the soldiers encamped there. An army of sixty thousand men was occupying a small city of twenty-five thousand, and it was very crowded. They noticed throngs of refugees as well, including perhaps as many as ten thousand runaway slaves. As they talked, Stanton turned to the central reason for his visit. "He talked to me a great deal about the negroes," Sherman wrote later, "for whom we all felt sympathy, but a sympathy of a different sort from that of Mr. Stanton, which was not of pure humanity, but of politics."[4]

Stanton insisted on meeting with leaders of Savannah's black community, so Sherman arranged a conference with "the most intelligent of the negroes." On January 12, 1865, twenty black men assembled upstairs in Charles Green's elaborate mansion on Madison Square. In what must have seemed an unreal setting, surrounded by gothic and rococo decorations, Stanton and the black leaders held a most unusual "conversation." All parties conducted themselves with extreme formality. The black men introduced themselves and then appointed Garrison Frazier, a sixty-seven-year-old retired Baptist minister, to speak for them. Stanton read from a prepared list of twelve questions about national politics, emancipation, the war, and the recruiting of black soldiers. Frazier responded in just as stilted a tone. In one crucial exchange, Stanton asked, "State in what manner you would rather live—whether scattered among the whites, or in colonies by yourselves?" Frazier answered, "I would prefer to live by ourselves, for there is a prejudice against us in the South that will take years to get over; but I do not know that I can answer for my brethren." All but one of the other black leaders indicated that they agreed with Frazier, laying the foundation for a unique plan to deal with the challenge of emancipation.[5]

The result was Sherman's Special Field Order No. 15, issued January 16, 1865. Whether or not Stanton participated directly in crafting the order, it clearly showed the impact of his meeting with the freedmen. Under this order, the coastal islands and the rice plantations along the rivers from Charleston south to the St. Johns River were set aside as a reservation for the freedpeople. Black heads of households could obtain forty-acre plots of tillable land, farm the land, and rely on the military to provide a steamer to carry their produce to market. These were to be independent black colonies, and "no white person whatever" would be permitted to live within the reservation. Finally, for those who claimed land under the order, it promised military protection "until such time as they can protect themselves or until Congress shall regulate their title." The editors of the *Savannah Republican* argued that Special Field Order No. 15 "sets forth very clearly what is to be done with the colored population." At the least, this was a unique solution to the problem of thousands of black refugees in the city; at best, it was a significant effort to secure autonomy for the freedpeople.[6]

On the afternoon of February 2, 1865, General Rufus Saxton, charged by Sherman with administering Special Field Order No. 15, met with perhaps a thousand black people at Savannah's Second African Baptist Church on Greene Square. The old wooden church was packed: the aisles and doorways were filled with people, and others gathered outside in the square. The choir sang "America," and the Reverend Ulysses Houston opened the meeting with a prayer. Then, General Saxton spoke, explaining that freedom brought the responsibility of work and that the government that had set them free had also "set apart the islands of the coast for their occupation, and that the head of each family was entitled to forty acres of land." Those who did not have work in Savannah should claim land in the coastal reservation, Saxton explained. The Reverend Mansfield French spoke next, proclaiming that freedom was a gift from God and that General Sherman had brought it to them. "Amen! Bless the Lord, yes, yes," the crowd responded. French continued, explaining that while the young men should enlist in the Union army and a few should continue to work for their old masters for wages, "all others should at once go to the islands." The emotional frenzy grew throughout the meeting as the exciting prospect of land and protection by the federal government seemed to promise true independence for the former slaves. As one observer reported to the American Missionary Association, it was "one of the most remarkable meetings ever held in the city of Savannah."[7]

If General Sherman and General Oliver O. Howard, commissioner of the Freedmen's Bureau, thought that Special Field Order No. 15 would send the black people of Savannah trooping off to the islands, thus solving Savannah's refugee problem, they were wrong. Some freedpeople did leave the city. Ulysses Houston led a group of several hundred freedpeople to settle on Skidaway Island, and others surely left the city as well. Those who left, however, could not offset the flood of refugees, mostly black, that continued to pour into Savannah. These refugees crowded into growing slums, particularly to the west and south of the city limits. Even those who left with Houston for Skidaway Island were back within a year, removed from the land after President Andrew Johnson nullified Special Field Order No. 15 on September 12, 1865.[8]

As a result, between 1860 and 1870 the white population of Savannah grew by about 9 percent, from 13,875 to 15,166, and the black population grew by about 65 percent, from 8,417 to 13,068. Figures for Chatham County were even more startling. In 1860, about half the county's 31,043 people were black. In 1870, almost 60 percent of the population of 41,279 was black. Savannah's and Chatham County's populations continued to grow throughout Reconstruction, and freed blacks substantially outnumbered whites in the county. Given that pattern of growth, freedpeople might eventually have outnumbered whites in the city as well. This demographic revolution posed not just a problem of order for a city crowded with refugees, but also a potential political crisis for Savannah's white elite.[9]

General Sherman's Special Field Order No. 15 is fairly well known, and often celebrated by historians. Less well known but ultimately more important for the experience of freedpeople in Savannah was his Special Field Order No. 143, issued December 26, 1864, which organized the municipal government of the newly conquered city. The order provided simply that "the Mayor and City Council of Savannah will continue to exercise their functions." If the capture of Savannah can be seen as an early Christmas present from Sherman to President Lincoln, then Special Field Order No. 143 was a Boxing Day gift to the city's white elite. While limitations were temporarily placed on the judicial and police powers exercised by Savannah's city government, Special Field Order No. 143 provided for a political continuity that undermined and ultimately destroyed freedpeople's efforts to become equal members of the Savannah community. While Special Field Order No. 15 had little long-term impact on the course of Reconstruction in Savannah, Special Field Order No. 143 had lasting and, ultimately, deadly consequences.[10]

In 1861, across the American South, a radical white elite had sought political independence and increased power through rebellion and a civil war. That effort failed on the battlefield. With defeat, many of these rebellious whites recast themselves as constitutional conservatives, seeking to preserve local political autonomy and what they defined as the proper relations of federalism. They hoped that their arguments would both prove politically palatable to the national government and permit the elites to maintain their power. In Savannah, General Sherman's Special Order No. 143 helped legitimate the local elites' continuing hold on political office. Through shrewd appeals to military authorities, court cases, and simple force, Savannah's political elite managed to avoid holding any meaningful local elections for the next four years. On December 6, 1865, white Savannah voters chose Edward C. Anderson as mayor. Anderson had served as mayor in the 1850s;

Coming Full Circle
Harriet Jacobs and the Crafts in Reconstruction-Era Savannah

After the Civil War, Harriet Jacobs, William Craft, and Ellen Craft arrived in Savannah to provide relief and create opportunities for recently freed people in the city. They supplied food, clothing, medicine, and other essentials to hospital patients and refugees; they opened schools and orphanages; and they established homes for the elderly. They solicited money to help enslaved blacks make the transition from slavery to freedom, and they reported on the conditions of life for the city's freed men, women, and children. Despite the extent of Jacobs's and the Crafts' labors in Savannah, that work is often overshadowed by the dramatic events of their earlier lives as fugitive slaves. All were renowned because they had published first-person accounts of the horrors of racial slavery and their harrowing escapes from bondage. The Crafts' *Running a Thousand Miles for Freedom* (1860) and Jacobs's *Incidents in the Life of a Slave Girl* (1861) propelled them to national and international prominence. By returning to the South, Jacobs and the Crafts were coming full circle. Savannah was at the center of their efforts to fight the social, political, and economic inequalities left in the wake of slavery.

Harriet Jacobs and her adult daughter Louisa Matilda Jacobs arrived in Savannah in November 1865. They had spent time in Washington, D.C., and Alexandria, Virginia, between 1863 and 1865, participating in relief efforts for refugee slaves, or contrabands, by providing health care and operating the Jacobs Free School. In Savannah, the Jacobs women immediately undertook similar kinds of work. At the city's poorhouse—converted to a temporary freedmen's hospital under the directorship of Major Alexander Augusta, an acquaintance of theirs from Alexandria—they distributed clothes, raised funds for a holiday dinner that they prepared, and opened a makeshift school. They volunteered to take charge of a planned orphanage and home for the elderly. Harriet continued amassing supplies and financial contributions from philanthropic associations in New York, Pennsylvania, and Massachusetts. During their time in Savannah, the Jacobses reported on the state of freedmen's affairs to supporters in the North and in England, stressing the importance of land ownership, economic opportunities, and adequate health care for blacks as means of securing autonomy; they also documented the city's simmering racial violence.

Harriet and Louisa Jacobs were actively involved in the education of freedpeople at a time when control of that endeavor was growing increasingly contentious. The organization of schools for freedpeople was an immediate concern of Savannah's black educators, who, after decades of operating clandestine schools, formed the Savannah Education Association in early 1865. But white northern missionaries, supported by the Freedmen's Bureau, believed that they should control schools for the newly freed. When Harriet and Louisa Jacobs reached Savannah, six black-led schools were in operation, and educator Aaron Bradley planned to open another. But by the early spring of 1866, the Reverend S. W. Magill and other officials of the American Missionary Association had gained control of the schools and reduced the Savannah Education Association to a mere "auxiliary" status. In the midst of this struggle, the Jacobses established the Lincoln School in the eastern section of the city, one of only two black-led and black-taught schools to survive the reorganization and remain independent. The Jacobses were interested also in the settlement schools established on the rice plantations that lined the Savannah River. But as violence surged in the countryside in the face of reduced military protection and a growing white backlash, they were unable to make inroads there. They left Savannah in July 1866, much to the delight of local whites, who characterized them as northern troublemakers, though Harriet continued to raise funds for black institutions in Savannah until as late as 1868.

In addition to scores of others who carried on the work of Reconstruction, Ellen and

Harriet Jacobs, 1894. Image courtesy of Documenting the American South, University of North Carolina at Chapel Hill Libraries.

William Craft succeeded the Jacobs women in Savannah. After nearly two decades of exile in England, the Crafts returned to the United States around 1869 and, like Jacobs, dedicated themselves to promoting the interests of freedpeople. After living in Boston for a short time, they resettled in Georgia in 1870, where they established the Southern Industrial School and Labor Enterprise with proceeds from lectures that William delivered in the North and the financial assistance of abolitionists. Members of the Ku Klux Klan burned it down that same year, however, revealing the deep hostility and intense violence that blacks faced during Reconstruction. Unwilling to yield to this intimidation, the Crafts relocated to Bryan County, just outside Savannah, and purchased an 1,800-acre plantation with their savings and with money raised from their northern supporters. In 1873, they opened the Woodville Co-operative Farm School, which provided education and employment for freed people. Sixteen families lived on the farm and grew rice, corn, and cotton for their collective benefit. Ellen headed the school and taught seventy-five children free of charge—thirty who resided on the plantation and the rest from the local community. In 1876, resentful whites coordinated a smear campaign against the Crafts, accusing William of squandering donated school funds on his family's personal expenses. Though he sued for libel, William was unsuccessful in clearing his name and could no longer raise money from outside supporters. That hardship, along with falling cotton prices and increasing hostility, forced the school and co-op to close in 1878. The Crafts remained at Woodville for some years afterward, struggling to keep the plantation operational, but eventually went bankrupt. They moved to Charleston to live with their daughter and her family. Ellen died in 1891, and shortly afterward, the farm that she had started with her husband was auctioned off to pay his debts; William died in 1900.

JENIFER L. BARCLAY

during the war, he commanded a blockade-runner and the city artillery batteries on the river. Along with Mayor Anderson, the aldermen elected in 1865 were old-line elites who had served previously on the city council. Anderson and most of these aldermen held their offices until October 1869, even though Savannah was supposed to hold municipal elections annually. To maintain their power and position, the mayor, aldermen, and other city officials believed they had to prevent freedmen from winning the right to vote or, failing that, to make their franchise meaningless. From 1865 through 1869, the Reconstruction effort in Savannah centered upon the possibility of political action by the emancipated slaves and the attempt by the old white elite to maintain control over local government and local courts. This struggle came to a head in the fall and winter of 1868–69.[11]

There had been significant conflict in Savannah between whites and blacks before 1868, but it did not become overtly political until freedmen received the right to vote

By telegraph from Fort Monroe

Head-Quarters Military Division of the Mississippi,

In the Field 186

Savannah, Dec 22 1864

To his Excellency,

President Lincoln,

I beg to present you as a Christmas Gift the City of Savannah with (150) heavy guns and plenty of ammunition, as also about (25000) bales of cotton

one hundred and fifty

twenty five thousand

W. T. Sherman
Maj Genl.

33 Col

Telegram from Maj. Gen. William T. Sherman to President Abraham Lincoln, announcing the surrender of Savannah, Georgia, as a Christmas present to the President, 12/22/1864. *Records of the Office of the Secretary of War, Record Group 107; National Archives Building, Washington, D.C. (online version available through the Archival Research Catalog [ARC Identifier 301637] at www.archives.gov).*

under the first Reconstruction Act, enacted on March 2, 1867. From the perspective of the white elite, the mass outdoor rallies, marching, and organization by freedpeople following passage of the act presented a frightening threat to social norms and political control. This public political activity was in great contrast to the relative public obscurity that enslaved blacks had maintained. Worse, blacks quickly signaled that they intended to challenge local leaders directly. Freedmen organized a petition drive in May 1867, calling for the federal government to remove the mayor and the aldermen of Savannah. The petition alleged that those political officers perpetrated "injustice to the colored people," particularly "at the courts." The Mayor's Court in particular was notorious in this regard. Black prisoners convicted of violating local ordinances or misdemeanors by the Mayor's Court were sentenced to work on the public streets for up to twelve months while wearing a ball and chain—an early version of a chain gang. White prisoners were usually assessed modest fines instead of being sentenced to hard labor, and those put to work did not have to wear a ball and chain. The freedmen's petition threw down the gauntlet, and it had genuine force behind it. By July 1867, there were 3,091 black men and only 2,240 white men registered to vote in Savannah. In Chatham County, the black majority was even larger. If allowed to vote openly and freely, blacks could control politics in the city.[12]

Savannah's white leadership did not know what to make of freedpeople's political activities. Slavery had largely been legitimated upon racial grounds. According to most nineteenth-century racial concepts, people of African heritage were slaves because of their natural inferiority. At best, as Mayor Anderson explained in December 1868, "Negroes are regarded by us as children." At worst, blacks were considered beasts. The limitations placed on the civil rights of slaves and free people of color before emancipation had been justified as necessary to protect society from their childlike or degraded natures. Suddenly, less than three years after emancipation, whites were told that members of this inferior race were due the rights of citizens, including the right to vote. Many white conservatives found such suggestions preposterous. At first, newspaper accounts reflected this, ridiculing freedmen's public political activities. By the fall of 1867, however, Savannah's newspapers were increasingly portraying political meetings involving blacks as disorderly, confused, and dangerous. Any black political activity was, by implication, a threat to public safety.[13]

On September 30, 1867, debate grew heated during a Republican rally in Chippewa Square. At one point, a "conservative negro pushed into the crowd and threatened Aaron A.

Bradley," a black political leader soon to be elected to the Georgia State Senate. Watching events closely, the Savannah police decided to halt the meeting. They moved in, assisted by U.S. soldiers, and began to arrest blacks attending the meeting. Ultimately, forty freedmen were arrested, along with two freedwomen who objected loudly to the arrests. All those arrested were later charged with offenses ranging from disorderly conduct to carrying weapons. The newspapers asserted that Savannah had been saved from a deadly riot.[14]

Searching for a solution to the problem of federally imposed black male suffrage, many of Georgia's white conservatives hoped that by boycotting the federally required election of October 29–November 2, 1867, for delegates to a state constitutional convention, they would discredit the results. Instead, the boycott simply ensured a Republican victory at the polls. Thus, a Republican-dominated convention created the Georgia Constitution of 1868. Under the new constitution, municipal and state elections were scheduled for the spring of 1868. Yet Savannah's elite managed to avoid holding a local election. In March 1868, city leaders contacted General George Meade, who was directing Military Reconstruction in Georgia, and used the conflict and arrests made in Chippewa Square the previous September as an example of the chaos to be expected if local elections were held in the city. General Meade postponed municipal elections in Savannah, and the existing slate of city officials retained their offices.

The election of state officers went forward in April, however, and white and black voters turned out in large numbers. Despite their best efforts, Democratic candidates were defeated in the city and overwhelmingly in Chatham County. All three of Chatham County's newly elected members of the state legislature were black Republicans. Thus, as the elections in the fall of 1868 approached, Savannah's conservative white leadership knew that Democratic candidates could not win free local elections.[15]

By August 1868, it had become clear that violent conflict was brewing in Savannah. Clashes grew more common between the city's police, dressed in "cadet" grey uniforms, and freedpeople. Blacks complained that they were arrested for little or no reason and often kept in the city jail for days or weeks without charge. When an arrest was made, other blacks often harassed the arresting officers, tried to free the prisoner, and followed along behind, complaining loudly, as the prisoner was taken to jail. On the night of August 30, 1868, police sergeant William Moran arrested a freedman for firing his pistol four times after dark. Dozens of blacks—Sergeant Moran said 150—surrounded the policeman and his prisoner. Only with the help of a local black leader was the sergeant

The Beach Institute and the American Missionary Association

Founded in Savannah, Georgia, in 1867, the Beach Institute served as a school for African American children. Operating until 1919, the school educated the first generations of African American children living in the postemancipation South. As a result, the stately white clapboard building became an important symbol of African American education in the city, which was built on a foundation established by Jane Deveaux and by the Savannah Education Association (SEA). Ongoing tensions between the American Missionary Association (AMA) and the African American community, though, demonstrated the complicated history of the Beach Institute and postbellum African American education in Savannah.

The Beach Institute emerged directly out of the Civil War–era struggles for African American education that began shortly after Savannah's surrender to Union troops. In late 1864, the Reverend William J. Campbell, the Reverend Ulysses L. Houston, the Reverend James Lynch (an African Methodist Episcopal minister from Baltimore), and other local African Americans organized the SEA to fund, establish, staff, and superintend schools for the newly emancipated. Former slaves desired to become literate, and eager students quickly filled the SEA schools, which soon outgrew their facilities throughout the city.

These early efforts attracted the attention of the AMA, an interdenominational abolitionist organization that worked to assist former slaves during and after the Civil War. Seeking to expand its efforts to include freedpeople in Savannah, the Reverend S. W. Magill, a white Georgia native and the superintendent of AMA schools, in mid-January 1865 opened a school in the Wesley Chapel on South Broad Street, using AMA teachers. The AMA soon moved to the larger Massie School on Gordon Street to accommodate the number of interested students. Yet even as the AMA was increasing the number of black-operated SEA schools, it was co-opting the fledgling educational system. In late February 1865, it attempted to provide experienced administrators for SEA schools. When the AMA went so far as to demote black SEA teachers, local African Americans mistrusted, resented, and lost confidence in the organization, viewing it as undermining African Americans' efforts to determine the educational needs of their community without white assistance. But financial considerations nonetheless forced many to enroll in the AMA schools rather than private schools established by African Americans. By 1866, the AMA had expanded its operations to Andrew's Chapel (a Colored Methodist Episcopal church), the lecture rooms of the First African and Bryan Baptist Churches, Sturtevant Hall, and other locations formerly operated by the SEA.

The early educational efforts of the SEA, the arrival of the AMA in Savannah, and the inability to provide adequate accommodations for the large number of African Americans desirous of education led the AMA to establish the Beach Institute in 1867. It named the new school after Alfred E. Beach, the editor of *Scientific American*. His large donation, along with funding from the Freedmen's Bureau and local citizens, facilitated the purchase of land and the construction and outfitting of the school. At the dedication, several visiting dignitaries emphasized the role of the school in the transition from slavery to freedom. John R. Lewis, a state Freedmen's Bureau agent, remarked that former slaves and their children "were not thoroughly emancipated or free until they . . . became educated and fit to enjoy the rights which had been conferred upon them." The school opened with an enrollment of approximately six hundred. Students daily passed under the inscription "Knowledge with Virtue," which was above the main entrance. They initially received instruction from a teaching staff that included eight white female teachers, one female African American teacher, and a white male principal. Despite the monthly fees and predominantly white teaching staff, student enrollment and daily attendance remained high throughout its early years. Competition with private African American schools, tuition costs, and ongoing tensions between the AMA and the African American community occasionally caused decreases in enrollment. Yet the Beach Institute overcame such obstacles because of its curriculum, reputation, and spacious accommodations. As a result, the large and stately school quickly became an

important fixture of African American education in Savannah and across the South.

In 1874, the Beach Institute became a free public school when the AMA rented the building to the Savannah Board of Education, which sought to develop a system of public schools for African American children. For four years, the Beach Institute provided a free education to Savannah's African American children. But a fire in 1878 temporarily closed the school. During the rebuilding efforts, the AMA again ran the Beach Institute as a private school; the organization wanted to implement a higher grade of instruction than the city thought feasible for African American children. After 1878, the Beach Institute continued to attract students from across the city, but it also competed with nearby educational institutions such as Georgia State Industrial College. To generate additional revenue, officials rented a single room and then the entire basement to Savannah Boys Club in 1917. Unfortunately, the effort was not enough to overcome the school's dwindling finances.

In 1919, a significant decline in enrollment and the opening of Savannah's first public high school for African American children forced the closure of the Beach Institute. Today, it serves as an educational and cultural center operated by the King-Tisdell Cottage Foundation. While no longer a school, the Beach Institute remains an important symbol of education and African American achievement in Savannah.

HILARY N. GREEN

able to leave the scene with his prisoner. In response, the next morning the *Daily News and Herald* editorialized, "Hardly an arrest of a negro is made now-a-days but an attempt is made to rescue him by negro mobs. Negro insolence is becoming more and more intolerable . . . The negroes are daily provoking the whites—by their acts saying 'we defy you.' It is time their insolence should be checked, and when it is done, let it be done in such a manner that the remembrance of it will strike terror to the heart of each member of the race so long as it is in existence."[16]

As the November election approached, the threatening language grew. On September 28, 1868, the *Daily News and Herald* changed its name to the *Morning News*, the editor harking back to his prewar secessionist newspaper of the same name. The *Morning News* reported again and again on "Radical pow wows" and "Union League plots" throughout September and October. Typical were the comments of the paper following a speech by the Reverend James M. Simms. Simms was one of the black assemblymen from Chatham County. In September 1868, the Georgia legislature expelled its black members, including Simms, claiming they could not serve because of their race. At an October rally in front of the Chatham County courthouse, Simms condemned the Democratic Party and the white Republicans who had cooperated with it to expel the black legislators. "He said," reported the *Morning News*, "that the blacks had gained the right to vote by a revolution, and that it would require a bloodier revolution to take it away."[17]

The next day, the *Morning News* editorialized on Simms's speech, calling his comments dangerous and incendiary. "He should know," the paper explained, "that he is putting the whites on their guard." The paper then reminded all freedmen of "the example of New Orleans." This was a direct threat of political violence. On June 30, 1866, in New Orleans, freedmen and white Republicans met to construct a new state constitution for Louisiana. They were attacked by a mob of whites, many of them ex-Confederates, that had clearly been organized by city officials using the fire department's signaling system. At least thirty-four freedmen and three Republican delegates died, and scores more were wounded. Some died when the mob fired indiscriminately and at length into the convention hall, massacring the delegates trapped there. In other words, warned the newspaper, freedmen who engaged in political activity in Savannah risked setting off a massacre like that in New Orleans.[18]

Through October, the political atmosphere in Savannah grew even more poisonous as the presidential election between Ulysses Grant (Republican) and Horatio Seymour

(Democrat) loomed. White leaders in Savannah embraced an idea circulating among Democrats across the state. They argued that officials could challenge black voters at the polls under a state constitutional provision that required a prospective voter to "have paid all taxes which may have been required of him, and which he may have had an opportunity of paying, agreeably to law, for the year next preceding the election." The idea of this poorly worded section of the Constitution of 1868 was that voters would have to pay the year's tax before the election in which they planned to vote. Democrats, however, chose to read the awkward wording as requiring voters to pay the tax for the year *preceding* the election year. The only tax required of all Georgians was an educational poll tax of one dollar a head. Thus, if a potential voter could not prove or swear that he had paid the tax, he could be prevented from voting. To forestall this, on October 20, Georgia's Republican governor, Rufus Bullock, issued a proclamation suspending the collection of all poll taxes. The intention, he stated explicitly in the proclamation, was to prevent voter challenges on the basis of the poll tax.[19]

The *Morning News* argued that the governor's proclamation had no effect, for two reasons. First, the governor did not have power to suspend operation of part of the state constitution. Second, the governor could not suspend the collection of past taxes, and since the constitution stated "year next preceding the election," this meant taxes for the preceding year, 1867, not 1868. Thus, Democrats planned to challenge every black voter in Chatham County, requiring them to swear and perhaps even prove that they had paid the poll tax in 1867. "Those who swear falsely *will be prosecuted for perjury*," threatened the *Morning News*.[20]

Before six a.m. on Tuesday, November 3, 1868, more than a thousand freedmen waited in line in front of the Greek Revival courthouse on Wright Square for their chance to vote. Governor Bullock had required by proclamation that there be at least three ballot boxes available to voters, meaning that there should have been three voting locations in Savannah. That was not the case, as James M. Simms, the black politician and minister, explained later to a congressional committee. There was only one polling location for the entire city; the three required ballot boxes were put inside the Chatham County courthouse. Voters were supposed to go to particular boxes based on the first letter of their last names. Those whose names began with the letters N–Z were to vote at the back door of the courthouse on York Street. The other two ballot boxes could be reached by coming down the front entrance hallway, which had been divided into two narrow passages by a newly constructed wooden wall; those with "A–G" names voted on the left, and those with "H–M M" names on the right. Those requirements were confusing enough, but once inside each of the narrow hallways, just before the ballot boxes, potential voters confronted three registrars backed by sheriff's deputies. Nine registrars worked the three lines of voters, and seven of the nine registrars were Democrats; as Colonel Amherst Stone later explained, "When I used the word Democrat there, I meant rebels." The Democratic registrars planned to require that black voters swear to a lengthy list of qualifying items, including that they had paid their poll tax for 1867. If a voter hesitated too long, said he could not remember, admitted he could not swear, or refused to swear, he would then be sent out of the courthouse without being allowed to vote.[21]

The long line began entering the courthouse to vote at just past six. The first few men were allowed to vote without challenge, and then the Democratic registrars began to challenge every Republican. Once that began, according to James M. Simms, registrars turned away nine out of every ten black voters. Two of the nine registrars were Republicans, and soon these men began to challenge Democratic voters. The voting process slowed to a crawl. Black men denied the chance to vote returned to the square in front of the courthouse to complain, talk, and try to decide upon a course of action. Meanwhile, the challenges grew ever more absurd. When Doctor Joseph W. Clift, a Republican and a sitting member of Congress, came to vote, the Democrats challenged him on the basis of residency for living in Washington, D.C., the previous six months.[22]

Simms was in the square in front of the courthouse. He explained later that freedmen denied the vote became increasingly numerous and excited as the morning wore on: "They came to me in large numbers and inquired what was to be done. . . . The excitement had become intense." Up to this point, white voters had waited in line with black voters in what must have been an increasingly chaotic scene in front of the courthouse. More white men arrived at the square as the morning progressed, many of whom would have read that morning's newspaper editorials. "Men are at some times masters of their fate," argued the *Morning News*. "This is that time. If we will, we can turn the tide of evil at this hour. But, it must be by action." The *Republican* urged, "Let every citizen of Savannah go forth to battle for his country and his-self today." As the *Morning News* had explained the day before, "No one doubts your bravery; it has been proved on many a bloody battle-field during long years of war." Clearly, the situation in Wright Square was very dangerous, filled with growing numbers of angry blacks denied the right to vote and with whites desiring action to "turn the tide of evil" and remembering their battlefield experience during the war.[23]

Two hours after the polls opened, around eight a.m., a group of about fifty white workers from the Central of Georgia Railroad yards entered the square. Seeing the long, slow-moving line and the crowded square, the railroad workers sent a message to county sheriff James Dooner in the courthouse, asking him to clear a path for the white workers so that the men could vote and return to work. According to the *Morning News*, blacks had deliberately blocked the front entrance to the courthouse, and "white men who attempted to reach the Court House doors were actually clubbed away by the insolent and excited blacks." Sheriff Dooner and his deputies went to the main door of the courthouse, facing the square, and "spoke to the crowd and endeavored to make them clear the entrance." Deputies moved forward to push the line of waiting black voters away from the entrance. The blacks resisted, using clubs according to the newspaper, and some white citizens went to assist the deputies. The *Republican* reported: "The shock of the encounter caused a break in the solid phalanx of negroes, and the whites commenced to go in to the polls."[24]

Meanwhile, the sheriff concluded that his deputies, the white citizens assisting him, and three policemen at the courthouse could not maintain order. According to plans made before the election, a force of policemen waited in the armory on Chippewa Square, just two blocks away. At least ten of those policemen, commanded by Lieutenant Howard, hurried to the scene. They arrived just as the line of black voters was pushed away from the entrance. The policemen helped consolidate the position, holding back the black voters as the white voters went in. Then, James M. Simms testified, "The colored men supposed they would be allowed to pass in as well as the whites, but as soon as the white men had passed in the colored men found that they were kept back and not allowed to go in through the passage." Sheriff Dooner recalled that after the entrance was cleared, he stood on the front porch of the courthouse for about a minute and then stepped around the north side of the courthouse, away from the crowd, to check on affairs at the rear of the courthouse. Samuel D. Dickson, a notary in the courthouse, estimated that there were three thousand people in the courthouse square. Then, according to the *Morning News*, "The negroes rushed forward to regain their ascendancy at the Court House door and a desperate fight ensued." A gunshot rang out.[25]

According to the *Morning News*, "The first shot was fired by a negro . . . This negro pulled out a pistol and fired deliberately into the crowd of white men." The shot, said the paper, hit Mr. John Haupt in the shoulder. The *Republican* agreed that a black man fired the first shot, but said it was into the abdomen of patrolman Richard A. Reed. U.S. Army captain J. Murray Hoag, who investigated the event for the Freedmen's Bureau, wrote, "It is impossible to state who fired the first shot." The newspapers suggested that most of the black voters were armed. Hoag's report contradicted that assertion: "Not one in fifty [blacks] were armed, while the democracy had one or more revolvers each." After the first shot, two more shots quickly followed, reported the *Morning News*. There was a lapse of a minute or two, during which "almost perfect silence prevailed." After that, the police officers "drew their revolvers and fired into the crowd."[26]

Pandemonium followed. For five to ten minutes, "the firing was continuous and unbroken." Black voters "scattered in every direction, seeking shelter from the shots wherever any protective covering could be found," reported the *Morning News*. Blacks were pursued by "officers and citizens" as "bullets filled the air." Another newspaper account added, "Many of our white citizens behaved with uncommon bravery and fought like men who knew their rights." The sheriff, utterly confused, tried to assist a wounded policeman, fetch water, and gain control of the wild situation all at the same time. He was successful in none of his efforts. While Benjamin Cole was walking from the east side to the west side of the courthouse, he heard gunfire erupt. Looking into the square, he saw blacks hurling brickbats at the police, and saw two black men with revolvers. The sheriff, observing from almost the same vantage, saw a white man with a revolver and ordered him to put it away. He also saw a black man with a sword, but mentioned no black men with guns. Samuel Dickson, a notary, was in the courthouse making sure the ballot boxes were secure. By the time he went to the front of the courthouse, "the crowd was dispersed, except a few colored men who were running out through the square and four or five policemen running after them and firing revolvers at them."[27]

There was confusion about the casualties. Four policemen were hit by bullets; two later died. One white citizen was shot. Two black men were found dead in the square, one shot in the head, the other through the heart. "We calculate that from fifteen to twenty negroes were wounded," reported the *Morning News*. City doctors reported treating many wounded black people, three of whom appeared to be in critical condition. Hoag later reported seventeen wounded and three dead among the freedmen.[28]

The army sent a company of soldiers to the courthouse square, but they found things to be orderly, with voting by whites underway. Assured that the violence was past and that the polls were once again open, the soldiers returned to their barracks. A few black men gathered on the far side of the square and considered trying to vote again, but James M. Simms convinced them to leave the area. Many blacks assembled for a meeting at the "New Street Church," probably the old location of the St. Philip AME Church. By ten a.m., Hoag reported, "They unanimously resolved to go to their respective homes rather than risk their lives or bring on a riot."[29]

Although the polls in Savannah stayed open, only whites voted. Captain Hoag went to the courthouse square and mingled with the whites gathered there. He contrasted the attitude of the freedpeople, who had gone home without voting in order to avoid violence, with that of the white men at the courthouse, who boasted that they wanted another chance to kill more blacks. At six o'clock, when the polls closed, "loud and pro-longed cheers . . . for Seymour and Blair" erupted in the courthouse, "which were taken up and re-echoed by the crowd outside." (Francis Preston Blair was the Democratic vice presidential candidate.) The celebration for the Democratic candidates continued as an excited crowd assaulted a cart bearing a banner for Grant and (Schuyler) Colfax. Young men ripped it to shreds, and then mounted men carried the pieces through the city as trophies of victory.[30]

The election returns broke down predictably. At the three Chatham County precincts outside the city, where blacks had for the most part voted freely, a total of 97 votes were cast for Seymour and Blair, and 1,922 for Grant and Colfax. In the city, Grant and Colfax received only 394 votes, while Seymour and Blair garnered 4,544. Chatham County went for Seymour and Blair by more than 2,300 votes. Since there were only about 3,000 reg-istered white voters in the county, and most of Savannah's blacks were prevented from voting, this was a truly remarkable tally.[31]

The night after the election, a "heavy force of citizens" patrolled the city. The news-papers reported two accidental shootings during the night. Another force of mounted men, led by the chief of police, former Confederate general Robert Anderson, rode south into the county to find and destroy any armed bands of blacks. They found one. On the Ogeechee south of the city, after the polls had closed, state senator Aaron Bradley and other freedpeople celebrating the apparent Republican victory set out for the city. Bradley rode in his carriage, and a black militia called the Ogeechee home guard accompanied him. These two armed groups met in the dark on the outskirts of the city. A gun battle erupted, and one white man, Samuel Law, the son of Judge William Law, was killed. The coroner's jury ruled that Aaron Bradley was responsible for Law's death, and warrants were sworn out for Bradley, who fled the state. Moses Bentley, another black leader, was arrested in Savannah and charged with the murder of a policeman at the courthouse.[32]

The disastrous presidential election of 1868 was a turning point for Savannah politics. The city's white elite, which controlled most local political offices, the courts, and the newspapers, learned that they could use government and the media to trick, manipulate, and intimidate blacks as well as rig elections. If necessary, they could use the police to shape politics with violence. Because the poll tax had played a crucial role in the Democrats' election victory, in March 1869 the city council imposed a local voter-registration tax. Thus, Savannah voters had to contend with both a state and a local poll tax. The local Democratic Party, now calling itself the Conservative Party, proposed a new system of committees to nominate candidates for local elections. The city council ratified the new system, which established a closed system of nomination by party-chosen delegates, creating an early version of a local white-only primary.[33]

The first municipal election in four years took place on October 11, 1869. In keeping with the lessons learned the previous November, there was only one polling place—the courthouse. One hundred armed white "special deputies" awaited voters in the courthouse square. Crowded inside the courthouse were seventy-five members of a Conservative Party "Challenging Committee" ready to bring wholesale challenges against black voters. Hundreds were turned away; others didn't even attempt to vote. The Conservative Party ticket crushed the Republicans by a margin of three to one. As the mayor-elect, John Screven, explained, the Conservatives kept control of the city "in their own hands."[34]

Savannah's African American political leaders learned from these events. The crucial lesson was that Savannah's whites would, if needed, kill blacks in order to maintain control over local politics. That reality posed a formidable challenge to sustaining black political activity. Similar sorts of violence and manipulation at the polls had spread statewide during 1868 and 1869. When Republican state representatives were reseated in the Georgia legislature in 1869 under a third Reconstruction, they attempted to engage these problems. The black minority introduced bills to end the chain gang, convict leasing, segregation in public accommodations, and the hated poll tax. Their efforts came to naught.[35]

In the state election in late 1870, all of Chatham County's black representatives were unseated by white conservatives. Black Savannahians were completely excluded from the city council, from juries, and even from the police force. Despite the vulnerability that

Bird's Eye View of Savannah
(St. Louis: Ruger, 1871).
Historic American Buildings
Survey, Historic American
Engineering Record, Historic
American Landscapes
Survey collection, Prints
and Photographs Division,
Library of Congress,
HABS GA,26-SAV,53—229.

resulted from this, blacks' political activities did not cease, but instead took on the nature of protest. In 1871, blacks participated in a strike that spread across the waterfront. In the summer of 1872, black resistance overturned local efforts to establish segregation on the city's new streetcar system, although their demonstrations cost the lives of three black men. Many blacks voted in the fall of 1872, but faced intimidation by not only white deputies at the polls, but also hordes of Savannah's newly reestablished white militia companies. By the fall of 1873, only about 400 black men were still registered to vote in Savannah. Overpowering dominance, however, was not enough for white leaders, who seemed intent on driving all African Americans from Savannah's political sphere. Black fire companies had been a source of pride and a means of civic participation for decades in Savannah. In 1872 the city council started disbanding the black companies, completing the process in 1875. Over the next three decades black Savannahians were increasingly pushed out of the public sphere. The state even disbanded the black militia units in 1904. By then there were virtually no public venues for black political activity in Savannah, and black politics often revolved around acquiring spoils through the local Republican Party.[36]

Ultimately, two parallel worlds developed in Savannah, as happened in cities across the South. One was the very visible white world of factors, lawyers, merchants, and workmen who controlled Savannah politics. The other was a barely visible world of black businessmen, ministers, longshoremen, and servants. Blacks had their own religious institutions, fraternal societies, and women's groups, all of which played a crucial role in Savannah's black community, but they were denied a political role in Savannah's government or an important place in the public realm. Through the 1870s, 1880s, and 1890s, a growing host of local, state, and federal laws and court decisions deepened and reinforced the system of segregation and disfranchisement. Some black leaders, such as Bishop Henry McNeal Turner, abandoned hope in the American system and proposed a return to Africa. Not until the 1940s, 1950s, and 1960s would black voters again become a force in Savannah politics.[37]

In December 1868, Assemblyman James M. Simms testified before Congress about the terror he had witnessed in Savannah and in Georgia generally during the presidential election. The Committee on Reconstruction, astonished by the story of events in Savannah, questioned Simms closely about how such things could have happened. "Many of the best citizens of the State," Simms explained, "have by their silence allowed them to be done." Dr. S. P. Powell had a blunter answer when questioned by the same committee: "In answer to the question by Mr. Norris, whether he thought any respectable democrat had anything to do with the matter . . . he replied that it was his impression that what were called 'respectable' democrats had the management of it."[38]

"The Fighting Has Not Been in Vain"
African American Intellectuals in Jim Crow Savannah
Bobby J. Donaldson

On the morning of January 2, 1893, the crowds gathered early along East Broad and Liberty Streets for Savannah's annual Emancipation Day parade and celebration. The processional of dignitaries, bands, fraternal groups, civic organizations, and military battalions moved toward Chippewa Square. They were led by James Middleton's famous band and Colonel John H. Deveaux, the highly respected leader of the "colored" state militia. Bystanders could watch notable figures go by in horse-drawn carriages, including James E. Whiteman, the grand marshal and the chairman of the Chatham County Republican Party, and Dr. J. J. Durham, the featured speaker and pastor of the Second African Baptist Church. They might have recognized other familiar faces, including Judge James Meriles Simms, the venerable minister and Reconstruction veteran, and the Reverend Alexander Harris, the aging Confederate army musician who had been part of the famed colloquy with Secretary Edwin Stanton and General Sherman in 1865.

As guests processed to Chippewa Square to take their seats inside the Savannah Theatre, some no doubt recalled the interruption of black Republican speaker Aaron A. Bradley and the arrest of forty-two freedpeople at an outdoor Republican political gathering there a little over two decades prior. But African Americans now spoke unmolested, even if behind closed doors. The public celebration of Abraham Lincoln's Emancipation Proclamation marked the importance of their continued efforts to reclaim access to the public sphere. Following the Reverend Harris's "patriotic and touching prayer" and the reading of the Emancipation Proclamation by the president of the Beach Institute's Youth Literary Club, Dr. Durham delivered the keynote address. Freed from slavery as a young boy in South Carolina, Durham was not only Second African's pastor but also an accomplished physician, with degrees from Fisk University and Meharry Medical College. In a deep and moving cadence, he mesmerized the crowd as he chronicled the

Colonel John H. Deveaux, *Savannah Tribune*, October 10, 1914. Courtesy of the Zach S. Henderson Library, Georgia Southern University, Statesboro.

monumental strides in education and industry achieved by African Americans since "freedom's natal day." Armed with historical details and statistics, Durham defended "the goodness and progress of the Negro" and repudiated the "despicable charges" that African Americans were "incapable of development" and otherwise marked for extinction.[1]

Durham's remarks drew "deafening cheers" from his enthusiastic audience. As he took his seat, Middleton's band played a "soul stirring" rendition of "Marching through Georgia," which dramatized Sherman's decisive trek between Atlanta and Savannah. Then, James M. Simms rose to present a resolution marking the formation of the Georgia State Industrial College, which he had assisted in developing.[2] To Simms's mind, the development of a school of higher learning for African Americans in Savannah seemed a fitting symbol to mark the "Day of Jubilee." At nearly seventy years old, the small bespectacled minister with his trademark Vandyke beard was the living embodiment of the hopes and aspirations of black emancipation. The annual commemorations permitted Simms to reflect on the sobering events he had experienced in his long career. He knew from experience the agonizing shifts "between *hope* and *fear*" that African Americans had endured in the three decades since slavery's demise. Indeed, while Durham focused on the "goodness and progress" of the race in his address, Simms could turn to contemporary articles in John Deveaux's *Savannah Tribune*, the city's first black newspaper, for stark signs of a bleak racial outlook. Indeed, months after the crowd in the Savannah Theatre dispersed, one writer decried a rising tide of racial violence, praying, "Let a new era of justice reign, and right, not might and prejudice rule."[3]

When James M. Simms died in July 1912, five months shy of the fiftieth anniversary of the Emancipation Proclamation, the *Savannah Tribune* hailed the former judge and state representative as a "Relict of the Days of Reconstruction." Once disparaged by white leaders as a "pestilent little mulatto tailor" and "a disgrace to the judiciary," Simms was eulogized by his African American colleagues as someone who had been "bold, fearless and ever contended for what he thought right." Members of the Savannah Ministerial Emancipation Association remembered him as "a preacher of rare parts and a noted historian; his life is worthy of emulation, from the reconstruction period till the day of his death."[4]

In the three decades between the first volleys of the Civil War and the closing years of the nineteenth century, Judge Simms (as he was affectionately called) bore witness to a time "full of activities and stirring events." He faced violence, persecution, and exile for secretly teaching black children to read and write before the Civil War. After quietly delivering a copy of the Emancipation Proclamation to church members months before it became official, he shared their "inward panting for the long-looked-for and often-prayed-for freedom." He stood in awe as "the victorious army of liberty" commandeered Savannah streets in December 1864. In the rice districts west of the city, he assisted freed laborers as they charted their uncertain futures. After electrifying crowds at what one observer hailed as the "Great Reconstruction Meeting," Simms secured elective office and political appointments. Along the way, he bristled against segregation and mobilized voters even as whites heaped recriminations upon him for encouraging blacks to resist encroachments upon their freedoms. He drew the scorn of other black leaders who questioned his objectives and methods. Yet in the face of seemingly insurmountable odds and opposition within and beyond his community, Simms remained, in the words of one of his contemporaries, "presumptuous and defiant."[5]

As the race problem exploded around 1900, Simms's Civil War and Reconstruction experiences remained a prism illuminating black Savannah's unfinished quest for freedom and equality. After being expelled from the Georgia General Assembly in 1868, Simms and his displaced colleagues petitioned Congress for readmission; he then joined his erstwhile friend Henry McNeal Turner in forming the Civil and Political Rights Association of Georgia, which met at the Macon City Hall in October 1868. Though denied seats in the Georgia legislature, Simms and his colleagues remained emphatic defenders of suffrage, equal rights, and education. Pledging to refrain from violence and "mortal combat," the leaders agreed to fight white repression "with words, with the press, on the stump, on our knees, in the courts, in the Congress, and wherever we can."[6]

Following the formation of the Civil and Political Rights Association, Simms and Turner appeared before a congressional hearing to testify about "outrages perpetuated" across the state to undermine black voting power. Subsequently, Simms traveled around the country and described the "bitter prejudice" that led whites to trample blacks' constitutional rights and privileges.[7]

Confronted by entrenched bigotry that went unmitigated by the federal government, Simms resigned himself to a protracted fight for "civil and political rights." In the spring of 1876, he assumed an active role in the national Convention of Colored Men in Nashville. Working closely with the Reverend Turner, a fellow Savannahian named Charles

The Postbellum Transition from Agriculture to Industry

Four years of Civil War and the defeat of the Confederacy brought tremendous changes to the urban economy of Savannah. Secession from the Union created new pressures on southern cities to be self-sufficient, evidenced in Savannah by the government's seizure of the Rose Brothers' iron foundry; the conversion of an old church into a cartridge manufactory; and the opening of a new leather tannery—the holder of Confederate States of America patent #9—that promised to turn sheep, goat, calf, and alligator hide into goods for Confederate soldiers. But such enterprises faced labor shortages, a Union blockade, and numerous other barriers to success. Even before Sherman and his army reached the city in December 1864, the urban economy was in free fall: the port was stagnant and buildings were dilapidated. Unkempt cemeteries symbolized the general state of collapse. And many enslaved persons eager to seek their freedom had escaped to Fort Pulaski, Hilton Head Island, and other areas under Union control.

Emancipation and the breakup of large plantations seemed to create new opportunities for African Americans and other small farmers. Between 1860 and 1870, the number of Chatham County farms of three to ten acres in size increased from 24 to 203. But tensions over land ownership, labor contracts, and political rights quickly emerged. When, in 1868, the "Ogeechee District" southwest of the city erupted in deadly violence, city officials allowed vigilante groups to restore order. Many former plantation owners, with the municipal government's cooperation, reclaimed their property and put African American workers under sharecropping contracts and other sorts of restrictive labor agreements. In general, the era of widespread black landownership proved tense and short-lived.

Truck farming emerged as the plantation system declined and postbellum agriculture was carried out on a smaller scale. Merchants understood that they could profit from African Americans' horticultural and agricultural expertise, and thanks to improving steamship connections, it was possible to move local produce to northern cities quickly. By the late 1880s, Chatham County led the state in the production of Irish potatoes and also grew cabbage, beans, cantaloupe, watermelon, and strawberries for commercial markets. Many residents complemented their seasonal work in fruit and vegetable fields by harvesting, packaging, and distributing seafood. With the arrival of new canning technologies in the 1890s, Savannah was soon among the nation's leaders in the production of canned oysters, canned shrimp, and even terrapin.

Meanwhile, Savannah's industrial economy experienced a rapid, though spotty, recovery. The Savannah and Ogeechee Canal and the Central of Georgia Railroad reopened in 1865 and 1866, at first mainly to transport raw lumber. By 1866,

Bay Street, Savannah, looking west from city hall. In Joseph Gray, Savannah: Founded 1733; Municipal, Financial, Commercial, Industrial, Agricultural, Residential, and Historical (Savannah: Savannah Chamber of Commerce, 1911), 13. Courtesy of the Georgia Historical Society, Rare Pamphlet Collection, RP F294-ST-G73-1911.

boosters proclaimed that "sawmills are springing up as if by magic" on the city's western edge. The success of the Savannah, Florida and Western Railroad fostered similar industrial development on the city's east side. Over the next few decades, several other new industries also emerged on the city's east side. During the postbellum era, Savannah was home to cotton presses, machine shops, foundries, gristmills, a locomotive works, a large textile mill, a carriage factory, a cigar company, a baking powder manufacturer, a candy company, and two breweries. In addition, there were two soap factories, a plant that produced "artificial stone" from Portland cement and Savannah River sand, a mill that manufactured brown wrapping paper from an unusual mix of seven parts rice stalks to one part palm fronds, and a cottonseed oil processor that eventually became part of Wesson Oil. Many of these firms were short-lived; the boom-and-bust cycles of the industrial economy meant that investors frequently went bankrupt and hundreds of low-wage employees were thrown out of work. In the Panic of 1893, for instance, some four thousand Savannah workers were unemployed, leaving another eight thousand dependents in jeopardy.

Another shift in the commercial economy came from a rising demand for naval stores: the tar, pitch, rosin, spirits of turpentine, and other products of the southern pine forests went into lubricants, medicines, paints, soap, paving materials, and lamp oils. As forests in North Carolina and South Carolina became depleted, the center of timber-related businesses shifted to Savannah. By 1900, Savannah's S. P. Shotter Company was the largest rosin works in the world, and Savannahians set daily prices and quality standards for the industry. But the production of naval stores led to the brutal exploitation of its largely African American labor force—they worked in remote forests and lived in temporary dwellings that generally were cruder and more overcrowded than the typical slave cabin. It is no surprise that many turpentine workers labored against their will, forced to do so as part of chain gangs used to reinforce racial hierarchies.

The city's postbellum commercial economy centered above all on its ever-expanding port facilities. As the Atlantic Coast Line Railroad connected Savannah with cities north and south, and the Central of Georgia extended its routes and branch lines further into western Georgia and neighboring states, ever more freight reached Savannah. Railroads and shippers built large new warehouses and set aside millions of square feet of wharf space to store guano fertilizers, cotton, timber, naval stores, and more. The Central of Georgia purchased the large Bradley and Giles lumber mill in 1870, and by 1883 the railway's subsidiary the Ocean Steamship Company had taken control of the western bank of the canal from the river to the railroad shops. The federal government helped fuel this type of transport, deepening the river channel and harbor from twenty-two to twenty-six feet in the 1890s, and then to twenty-eight feet in 1913.

Changes in social relationships accompanied transitions in the industrial economy. Some interracial mingling certainly continued in low-income neighborhoods such as Oglethorpe Ward, where mixed-race brothels, taverns, and corner groceries remained common. But racial lines were hardening in the late nineteenth century. African Americans who challenged white authority figures often found themselves victims of discrimination, violence, or arrest (which could lead to performing unpaid labor on a chain gang). Labor tensions were especially fierce on the railroads. Employers sought to hire African Americans for some jobs at half the standard pay for white workers, and many whites formed labor brotherhoods that restricted certain jobs only to them. The railroads contributed to racial tension in another way when many African Americans sought to leave the segregated South for good when World War I presented work opportunities in northern cities. Despite concerted efforts to stop the exodus, some three thousand Africans Americans left Savannah in the first half of 1917 alone.

Overall, the region's economy changed considerably in the decades after the Civil War. In 1860, Chatham County produced twenty-five million pounds of rice and a thousand bales of Sea Island cotton; in 1900, the figures were a million pounds of rice and ten bales of Sea Island cotton. Savannah fell from the nation's forty-first largest city in 1860 to the eighty-sixth in 1910. Although its standing as a railroad center and port improved, commercial success depended largely on soil-depleting cotton, tree-killing naval stores, and commons-depleting shrimping and oystering. For the thousands of African Americans who worked in the low-paying jobs associated with those industries, the decades after emancipation brought a degree of freedom, but not much in the way of prosperity.

MARK R. FINLAY

William E. Wilson, Young Black Woman with Basket of Cotton, c. 1884–91. Courtesy of the Georgia Historical Society, MS 1375-113(249).

DeLaMotta, and Jefferson Long of Macon, Simms sought to advance Reconstruction's "unfinished mission" by refuting "the unhealthy condition of the public mind relative to the colored people in the South." In the weeks leading up to the convention, the *Savannah Tribune* ran a strong endorsement of the gathering and pointed to "the condition of the colored people" in Georgia as reason enough for Simms to interact with "some of the ablest men of our race." The newspaper's founder, John Deveaux, accused politicians and elected officials of displaying "the most wanton disregard for any rights of the negro, human or divine."[8]

Like Simms, Deveaux took great pride in leading Savannah's annual Emancipation Day commemorations. And as in the case of Simms, Deveaux's personal and professional journey highlighted both the promises of Reconstruction and the "hateful prejudice" that attended white redemption in the waning decades of the nineteenth century. (White southerners used the term *redemption* to indicate a return to antebellum social conditions in every way except outright slavery; they saw this as an attempt to "redeem" the South.) Deveaux was a member of the city's "colored aristocracy" by virtue of his grandmother Catherine Deveaux and his aunt Jane Deveaux, who ran secret schools in the antebellum period; and his grandfather John Benjamin Deveaux, pastor at the Third African Baptist Church. Deveaux rose to the rank of colonel in the Savannah-based black militia unit established during Reconstruction; he was also an influential Republican Party operative. And by continuing as a newspaperman long after the Republican Party had been driven out of electoral politics and blacks removed from the militia in Georgia, Deveaux revealed the "devastating and liberty-destroying effects" that white supremacy had upon his neighbors.[9]

As the accomplished editor and publisher of the *Savannah Tribune* and the short-lived *Savannah Echo*, Deveaux was uniquely poised to chronicle the growing despair that he and other black leaders experienced in the aftermath of Georgia's brief Reconstruction period. At the launch of the *Tribune* in 1875, Deveaux informed readers that he was committed to defending "the rights of the colored people" and elevating them "to the highest plane of citizenship." Positioning the newspaper as the "great educator and moulder of public sentiment," Deveaux contended, "The wrongs upon our people must be constantly exposed, and this cannot be done unless you have your own medium. . . . We must fight against this hateful prejudice, and for equal rights in every respect; and this cannot be effectively done without the aid of a newspaper."[10]

Black Militia Units in Postbellum Georgia

During Reconstruction, black militia units came into being on the sole initiative of local African Americans. They were part of the Union League and Loyalty League organizations, which supported the Republican Party in Georgia, yet no formal militia existed, white or black, during Reconstruction. The federal government reauthorized an official state militia for Georgia in 1872–73, insisting that there be black militia companies alongside white ones. State leaders acceded to the demand while segregating the militia into all-white and all-black companies; officers of the same color or race as their men led each unit. By 1892, the state was second only to South Carolina in the total number of militia units.

Although black units evoked the ire of their white counterparts and others angered by the increasing political power and public presence of African Americans, whites saw black militiamen as somewhat less threatening than the black Union soldiers who had occupied the South during the war. While many African Americans likely saw the military training as useful for self-defense purposes in the increasingly violent South, military preparedness was not the primary mission of the state militia. Black militias served a largely ceremonial function, taking the lead in setting the agenda for such important commemorations of black freedom as Emancipation Day, the Fourth of July, Thirteenth, Fourteenth, and Fifteenth Amendment Days, and Abraham Lincoln's birthday. Likewise, white militias oversaw celebrations reinforcing their commitment to the former Confederacy and its leaders.

Eight black units were based in Savannah from the 1870s to the 1890s. Militia units were subject to state laws and received accoutrements from the state. Militia members paid for their own uniforms and donated their time, including for the annual training encampment in Atlanta's Piedmont Park. The law limited black militias to one for every three of their white counterparts. Despite all the impediments and restrictions, in the end Savannah was home to eight black infantry companies, one cavalry company, and the only black artillery unit in the nation.

Disparity between white and black militia units became more and more apparent at the end of the 1880s. As segregation increased statewide, white militia units in Savannah challenged the right of black units to use public parade grounds in what became Forsyth Park. White militias, but not black ones, had medical units, machine guns, and signal corps. Black militiamen across Georgia, including Lieutenant Colonel John Deveaux, petitioned in the 1890s for their fair share of state and federal resources, equipment, and professional training; their petitions were received but ignored.

The Spanish-American War found black militiamen willing to serve, even though they had been denied access to the training that U.S. Army personnel had provided their white counterparts. Georgia allowed white and black militiamen to volunteer to serve in the war, but did not allow its militia companies to serve as units. War-mobilization problems led to a reorganization of the Georgia militia in 1899. That restructuring, combined with the growth of segregation, attempts at disfranchising the black population, and national military and militia reorganization, resulted in the termination of most black militia companies, decreasing their number statewide to seven, with three or four in Savannah. The final disbanding of those units occurred during the summer of 1905.

GREGORY MIXON

Deveaux remained vigilant in documenting incidents of racial violence and political terror. In October 1875, he served as an energetic and active participant in a "Colored Convention" in Augusta. As the chair of the Committee on Recent Troubles, he secured affidavits from constituents who had endured intimidation and assault at the hand of the Klan and other vigilante groups. A decade later, Deveaux demanded an end to Georgia's "cut throat, murderous" convict-lease system. When the state and federal governments did little to "put a stop to ku kluxism in Georgia," an editorial warned that black people would be "compelled to organize themselves into vigilance committees sure enough, and scour the country on behalf of the poor defenseless colored people in the interior who seem to be at the mercy of the most desperate outlaws in existence."[11]

Deveaux was committed to exposing the hypocrisy among white southerners who feigned gentility and paternal benevolence while enabling terror groups to "kill and outrage our people with impunity."[12] "The white people of the South," Deveaux observed, "are brutal in their instincts and blunted in their perceptions of morality and right. They make laws, but subordinate them to the violence of lawless mobs. . . . Where colored men are concerned their courts are travesties of justice and their elections are mockeries of popular government."[13] In late 1899, amid an aggressive effort by white Georgia politicians to pass a disfranchisement bill aimed at ridding "the state of the illiterate and purchasable negro vote," Deveaux held press conferences, generated petition drives, and successfully undermined the "manifestly unjust" legislation, which sought to disqualify the vast majority of black voters around the state.[14]

Deveaux's multilayered activism inspired Savannah's black community. When the Savannah Cotton Exchange and the Board of Trade objected to his federal appointment as the Savannah collector of customs in December 1897, a determined group of African Americans followed his example of public protest and successfully fought white opposition. They distributed handbills throughout the city that read, "Do not allow an insult to your race to go without resenting it." In a meeting held at the Odd Fellows Hall before a crowd of nearly a thousand people, the Reverend Leigh B. Maxwell, Captain R. W. White, and Dr. Cornelius McKane defended their colleague with resolutions that repudiated the Cotton Exchange's claims: "We feel that fitness should be the qualification for office and that it should not be controlled by prejudice, and we earnestly desire that such a spirit will soon be a thing of the past and every race co-operate for the advancement and best interest of developing this south land." In the end, Deveaux took office.[15]

In many respects, Reverend Simms and Colonel Deveaux represented the vanguard of black leaders in Savannah who worked vigorously to keep the memory and principles of Emancipation and Reconstruction alive into the early twentieth century. Although denied political office and confined to a segregated world behind the color line, Simms and Deveaux collaborated with an enterprising circle of community activists and leaders who amplified their political voices in the face of virulent opposition. In sermons, essays, literary works, petitions, minutes, and other publications throughout the late nineteenth and early twentieth centuries, Simms, Deveaux, and other African American intellectual leaders confronted prevailing ideas about "Negro inferiority" and labored to dislodge the social and ideological impediments that thwarted the "progress of the race." They regularly refuted accusations like those of Savannah judge and former U.S. senator Thomas Norwood, who remained unapologetic in his declaration that "God has set an impossible limit to the Negro's intellect."[16]

Unfazed by distorted assertions such as Norwood's, Emanuel K. Love, the pastor of Savannah's First African Baptist Church, championed education and regularly used his writings and sermons to attack the "reign of terror" and the racist vitriol that had dashed the political and economic promises of the Emancipation era. Born into enslavement near Marion, Alabama, in 1860, Love completed his educational training at the Augusta Baptist Institute (today Morehouse College) in 1877. He was described by one of his classmates as having a "well developed and richly cultivated intellect." After leading small congregations and working as a journalist in Augusta, Love assumed the pulpit

of Savannah's First African Baptist Church on Franklin Square in October 1885. As a prolific writer and the charismatic leader of the Missionary Baptist Convention of Georgia, Love commanded a strong following across the state.

Three years before he secured First African's pulpit, Love had impressed congregation members with a spirited sermon on education. In a meeting of the Missionary Baptist Convention at First African in May 1882, Love drew from his own autobiography and preached that "education is power." Mindful of the "damning evils" of illiteracy, Love believed that African Americans and especially their religious leaders "should wage uncompromising war on ignorance, which has so long enthralled our people." "We must encourage our people to get an education," Love insisted, "or must be content with our woeful fate."[17]

Not long after Love began his pastorate in Savannah, he gained widespread notoriety for his vehement denunciations of lynching and for his incessant calls for black pride and self-respect. Drawing on his vivid childhood memories of Reconstruction, Love outlined socially conservative strategies for African Americans to "get all the respect, rights and recognition we want." At an Emancipation Day address in 1888 attended by Colonel Deveaux and Judge Simms, Love stated that blacks should "get an education, save their money, live within their income, buy homes, be honest and virtuous . . . have confidence in each other[,] be true to the race, have faith in our great possibilities, have undying love for race pride." He reminded his audience that a "determined resolution" to advance self-help and "race elevation" was a meaningful way "to celebrate the Emancipation Proclamation."[18]

In addition, Love encouraged black leaders to be more forthright in speaking out against racism. In late January 1888, Love joined over three hundred delegates of the Union Brotherhood of Georgia in Macon to map out a "wise course of future action for the promotion of the race's welfare." Among leaders such as William J. White of Augusta and Henry McNeal Turner of Macon, Love counseled against public equivocation and shuffling dissemblance among African American leaders: "The time used to be when the

George Gibbons, 1819–1884

The life of George Gibbons exemplifies the experiences of a small group of nineteenth-century African Americans who remained closely affiliated after the Civil War with the white families that had owned them as slaves. George Gibbons's connection with the Telfair family gave him an education and economic advantages that he would not have had otherwise. But it may also have limited his relationships in Savannah's African American community.

Rev. George Gibbons. From E. K. Love, History of the First African Baptist Church, *82. Courtesy of Documenting the American South, University of North Carolina at Chapel Hill Libraries.*

On November 13, 1819, a female slave gave birth to George Gibbons on the Telfair family's Thorn Island Plantation, located in the Barnwell District of South Carolina. By the time he was a boy of ten or twelve, Gibbons was living with the Telfairs in their Savannah mansion, where his older brother Friday (1809–74) was a house servant. The relationship between the Telfairs and George was depicted before and after the Civil War as one in which the family's paternalistic care of him engendered his devotion. An intimate friend of the Telfair family in the antebellum years recalled in a letter how Friday served tea to those assembled in the Oak Room while young George stood nearby acting the part of the "little page in devoted attendance." And George was, no doubt, among the guests on Christmas Day when the Telfairs reversed roles with their servants. Writing after the Civil War about the continuing relationship between George and the Telfairs, the African American minister Emanuel Love noted his dedication to the "white people who raised him." Because paternalistic thinking informed the Telfairs' understanding of their roles as slaveholders, they probably believed that they had "reared" rather than "trained" George. And indeed, the Telfairs had a reputation for noblesse oblige, and not just in the South. As the *New York Home Journal* put it in 1871, the well-known consideration of Telfair family members "for their inherited Africans has associated their names with humanity."

The Telfairs took George with them on a trip to Europe that extended from May 1851 until the summer of 1852. Few Americans of his epoch experienced the grandeur of European culture. But George's privileged position in the Telfair mansion in Savannah came at the expense of his relationship with his own parents; we have no evidence of his feelings about being removed from them as a child. And as a house servant who appears to have spent his life largely in the city rather than traveling to the countryside, George may have had little contact with enslaved people in Savannah or the hinterlands. As for Mary Telfair, she represented herself as an indulgent mistress, sidestepping the word *slave* by substituting *servant*. But she was very much aware that these human beings were her property. When planning a yearlong trip to Europe in 1841, she looked for ways to occupy her house slaves and defray the expense of maintaining them in Savannah during her absence. She proposed that a friend hire George, his wife, Coomba, and her mother, Juddy, until her return.

Not all of George's life was tied up with the Telfairs. Both Friday and George were baptized, in 1830 and 1844. In 1860, while still enslaved, both became deacons of the First African Baptist Church. Around 1870, the church licensed George to preach; he served as an assistant there to Pastor William J. Campbell until he was called to the pastorate of Bethlehem Baptist Church in 1875. In 1878, he returned to the First African Baptist Church as pastor, where he served until his death.

Although his congregation at Bethlehem apparently appreciated his leadership, George's time at First African was less comfortable. He ascended to the pastorate as a replacement for the popular Campbell, who had succeeded

Andrew Marshall and raised $26,000 to build the first brick building for the church, in 1859—the only brick building owned by blacks in the city or state. In 1877, the church split over public accusations of financial malfeasance, and Campbell, by then elderly and feeble, left with a small faction to form a separate congregation. George assumed the pastorate. Becoming pastor under such circumstances would have been difficult for anyone. But according to Emmanuel Love, the historian of the church, George's life in the Telfair household, while it provided him with a wealth of opportunities, had distanced him from the broader Savannah black community: "He had been so confined at home with the affairs of the old white people who raised him that he knew next to nothing of what was going on among the negroes in everyday life."

Indeed, George maintained his connection to the Telfair family long after the Civil War. He remained employed by Mary Telfair, who never married. Upon her death, in 1875, he received a bequest of twenty-five shares of railroad stock, believed at the time to be worth seven thousand dollars. This enabled him to become a substantial property holder. But he remained caretaker of the Telfair house until the Telfair Academy of Arts and Sciences opened there in 1883. He continued to serve as pastor of First African Baptist Church until his death, in 1884. He remained committed to both occupations even though his personal wealth meant he needed neither:

at the time of his death, he was reported to hold property worth twelve thousand dollars.

After George Gibbons's death, blacks and whites in Savannah's segregated society remembered him differently. Whites passed over him with a comment that he was the "janitor" who had looked after Mary Telfair's house and collections from the time of her death until the Telfair Academy opened. The African American pastor Emanuel Love memorialized Gibbons for his "fine mind," "sublime thoughts," and "dignified bearing," but also lamented that while pastor of the First African Baptist Church, he lacked empathy for the hardships that members of his congregation faced in their daily lives. We do not hear Gibbons's own voice in these characterizations, but rather the voices of contemporaries who wrote about him. As a result, what we know about his life says as much about the society of nineteenth-century Savannah as it does about Gibbons as an individual. People who crossed racial boundaries found themselves straddling two cultures. George Gibbons's life is a clear example of this. Born a slave who remained a servant of the elite Telfair family throughout his life, Gibbons was excluded from the white society he served. Simultaneously, his immersion in the world of elite whites distanced him from the African American community he served in his ministry.

FEAY SHELLMAN COLEMAN

negro mumbled and cussed behind his master's back. He mustn't do that now. He is a man and must speak out and do his cussing before him."[19]

Despite Reverend Love's strong advocacy of self-help, temperance, frugality, and forthright leadership, he painfully discovered that these qualities would not spare black people from the lash of racial violence. In 1889, Love and a Baptist delegation sitting in first-class accommodations on a train near Baxley, Georgia, came under attack by a "dozen rough-looking men" who brandished pistols and demanded that they move to the Jim Crow compartments. When Love adamantly refused, the white "band of ruffians" severely beat the minister, along with others in his entourage, and then ejected them from the train. Confounded by the assault, Love and his companions penned a letter to the *National Baptist* magazine and raised a searching question: "We look to God and ask what are we to do? . . . It does seem that the glory of American citizenship means no glory for us. What are we to do?"[20]

Negro Baptising—Banks of Ogeechee Canal.

Unknown artist, Negro Baptising—Banks of Ogeechee Canal, *from an undated postcard. Courtesy of Mark Finlay.*

Yet Love continued to preach his message of self-help, moral reform, and racial pride. In an Emancipation Day address delivered in Augusta in 1891, he reminded his audience that the legal and political promises of Reconstruction would remain out of reach until African Americans exercised greater vigilance against "the Godless outrages" and tackled the "vexed and intricate Negro Problem." As he disparaged an ingenious Mississippi plan to disfranchise black voters and described the bleak social landscape African Americans faced, he underscored African Americans' shared history of resistance in the face of grave odds. In a well-crafted speech lined with historical references and allusions to news headlines and federal legislation, Love reminded audience members that their "peculiar vitality" meant that they could not be "lawed out, starved out, murdered out, lynched out, burned out, migrated out and if the Force bill is passed they will not much longer be counted out."[21]

Many of Savannah's black intellectuals joined Love and peers across the state in navigating a fine and often precarious line between open criticism of racial injustices perpetrated by whites and strong advocacy for racial uplift through self-help and respectability. In the city, black journalists, clergy, and civic leaders grimaced at the offending behavior, language, or dress that young people displayed before the judgmental gaze of white onlookers. A Savannah resident named J. B. Young called on "every law-abiding, self-respected hard working, colored citizen" to denounce "young men of the race" who "do everything to degrade and disgrace the race." Alarmed by the number of "boys and girls that are roaming aimlessly about the streets," black leaders in Savannah coupled their pleas for propriety and uprightness with explicit campaigns for community outreach, reform training, and improved school facilities and resources.[22] In a series of Emancipation Day addresses in 1897, Richard R. Wright, the influential president of the Georgia State Industrial College for Colored Youth (today Savannah State University), regularly emphasized "patience and honest labor" as the key to racial progress. He identified "good homes, properly reared children, faithful citizenship and an intelligent trust in God" as "the everlasting foundation stones of stable national progress."[23]

Such speeches inspired black women to perform missionary work to poor areas of the city. In the summer of 1899, Mrs. A. A. Whitman of St. Philip AME Church formed a group called the Mothers of the 19th Century Club. Rather than ridiculing the urban poor from a distance, Anna B. G. Carr, Whitman's colleague and a nurse at the McKane Hospital for Women and Children, encouraged greater service to the community: "Let us all awake from the stool of do nothing and arise to a sense of duty." Carr, Whitman, and their group of "race loving women" believed they could improve "the future of the race" by rehabilitating behavior and vice that proved "damaging to moral and intellectual society."[24]

But the continuing violence against African Americans in Georgia demonstrated the limits of self-help. In 1899, Wright heard the wrenching details of the lynching and dismemberment of Sam Hose in April 1899, an itinerant laborer on the outskirts of Atlanta. Bewildered by the increasingly volatile state of race relations, as expressed in the carnival glee that attended Hose's public torture, Wright wrote to a close friend, the Presbyterian minister Francis J. Grimke: "I, myself, am very discouraged. In fact, the colored people all

Mother Mathilda Beasley
Georgia's First Black Nun

Mother Mathilda Beasley was instrumental in helping African Americans move from slavery to freedom, not least in her social concerns. She established one of Savannah's first black orphanages and paved the way for education among African Americans in the city. In addition, she established herself as a key figure in the Catholic Church by becoming Georgia's first black nun.

Born Mathilde Taylor on November 14, 1834, in New Orleans, Louisiana, she was the daughter of an enslaved woman named Caroline Taylor (owned by James C. Taylor) and an unknown father, who was believed to be Native American. Orphaned as a young girl, Mathilde eventually made her way to Savannah as a free black, perhaps as early as 1859. The circumstances surrounding her freedom and subsequent journey to Savannah are unknown, but at some point in her early life, the spelling of her name was changed to "Mathilda."

In Savannah, she started a clandestine school at her residence. At the time, educating African Americans, enslaved or free, was a crime punishable by fine; if you were African American, the penalty included a whipping. In 1860, Mathilda worked also as a seamstress, a common occupation for free black females in the city.

There were 705 free blacks in Savannah in 1860, some of whom owned property and operated businesses. Abraham Beasley, a noted free black businessman and landowner, owned The Railroad House, which combined a restaurant, boardinghouse, saloon, and produce market. Mathilda met him when she began working in the restaurant, which was located on Bryan Street. In 1869, Mathilda and Abraham married. In preparation for the union, Mathilda was baptized conditionally in the Catholic Church, suggesting that there was some doubt about her involvement with the church.

Georgia in general and Savannah in particular had a challenging relationship with Catholicism, which had been banned during the colonial era. It was not until 1789 that the state gave Catholics equal rights. French Catholics settled in Savannah beginning in the 1790s. The Diocese of Savannah was not organized until 1850.

Although the Beasleys had no children of their own, Abraham had one child from a previous marriage, who was his namesake. Abraham died in 1877 and was buried in Savannah's Catholic Cemetery on Wheaton Street. He left all his possessions and money to Mathilda, including five acres of property worth three hundred dollars as well as other land on the Isle of Hope and on Skidaway Island.

In 1885, rather than enjoying her inheritance or continuing Abraham's business activities, Mathilda traveled to England to join a Franciscan novitiate in York. The motivation behind this

drastic move to strengthen her faith is unknown, but it is likely that she had had an opportunity to meet some members of the Poor Clares, an order of Franciscan nuns, when they traveled from York in 1884 to work with African Americans living on Skidaway Island.

Mathilda remained at the novitiate for a year before journeying back to Savannah. Upon her return, she donated her property to the Sacred Heart Church of Savannah to establish an orphanage. The St. Francis Home for Colored Orphans was founded in 1887 as the city's first such institution for African American girls. The orphanage was originally located near the Sacred Heart Church, but in 1890 was moved to St. Benedict the Moor's Parish on East Broad Street. Beasley faced a series of trials in trying to operate the orphanage. In 1895, teenage residents of the home made several attempts to destroy it. In addition, the home was always in need of funds. Beasley made several successful pleas to the Catholic Church for financial support and on at least two occasions received funding from Mother Katherine Drexel, a Pennsylvania nun who founded the Sisters of the Blessed Sacrament, a predominantly white religious order with a mission to African Americans and Native Americans.

In 1889, Beasley established the first community of African American nuns in Georgia, under the Third Order of St. Francis. From that point she was addressed as Mother Mathilda. But despite her service and contributions to the church, not all Catholics were willing to accept Beasley as an equal. Bishop Becker of Savannah wrote to Mother Drexel in 1891, asking her to assist Mother Mathilda with the orphanage. The bishop wanted the Pennsylvania order to incorporate Mother Mathilda and her group of nuns into their organization, albeit in a subordinate role. Mother Drexel did not honor the bishop's request.

Beasley's pleas for assistance eventually reached the Franciscan motherhouse in Italy, and the first of three Franciscan sisters from that country arrived in Savannah in 1897. Two others followed in 1898 to operate the orphanage and head the Savannah mission. Upon their arrival, Beasley moved out of the orphanage and into a small house at 1511 Price Street that had been built for her by the Sacred Heart Church. She continued to work at the orphanage, and she donated the money she earned from sewing to charity.

On December 20, 1903, Mother Mathilda Beasley was found dead at her private altar, wearing the habit of her order. She was in position, suggesting that she was kneeling in prayer at the time of her death. Next to her lay her clothing for burial and the instructions for her funeral, which specified that there be no eulogy. The ceremony, at Savannah's Catholic Cemetery, was attended by African American and white mourners, Protestants and Catholics.

ANNE ROISE

over the state are greatly depressed. We stand almost appalled at what our ears hear and what our eyes see. Our only hope is in God."[25]

Although classically trained in the liberal arts curriculum at Atlanta University and deeply versed in philosophy, history, and literature, Richard Wright emerged as a compelling voice on behalf of agricultural and industrial education. In the spring of 1906, Wright found himself in the middle of a heated battle about the political and professional opportunities available to college-trained men and women who came of age in the aftermath of Reconstruction. During Georgia Industrial's commencement exercises in May 1906, Wright listened nervously as Atlanta judge William R. Hammond disparaged African

American voters as a "threatening menace" and cautioned the graduating class that their newly minted diplomas would never make them the social or political equals of white citizens. Following Hammond's remarks, Wright looked at the baffled expressions around him and responded haltingly: "I know that Judge Hammond cannot expect us to endorse all that is contained in his address." In the days after the commencement, Dr. J. A. Brockett, the pastor of St. James Tabernacle, issued a blistering critique of Hammond's text. Incensed by Hammond's patently false depiction of African American civic and political capabilities, Brockett demanded that the judge fulfill the broken promises of Reconstruction and "abolish the white primaries—abolish the chain gang—blot out the stockades, their gross iniquities—restore to us that which the chattel mortgage has robbed us of and patiently and loyally obey the law as declared in the fifteenth amendment."[26]

Although the debate over Hammond's controversial remarks subsided, the fight for a "second Emancipation" continued. Emboldened by the Atlanta race riot of September 1906, which stoked fear and contempt among the state's black residents, white state legislators introduced the contrived specter of vindictive black bandits as justification for comprehensive disfranchisement policies aimed at African American voters. A group of black Savannahians characterized such efforts as "a cruel stab upon a weaker, by a stronger race" and an "unwise, prejudicial, and unwarranted" measure designed to circumscribe African American progress by stripping away the basic rights and privileges of citizenship: "It is class legislation, pure and simple, and should not be tolerated in a republican form of government, especially affecting, as it does, so large a per cent of loyal, worthy and desirable citizens."[27] When legislators ultimately approved the disfranchisement measure, the *Savannah Tribune* echoed the disappointment of African Americans around the state: "The bill is designed to disfranchise the venal, ignorant, illiterate and vicious negro, preserving to the white man the right of suffrage, regardless of educational or property qualifications." In the aftermath of the measure, disgruntled Savannah residents formed the Golden Rule Association expressly to fight disfranchisement, sought legal counsel to question the constitutionality of the bill, and passed resolutions that censured the governor and the Georgia General Assembly.[28]

Like campaigns in other southern communities, the battle to safeguard African American voting rights in Savannah constituted one phase of a protracted struggle to circumvent white-supremacist policies. While the Reverend Brockett and Sol C. Johnson, who became the *Tribune*'s editor and owner following the death of John Deveaux, in 1909, defended their constitutional rights as voters, they enjoined colleagues to "agitate in a dignified way for your rights" as they battled discrimination on Savannah streetcars.[29] Johnson, a seasoned civil rights veteran, likely harked back to his protest in 1899 against segregation on local trains. "The colored people of Savannah will never consent to be herded as cattle on the street cars," read an editorial in the *Savannah Tribune*. "When Jim Crowism commences colored people will walk."[30] With editorials, petitions, sermons, and mass meetings, grassroots organizers and noted civic leaders led an eighteen-month boycott. Throughout the public demonstrations, Johnson never swayed in his commitment to the protest, insisting that "leaders in thoughts should be leaders in action."[31]

Savannah's streetcar boycott and disfranchisement protests garnered the support of the Men's Sunday Club, a remarkably successful social, literary, and political forum created in April 1905 by Monroe W. Work, a sociologist at Georgia Industrial College and a protégé of W. E. B. Du Bois. In lectures, debates, and public programs, participants explored subjects of "vital importance to the life and progress of the colored citizen."[32] Members, lecturers, and invited guests (including participants in the women's auxiliary and members of the Frances E. W. Harper Literary and Social Circle) gathered weekly to debate such topics as "The Effects of the Policy Shops Upon the Community," "The

Unreliability of Negro Labor," "Negro Education in Chatham County," "Lynching Evils,"
"The Negro as a Political Factor," and Franz Boas's theories of racial difference."[33]

When Monroe Work left Savannah in 1908 to join the faculty of the Tuskegee Institute,
the Men's Club struggled to stay afloat. Despite the group's decline, political organizing
and public debates among black leaders in Savannah continued in a variety of venues
and locations. Following Work's departure, J. C. Lindsay, who was the manager of the
city's branch of the Atlanta Mutual Insurance Company, a writer for the *Tribune*, and a
member of the Negro Business League, emerged as one of Savannah's most impassioned
and prolific public intellectuals. In speeches and writings, he advanced a firm civil rights
agenda.

During an address in February 1917 on Abraham Lincoln at Savannah's First Congre-
gational Church, Lindsay chronicled the political and social shifts caused by the Emancipation Proclamation and Reconstruction legislation. As a flurry of books and pamphlets
lambasted the alleged corruption of African American officeholders, Lindsay advanced
a revisionist assessment of the era that hailed its educational and political advances:
"Those opportunities which were offered [then], coupled with the eagerness for learning

have been at the root of the progress of the race, have in fact, brought the Negro where he is today." He reminded his audience that "full emancipation" would remain a distant dream until African Americans could safely free themselves from "unjust discrimination, from unrighteous treatment, from invisible bonds that forbid one to live freely, to act freely, to enjoy freely."[34] Although Lindsay acknowledged that "we have had to fight every inch of the way to the present," he believed that "the fighting has not been in vain." Months later, Lindsay called upon the "thinking men of the race" to continue an "uncompromising warfare" against "racial discrimination, jim-crow laws, unfair and inhuman treatment, disfranchisement and mob violence."[35]

J. C. Lindsay's commitment to waging "uncompromising warfare" against racial injustice and segregation drew the attention of James Weldon Johnson, an Atlanta University graduate and the indefatigable field secretary of the National Association for the Advancement of Colored People (NAACP). When Johnson came to Savannah on February 16, 1917, to solicit support for an NAACP chapter in the city, he found an enthusiastic response among Lindsay and other "thinking men and women of our race." Before a captive audience at the St. Paul CME Church, Johnson outlined the NAACP's primary goals: "We cannot hope to win out against the forces that would circumscribe our already narrow sphere of opportunity and perhaps, eventually, almost re-enslave us, unless we can learn to mobilize our forces."[36] When Johnson returned to Savannah weeks later to finalize plans for the new chapter, he facilitated a public forum on "racial unity for racial self-defense and self-preservation" at St. Paul's. The *Savannah Tribune* reminded readers of the NAACP's broad mission and implored them to support the "causes it is fighting for."[37]

When the Savannah NAACP met at the St. Philip AME Church in April 1918, Dr. W. G. Alexander, a gifted writer and the presiding elder of the church, encouraged supporters to denounce any "sycophants and boot-licks" in their communities who seemed strangely content with the racial status quo. He insisted that World War I, which the United States had entered a year earlier, served as a fitting juncture for African Americans to "marshal their intelligence, and their character, their organizing power and their wealth in one determined and unrelenting attack" against the "damnable institution of Jim Crowism."[38] With the Savannah chapter's growing membership, its talented leadership, and the strong endorsement of the *Savannah Tribune*, James Weldon Johnson remained extremely hopeful that the city branch would broaden the NAACP's influence throughout southern Georgia. "The time is now ripe," he said, "for spreading the Association through the south."[39]

But Johnson's expectations were only half-realized. Dr. Alexander, along with Mrs. Pearl Smith, who served as the "Captain of Women" for the NAACP's membership drive, continued to bring intellectual heft and organizational skills to the chapter's operations, but the escalating war effort, the continued exodus of valuable workers (including J. C. Lindsay to Atlanta), and Alexander's own departure in 1922 to serve as president of Atlanta's Morris Brown College limited the NAACP's impact as a force "for equal justice and equal opportunity."[40]

But the NAACP was not the only force for black political activism in Savannah. Black women were key to other forms of activism in the city on behalf of the race, and on behalf of themselves. In addition to canvassing Savannah for NAACP members, Pearl Smith devoted her time and energies to the Chatham County Republican League, the City Federation of Negro Women's Clubs, and auxiliaries in the African Methodist Episcopal Church. A stalwart defender of women's rights and the women's suffrage amendment, Smith conducted literacy training schools, held mock elections, engaged in uplift work, and devised a litany of plans to open "the eyes of all Americans to the rights of true womanhood."[41]

Like Smith's, Rebecca Stiles Taylor's résumé was replete with a long list of associations, including the Urban League, the NAACP, the National Association of Colored Women, the *Savannah Journal* newspaper, and the Toussaint L'Ouverture Branch of the Savannah Chapter of the American Red Cross.[42] During a meeting of the State Federation of Colored Women's Clubs in June 1918, Taylor led the charge as club members condemned "unwarranted lawlessness" and the "spirit of humiliation and dread" that haunted families and communities, including black women. In 1918, the brutal death of Mary Turner, a pregnant African American laborer who was lynched near Valdosta, Georgia, highlighted the fact that black women were not safe from the racial violence rampaging throughout the South. After the crowd hanged Turner upside down, someone cut her eight-month-old fetus from her; the baby made two cries before its head was crushed. In response to those horrific murders, the Savannah women's delegation declared, "We feel that our lives are unsafe as long as this iniquitous institution [lynching] exists." Yet amid the terror and anxiety generated by these and other lynchings, Taylor and other Savannah women remained steadfastly committed to uplifting the race and working with others to improve

Staff of the Savannah Tribune. *Savannah Tribune, October 3, 1914. Courtesy of Zach S. Henderson Library, Georgia Southern University, Statesboro.*

"the standard of Negro womanhood intellectually, industrially, spiritually and politically in Georgia."[43]

In March 1922, Mary L. Ayers, a leader of the Negro National Women's League and an active member of the Order of the Eastern Star, called a recruiting meeting at Tabernacle Baptist Church. There she encouraged audience members to join the league in its push for "the political and civil rights of the Negro women." She emphasized that "liberty, equality, and justice" required constant "organization, cooperation, and unity." By locating the origins of the black freedom struggle in the Emancipation era, Ayers paid homage to pioneering "race giants" like Frederick Douglass and Henry McNeal Turner, who "began the fight for Negro citizenship." Since women's suffrage had been achieved (the Nineteenth Amendment was ratified in 1920), Ayers enjoined the audience to "bend every effort to clear the path of injustice." "To wail and mourn and pray for success without action will be of no avail," she cautioned. "We must buckle on our armor and fight for liberty."[44]

Five years later, as Rebecca Stiles Taylor traveled to Birmingham, Alabama, and contemplated her parting words as the outgoing president of the Southeastern Federation of Colored Women's Clubs, she too drew lessons from studying the Emancipation period.

Born in Savannah in 1881, Taylor came of age during the height of white redemption. Opting to sidestep a historical narrative of "trials and sorrows," Taylor articulated a radical vision for the future. From the perspective of four decades, she remarked, "We stand on the threshold of a new era—a new South." But she cautioned her attentive audience that a "new world of opportunity and power" could not be achieved by following traditional paths of civic organizations, interracial dialogues, and what she described as a focus on "constructive citizenship" alone. Like her associate Mary Ayers, Taylor did not devalue the critical need for civic engagement and increased cooperation across the color line. While those tools were important, time, wars, and migration had convinced Taylor that the "path of injustice" would prove insurmountable until the "minds of black and white" southerners became "mentally emancipated." Although the "Emancipation Proclamation broke the chains of chattel slavery," Taylor explained in concrete terms how self-doubt, low self-esteem, crass materialism, narrow outlooks, and "mental slavery" held a paralyzing grip on "the minds of both black and white" people.

Taylor's sharply worded call for "intellectual liberty" and her insistence that the "Negro's freedom is not complete" reverberated throughout the Birmingham sanctuary where the Southeastern Federation met. One audience member commended her for "standing firm in her convictions, not afraid to voice them in the heart of the Southland."[45]

Like many social activists who preceded her, Rebecca Stiles Taylor had a keen knowledge of history, and she well understood that the long fight for freedom required constant study, recalibration, and negotiation. While she held out hope that "true freedom" would be reached when African Americans achieved "mental emancipation," others in Savannah were not easily convinced that black pride and race consciousness could root out the entrenched forces of white supremacy. Bewildered by the South's dogged commitment to "Jim Crowism, disfranchisement and the unfairness of courts to Negroes," one Savannah resident who did not share Taylor's hope for a "new South" instead depicted the region as "depraved and demoralizing, and becoming more so each day."[46]

It may well be that the optimism that Mary L. Ayers, Rebecca Stiles Taylor, Richard R. Wright, and J. C. Lindsay shared about the future of African Americans extended from their interest in the complex lessons of the past. Through conversation, reading, research, and correspondence, they understood that they were part of an extraordinary intellectual legacy—heirs of men and women who were unwavering in their commitment to keeping the hopes and aspirations of Emancipation and Reconstruction alive.[47]

Sol C. Johnson was also a keen student of history. Born in 1869 in Savannah's Yama-craw community, Johnson came up under the tutelage of Judge James M. Simms and Colonel John H. Deveaux. By the early 1950s, he had a wealth of information about much that had transpired in Savannah over seven decades. In his office at the *Savannah Tribune*, visitors could find bound volumes of the newspaper dating back to the nineteenth century, along with photographs on the walls of Sojourner Truth, Frederick Douglass, Phillis Wheatley, Abraham Lincoln, and his boyhood friend Robert S. Abbott. One prized image was a photograph of the nattily dressed editor posing near his printing press with two young admirers—the grandsons of James Simms.

Johnson died in 1954 at the age of eighty-seven, a few months before the U.S. Supreme Court issued its decision in *Brown v. Board of Education*. The historical connections between the editor's life work and the civil rights struggle were not lost on Louis E. Martin, a former writer for the *Savannah Tribune*. Then an editor for the *Chicago Defender*, Martin commended Johnson's generation for overcoming the "crippling conditions created by color prejudice." Convinced that civil rights gains accrued incrementally, Martin credited Johnson and the men and women who came of age in the shadow of Reconstruction for helping "force the issue of first class citizenship in our time."[48]

During the 1950s, Rebecca Stiles Taylor Dodson, a colleague of Martin's at the *Defender*, was one of the few surviving participants who had collaborated with Sol Johnson in Savannah's early "race struggles." Two weeks after *Brown* was decided, the seventy-four-year-old columnist informed her readers that she regarded the decision as an affirmation of her half century of work as a clubwoman and teacher in Jim Crow Savannah and rural Georgia. Still an advocate for "mental emancipation," she recalled how she aimed to "awaken Negroes as to their needs and opportunities." She chronicled in moving detail the profound financial and material inequities that stymied black education and progress in Georgia. Voicing the sentiments of contemporaries with stark memories of life "behind the veil," Taylor began her reflections on the landmark Supreme Court ruling with a fitting epigram: "It has been a long time a-coming but it is here at last."[49]

Notes

INTRODUCTION

1. For major overviews of U.S. slavery, see Ira Berlin, *Many Thousands Gone: The First Two Centuries of Slavery in North America* (Cambridge, Mass.: Harvard University Press, 1998); and *Generations of Captivity: A History of African American Slaves* (Cambridge, Mass.: Harvard University Press, 2003). Books on slavery and nineteenth-century African Americans in North American cities are too numerous to name. Works on Savannah referred to in this volume are in the Further Reading section. Books on slavery in cities include Richard Wade, *Slavery in the Cities: The South, 1820–1860* (New York: Oxford University Press, 1964); and Claudia Goldin, *Urban Slavery in the American South, 1820–1860: A Quantitative History* (Chicago: University of Chicago Press, 1976). Slavery in New York, Baltimore, and New Orleans is the subject of the richest recent literature. See Ira Berlin and Leslie M. Harris, *Slavery in New York* (New York: New Press, 2005); Leslie M. Harris, *In the Shadow of Slavery: African Americans in New York City, 1626–1863* (Chicago: University of Chicago Press, 2003); Graham Hodges, *Root and Branch: African Americans in New York and East Jersey, 1613–1863* (Chapel Hill: University of North Carolina Press, 1999); Shane White, *Somewhat More Independent: The End of Slavery in New York City, 1770–1810* (Athens: University of Georgia Press, 1991); Craig Steven Wilder, *In the Company of Black Men: The African Influence on African American Culture in New York City* (New York: New York University Press, 2002); Thelma Wills Foote, *Black and White Manhattan: The History of Racial Formation in New York City* (New York: Oxford University Press, 2004); T. Stephen Whitman, *The Price of Freedom: Slavery and Manumission in Baltimore and Early National Maryland* (Lexington: University Press of Kentucky, 1997); Christopher Phillips, *Freedom's Port: The African American Community of Baltimore, 1790–1860* (Urbana: University of Illinois Press, 1997); Seth Rockman, *Scraping By: Wage Labor, Slavery, and Survival in Early Baltimore* (Baltimore: Johns Hopkins University Press, 2009); Gwendolyn Midlo Hall, *Africans in Colonial Louisiana: The Development of Afro-Creole Culture in the Eighteenth Century* (Baton Rouge: Louisiana State University Press, 1992); Lawrence Powell, *The Accidental City: Improvising New Orleans* (Cambridge, Mass.: Harvard University Press, 2012); Judith Kelleher Schafer, *Becoming Free, Remaining Free: Manumission and Enslavement in New Orleans, 1846–1862* (Baton Rouge: Louisiana State University Press, 2003); Jennifer Spear, *Race, Sex, and Social Order in Early New Orleans* (Baltimore: Johns Hopkins University Press, 2009).

2. See Jennifer Pustz, *Voices from the Back Stairs: Interpreting Servants' Lives at Historic House Museums* (DeKalb: Northern Illinois Uni-

versity Press, 2009); Jennifer Eichstedt and Stephen Small, *Representations of Slavery: Race and Ideology in Southern Plantation Museums* (Washington, D.C.: Smithsonian Books, 2002).

3. See James Oliver Horton and Lois E. Horton, eds., *Slavery and Public History: The Tough Stuff of American Memory* (Chapel Hill: University of North Carolina Press, 2006).

4. See James Oliver Horton, "Slavery in American History: An Uncomfortable National Dialogue," in Horton and Horton, *Slavery and Public History*, 49–54.

Chapter 1.

THE TRANSATLANTIC SLAVE TRADE COMES TO GEORGIA

1. Betty Wood, *Slavery in Colonial Georgia, 1730–1775* (Athens: University of Georgia Press, 1984), 1–23, 74–87; Julia Floyd Smith, *Slavery and Rice Culture in Low Country Georgia, 1750–1860* (Knoxville: University of Tennessee Press, 1985), 98; Louis De Vorsey Jr., ed., *DeBrahm's Report of the General Survey in the Southern District* (Columbia: University of South Carolina Press, 1971), 162; Harold E. Davis, *The Fledgling Province: Social and Cultural Life in Colonial Georgia, 1733–1776* (Chapel Hill: University of North Carolina Press, 1976), 7–32.

2. Wood, *Slavery in Colonial Georgia*, 1–23.

3. Davis, *Fledgling Province*, 8.

4. Allen D. Candler and Lucian Lamar Knight, eds., *The Colonial Records of the State of Georgia*, 26 vols. (Atlanta: Franklin Printing and Publishing Co., 1904–37), 1:11.

5. Darold D. Wax, "'New Negroes Are Always in Demand': The Slave Trade in Eighteenth-Century Georgia," *Georgia Historical Quarterly* 68, no. 2 (Summer 1984): 193–220; Wood, *Slavery in Colonial Georgia*, 1–23; and Kenneth Coleman, *Colonial Georgia: A History* (New York: Scribner's Sons, 1976), 36–54.

6. Davis, *Fledgling Province*, 7–32; Wood, *Slavery in Colonial Georgia*, 4–5.

7. Milton L. Ready, "Land Tenure in Trusteeship Georgia," *Agricultural History* 48, no. 3 (July 1974): 353–68.

8. Wood, *Slavery in Colonial Georgia*, 24–43; Wax, "'New Negroes,'" 196.

9. Thomas Stephens, *A Brief Account of the Causes That Have Retarded the Progress of the Colony of Georgia* (London, 1743), 7.

10. Davis, *Fledgling Province*, 7–32; Wood, *Slavery in Colonial Georgia*, 4–5.

11. Quoted in Wood, *Slavery in Colonial Georgia*, 31.

12. Ibid., 74–87.

13. Frank Lambert, *James Habersham: Loyalty, Politics, and Commerce in Colonial Georgia* (Athens: University of Georgia Press, 2005), 76–79.

14. Quoted in Lambert, *James Habersham*, 78.

15. Quoted in Paul S. Taylor, *Georgia Plan, 1732–1752* (Berkeley and Los Angeles: University of California Press, 1972), 266.

16. Wood, *Slavery in Colonial Georgia*, 92; and Wax, "'New Negroes,'" 196–97.

17. Wood, *Slavery in Colonial Georgia*, 98; Wax, "'New Negroes,'" 196–97.

18. W. Robert Higgins, "The South Carolina Negro Duty Law" (master's thesis, University of South Carolina, 1967), 149.

19. Located southwest of Savannah on the Georgia coast, Sunbury received eleven known transshipments of African captives from the West Indies, totaling 133 captives in the 1760s. Most of the shipments were small, numbering fewer than 10 people; however, one large cargo of 50 Gambian slaves arrived in 1765, and another group of 24 Africans were disembarked in the following year. For information on Sunbury shipments, see Elizabeth Donnan, ed., *Documents Illustrative of the History of the Slave Trade to America*, 4 vols. (Washington, D.C.: Carnegie Institute of Washington, 1930–35), 4:609–25.

20. *Georgia Gazette*, August 15, 1765.

21. W. Robert Higgins, "Charleston: Terminus and Entrepôt of the Colonial Slave Trade," in *The African Diaspora: Interpretive Essays*, ed. Martin L. Kilson and Robert L. Rotberg (Cambridge, Mass.: Harvard University Press, 1976), 129–30.

22. Donnan, *Documents of the Slave Trade*, 4:612.

23. Voyages: The Trans-Atlantic Slave Trade Database, accessed January 1, 2011, http://www.slavevoyages.org. In 1755 more than sixty slavers disembarked African captives in Jamaica.

24. Donnan, *Documents of the Slave Trade*, 4:609–25.

25. Equiano, *Interesting Narrative of the Life of Olaudah Equiano, or Gustavus Vassa, The African. Written by Himself*, ed. Werner Sollors (New York: Norton, 2001), 102; Vincent Carretta, *Equiano, the African: Biography of a Self-Made Man* (Athens: University of Georgia Press, 2005), 165.

26. Equiano, *Life of Equiano*, 96–97, 108.

27. Ibid., 96–121, 122.

28. Donnan, *Documents of the Slave Trade*, 4:609–25; Wax, "'New Negroes,'" 196–200.

29. Wax, "'New Negroes,'" 199–202.

30. Wood, *Slavery in Colonial Georgia*, 103–5.

31. Wax, "'New Negroes,'" 198–206; Gregory E. O'Malley, "Beyond the Middle Passage: Slave Migration from the Caribbean to North America, 1619–1807," *William and Mary Quarterly* 66, no. 1 (January 2009): 150–51.

32. Quoted in Lambert, *James Habersham*, 59–80.

33. Equiano, *Life of Equiano*, 107; George C. Rogers Jr., *Charleston in the Age of the Pinckneys* (Norman: University of Oklahoma Press, 1969; reprint, Columbia: University of South Carolina Press, 1980), 8, 11–12; Frances Harrold, "Colonial Siblings: Georgia's Relationship with South Carolina during the Pre-Revolutionary Period," *Georgia Historical Quarterly* 73, no. 4 (Winter 1989): 707–44.

34. Kenneth Morgan, "The Organization of the Colonial American Rice Trade," *William and Mary Quarterly* 52, no. 3 (July 1995): 443–48.

35. Wood, *Slavery in Colonial Georgia*, 88–109.

36. Smith, *Slavery and Rice*, 15–29, 213; Davis, *Fledgling Province*, 123–24; Wood, *Slavery in Colonial Georgia*, 98.

37. Donnan, *Documents of the Slave Trade*, 4:608–30; *Georgia Gazette*, July 2, July 30, August 6, and October 22, 1766; September 9, November

25, and December 25, 1767; June 1, August 10, September 14, October 5, and October 12, 1768; April 19, May 3, June 7, and August 9, 1769; March 21, May 2, May 9, and May 23, 1770; *South Carolina Gazette*, May 9 and July 18, 1771; and Voyages: The Trans-Atlantic Slave Trade Database.

38. Voyages: The Trans-Atlantic Slave Trade Database.

39. Joseph Clay to Michael Collins, April 8, 1775, quoted in Wax, "'New Negroes,'" 213.

40. Quoted in James McMillin, *The Final Victims: Foreign Slave Trade to North America, 1783–1810* (Columbia: University of South Carolina Press, 2004), 5. A snow is a small sailing vessel, something like a brig.

41. Voyages: The Trans-Atlantic Slave Trade Database. The *Amelia* and the *Nelly* probably disembarked their cargoes surreptitiously south of Savannah along the coast of Georgia.

42. Philip D. Morgan, *Slave Counterpoint: Black Culture in the Eighteenth-Century Chesapeake and Lowcountry* (Chapel Hill: University of North Carolina Press, 1998), 60–68.

43. Donnan, *Documents of the Slave Trade*, 4: 609–25; Wax, "'New Negroes,'" 193–220; Wood, *Slavery in Colonial Georgia*, 88–109; Smith, *Slavery and Rice*, 93–112; Voyages: The Trans-Atlantic Slave Trade Database.

44. Telfair to Robert Mackmillan, September 2, 1773, Telfair Papers, Georgia Historical Society (GHS), Savannah; Wood, *Slavery in Colonial Georgia*, 104–106.

45. Cowper and Telfair to Samuel Sandys, October 28, 1774, Telfair Papers, GHS.

46. Wood, *Slavery in Colonial Georgia*, 105.

47. Morgan, *Slave Counterpoint*, 146–59.

48. Cowper and Telfair to Samuel Sandys and Company, November 10, 1774, Telfair Papers, GHS.

49. Voyages: The Trans-Atlantic Slave Trade Database; Wood, *Slavery in Colonial Georgia*, 101–102.

50. McMillin, *Final Victims*, 50.

51. Clay to Jones and Erving, September 2, 1775, quoted in McMillin, *Final Victims*, 53.

52. Henry Laurens to Richard Oswald, May 17, 1756, quoted in Daniel C. Littlefield, *Rice and Slaves: Ethnicity and the Slave Trade in Colonial South Carolina* (Baton Rouge: Louisiana State University Press, 1981), 8.

53. Henry Laurens to Smith and Clifton, July 17, 1755, quoted in Littlefield, *Rice and Slaves*, 8.

54. Ibid., 8–10; McMillin, *Final Victims*, 52–53.

55. Philip D. Morgan, "Black Society in the Lowcountry, 1760–1810," in *Slavery and Freedom in the Age of the American Revolution*, ed. Ira Berlin and Ronald Hoffman (Urbana: University of Illinois Press, 1986), 83–141; Wood, *Slavery in Colonial Georgia*, 103.

56. Philip D. Curtin, *The Atlantic Slave Trade: A Census* (Madison: University of Wisconsin Press, 1969), 150, 160.

57. Clay and Company to Messrs. Scott, Mackie, and Dover, December 19, 1772, MS 153, Clay & Co. Papers, GHS. For discussions of slave prices, see Wood, *Slavery in Colonial Georgia*, 95–98, and Smith, *Slavery and Rice*, 96–98.

58. Telfair to Basil Cowper, August 11, August 14, and September 2, 1773, Telfair Papers, GHS.

59. Wax, "'New Negroes,'" 211.

60. Quoted in McMillin, *Final Victims*, 74.

61. Edward Telfair to William Thompson, August 11, 1773, Telfair Papers, GHS.

62. Edward McCrady, *South Carolina under the Royal Government, 1719–1776* (New York, 1899), 649.

63. Smith, *Slavery and Rice*, 99; Paul M. Pressly, "Scottish Merchants and the Shaping of Colonial Georgia," *Georgia Historical Quarterly* 91, no. 2 (Summer 2007): 5.

64. Pressly, "Scottish Merchants," 11.

65. Ibid., 17. The firm of Cowper and Telfair used several different names during the royal period, including Cowper and Telfair; Cowper and Telfairs; William and Edward Telfair; Edward Telfair and Company; Telfair, Cowper, and Telfair; and Edward Telfair of Antigua, Merchant.

66. Coleman, *Colonial Georgia*, 214–15.

67. Pressly, "Scottish Merchants," 10–12.

68. E. Merton Coulter, "Edward Telfair," *Georgia Historical Quarterly* 20, no. 2 (June 1936): 101–24.

69. Wax, "'New Negroes,'" 206; Donnan, *Documents of the Slave Trade*, 4:608–29.

70. McMillin, *Final Victims*, 80.

71. Wood, *Slavery in Colonial Georgia*, 99; Henry Laurens to Wells, Wharton, and Doran, May 27, 1755, quoted in Elizabeth Donnan, "The Slave Trade into South Carolina before the Revolution," *American Historical Review* 33, no. 4 (July 1928): 815.

72. Wax, "'New Negroes,'" 210–15; McMillin, *Final Victims*, 73–75.

73. Wax, "'New Negroes,'" 208–209; *Georgia Gazette*, November 22, 1764, January 3, 1765, and July 2, 1766.

74. Wood, *Slavery in Colonial Georgia*, 101–103.

75. Telfair, Cowper, and Telfair to Messrs. Samuel, Sandys & Co., October 12, 1774, Telfair Papers, GHS.

76. Equiano, *Life of Equiano*, 77.

77. Telfair, Cowper, and Telfair to Samuel, Sandys & Co., October 12, 1774.

78. Ira Berlin, *Many Thousands Gone: The First Two Centuries of Slavery in North America* (Cambridge, Mass.: Belknap Press of Harvard University Press, 1998), 43.

79. McMillin, *Final Victims*, 31–32.

Chapter 2.

"THE KING OF ENGLAND'S SOLDIERS"

1. See Benjamin Quarles, *The Negro in the American Revolution* (Chapel Hill: University of North Carolina Press, 1961), 144; *New England Chronicle*, November 11, 1779. For an additional example of a black woman leading British troops to valuable targets in the South Carolina Lowcountry in 1782, see Caroline Gilman, ed., *Letters of Eliza Wilkinson: During the Invasion and Possession of Charlestown, S.C., by the British in the Revolutionary War* (New York: Colman, 1839), 24.

2. Sylvia Frey, *Water from the Rock: Black Resistance in a Revolutionary Age* (Princeton, N.J.: Princeton University Press, 1991), 97–98; "Abstract of the Number of Men women and children, Negroes and prisoners victualled at the commissary general's stores at Savannah from 11th to 20th October 1779," in Clinton Papers, William L. Clements Library, University of Michigan; see also Robert Olwell, *Masters, Slaves, and Subjects: The Culture of Power in the South Carolina Low Country, 1740–1790* (Ithaca, N.Y.: Cornell University

Press, 1998), 243–81; Minutes of the Governor in Council, October 25, 1779, in Allen D. Candler, *The Colonial Records of the State of Georgia*, (unpublished typescript, Georgia Archives), vol. 38, pt. 2, 230.

3. Betty Wood, "'High notions of their liberty': Women of Color and the American Revolution in Lowcountry Georgia and South Carolina, 1765–1783," in *African American Life in the Georgia Lowcountry: The Atlantic World and the Gullah Geechee*, ed. Philip Morgan (Athens: University of Georgia Press, 2010), 63; George F. Jones, "The Black Hessians: Negroes Recruited by the Hessians in South Carolina and Other Colonies," *South Carolina Historical Magazine* 83 (October 1982), 287–302, especially 299n25.

4. Thomas Bee to Governor John Matthews, Goose Creek, December 9, 1782, in Thomas Bee Papers, South Caroliniana Library, and Olwell, *Masters, Slaves, and Subjects,* 258–60; George F. Tyson, "The Carolina Black Corps: Legacy of Revolution (1782–1798)," *Revista/Review Interamericana* 5, no. 4 (Winter 1975–76), 651.

5. Frey, *Water from the Rock,* 174

6. William Bartram, *Travels through North and South Carolina, Georgia, East and West Florida* (London: J. Johnson, 1792), 467–68.

7. Betty Ford Renfro, *River to River: The History of Effingham County, Georgia* (Saline, Mich.: McMaughton-Gunn, 2005), 10.

8. *Gazette of the State of Georgia*, May 3, 1787. See also Louis De Vorsey, *The Georgia–South Carolina Boundary: A Problem in Historical Geography* (Athens: University of Georgia Press, 1982).

9. Frey, *Water from the Rock,* 212.

10. Robert Watkins and George Watkins, eds., *A Digest of the Laws of the State of Georgia: From Its First Establishment as a British Province down to the Year 1798* (Philadelphia: Aitken, 1800), 163–79.

11. Johann David Schoepf, *Travels in the Confederation* (New York: Bergman, 1968) 1:220.

12. *Gazette of the State of Georgia*, December 18, 1783.

13. Ibid., October 19, 1786.

14. Chatham County Superior Court Minutes, grand jury, October term, 1786; *Gazette of the State of Georgia*, October 19, 1786.

15. *Gazette of the State of Georgia*, October 19, 1786.

16. Joseph Vallence Bevan Papers, Georgia Historical Society, folder 10, item 86. There is a slightly different copy in the Telamon Cuyler Collection, Hargrett Library, University of Georgia, box 82, folder 1: Slave Rebellion 1786.

17. Either Union Creek south of Purrysburgh or the Union causeway nearer to Savannah.

18. Joseph Vallence Bevan Papers, folder 10, item 87.

19. Proclamation Book AAA, 1782–1823, 10–11, Georgia Archives; *Gazette of the State of Georgia*, January 4, 1787.

20. Governor's Messages, 1786–1788, no. 459, South Carolina Department of Archives and History.

21. Thomas Pinckney letter book, 1787–1789, South Carolina Department of Archives and History.

22. The National Archives (UK), CO 5/378, 54v/55r; *South Carolina Council Journal*, April 4,

1769, South Carolina Department of Archives and History, 32, 145–46.

23. *Gazette of the State of Georgia*, April 26, 1787.

24. Joseph Vallence Bevan Papers, folder 10, item 84.

25. Frey, *Water from the Rock*, 52. On the Georgia slave trade, see Darold D. Wax, "'New Negroes Are Always in Demand': The Slave Trade in Eighteenth-Century Georgia," *Georgia Historical Quarterly* 68, no. 2 (1984), 193–220.

26. *Gazette of the State of Georgia*, May 10, 1787.

27. Ibid., May 24, 1787.

28. Trial of Lewis, Telamon Cuyler Collection, box 71, folder 12: Georgia Slavery Trials, Hargrett Library, University of Georgia.

29. Sharper's background comes from the advertisement of William Woodard, *Gazette of the State of Georgia*, July 24, 1783.

30. All quotations are from the Trial of Lewis.

31. *Gazette of the State of Georgia*, April 28, 1785. Gunn stated that most of the slaves he sought "have been absent 18 months, or two years" (*Gazette of the State of Georgia*, May 17, 1787). For more on gendered resistance, see Betty Wood, "Some Aspects of Female Resistance to Chattel Slavery in Low Country Georgia, 1763–1815," *Historical Journal* 30, no. 3 (1987), 603–22.

32. Watkins and Watkins, *Digest of the Laws of Georgia*, 167.

33. Georgia Executive Council Minutes, 1786–1789, May 26, 1787, Georgia Archives; *Gazette of the State of Georgia*, June 14, 1787.

34. *Georgia House Journal*, 1788, 285–87,

Georgia Archives. South Carolina operated a similar policy; see Timothy James Lockley, *Maroon Communities in South Carolina: A Documentary Record* (Columbia: University of South Carolina Press, 2009), 79–86.

35. *Georgian*, March 13, 1823.

36. Governor's Messages, 1788, no. 459, South Carolina Department of Archives and History; *Gazette of the State of Georgia*, May 31, 1787.

37. *Gazette of the State of Georgia*, May 10, 1787.

38. Governor's Messages, 1788, no. 459, South Carolina Department of Archives and History.

Chapter 3.

AT THE INTERSECTION OF

COTTON AND COMMERCE

A note on tables. The following sources were used to compile the tables in this chapter: J. L. Agnew and F. D. Lee, *Historical Record of the City of Savannah* (Savannah: Morning News Steam-Power Press, 1869), 137–40; Joseph Bancroft, *Census of the City of Savannah, together with Statistics relating to the Trade, Commerce, Mechanical Arts and Health . . .* (Savannah: Edward C. Councell, 1848), 37–38; Joseph Bancroft, *Census of the City of Savannah, together with Statistics relating to the Trade, Commerce, Mechanical Arts and Health of the Same . . .*, 2nd ed. (Savannah: Edward J. Purse, Printer, 1848), 39; "Commercial Cities of the U.S.: Savannah, Ga.," *Hunt's Merchants' Magazine* (April 1849), 376–87, in "Savannah's Commerce Volume 1," Thomas Gamble Collection, Kaye Kole Genealogy and Local History Room, Bull Street Branch, Live Oak Public Libraries (LOPL); Thomas Gamble, Jr., comp., "Chronological Record of Shipping through Savannah," in "Savannah's Commerce Volume 2," Thomas Gamble Collection, LOPL; Joseph F. Greenough, "The City of Savannah, Georgia," *Hunt's Merchants' Magazine* (July 1853), 57–63, in "Savannah's Commerce Volume 2"; William Harden, *A History of Savannah and South Georgia Volume 1* (1913; repr., Atlanta: Cherokee Publishing Co., 1981), 473; Richard H. Haunton, "Savannah in the 1850s" (PhD diss., Emory University, 1968), 144–48; *The Industries of Savannah, Ga.* (Savannah: J. M. Elstner & Co., 1886), 12; *Mayor's Annual Reports, 1855–1857, 1860, 1867–1870*, Record Series #5600MY-50/60 City of Savannah, Mayor's Office — Mayor's/Municipal Annual Reports, City of Savannah, Research Library and Municipal Archives; "A Statement of the trade for one year of the port of Savannah, in the State of Georgia, exhibiting the value of the foreign & coastwise exports . . . from the 1st of 1803 to the 30th of September 1804 . . . ," Item 5, Folder 2, Collection #MS 704 Savannah Ports Records, Georgia Historical Society; and George White, *Statistics of the State of Georgia . . .* (Savannah: W. Thorne Williams, 1849), 154–59.

1. See Betty Wood, *Women's Work, Men's Work: The Informal Slave Economies of Lowcountry Georgia* (Athens: University of Georgia Press, 1993); Timothy James Lockley, *Lines in the Sand: Race and Class in Lowcountry Georgia, 1750–1860* (Athens: University of Georgia Press, 2001); Robert Olwell, "'Loose, Idle, and Disorderly': Slave Women in the Eighteenth-Century Charleston Marketplace," in *More than Chattel: Black Women and Slavery in the Americas*, ed. David Barry Gaspar and Darlene Clark Hine (Bloomington: Indiana University Press, 1996), 97–110.

2. Ulrich Bonnell Phillips, *A History of Transportation in the Eastern Cotton Belt to 1860* (New York: MacMillan, 1913), 31; Lewis Cecil Gray, *History of Agriculture in the Southern United States to 1860*, 2 vols. (Gloucester, Mass.: Peter Smith, 1858), 2:1021–24; Robert B. Outland III, *Tapping the Pines: The Naval Stores Industry in the American South* (Baton Rouge: Louisiana State University, 2004), 29.

3. Gray, *Agriculture in the Southern United States*, 2:680.

4. Brian Schoen, *The Fragile Fabric of Union: Cotton, Federal Policies, and the Global Origins of the Civil War* (Baltimore: Johns Hopkins University Press, 2009), 43, 255.

5. Gray, *Agriculture in the Southern United States*, 2:683; Walter J. Fraser Jr., *Savannah in the Old South* (Athens: University of Georgia Press, 2003), 246–48, 251–54; Erskine Clarke, *Dwelling Place: A Plantation Epic* (New Haven, Conn.: Yale University Press, 2005), 60.

6. Wm. F. Switzler, Treasury Department, *Report on the Internal Commerce of the United States* (Washington, D.C.: Government Printing Office, 1886), lxxi; D. W. Meinig, *The Shaping of America: A Geographical Perspective on 500 Years of History*, vol. 2: *Continental America, 1800–1867* (New Haven, Conn.: Yale University Press, 1993), 285–86; "Courier Letter-Sheet Review of the Market and Prices Current, Charleston," *Charleston Daily Courier*, October 8, 1858.

7. C. G. Parsons, *Inside View of Slavery; or, a*

Tour among the Planters (Boston: Jewett, 1855), 23; Edward C. Anderson, *Report of Edward C. Anderson, Mayor of the City of Savannah, for the Year Ending October 31st, 1855* (Savannah, Ga.: Power Press of Geo. N. Nichols, 1855), 14. For a general overview of transportation in the antebellum South, see Phillips, *Transportation in the Eastern Cotton Belt*; on the development of southern railroads in particular, see Aaron W. Marrs, *Railroads in the Old South: Pursuing Progress in a Slave Society* (Baltimore: Johns Hopkins University Press, 2009).

8. Vessels along the lower Savannah carried as many as a thousand bales of cotton at a time; see Phillips, *Transportation in the Eastern Cotton Belt*, 123, and Wilma Dunaway, *Slavery in the American Mountain South* (Cambridge: Cambridge University Press, 2003), 88–96. For more information on enslaved watermen in the antebellum South, see Thomas C. Buchanan, *Black Life on the Mississippi: Slaves, Free Blacks, and the Western Steamboat World* (Chapel Hill: University of North Carolina Press, 2004); David S. Cecelski, *The Waterman's Son: Slavery and Freedom in Maritime North Carolina* (Chapel Hill: University of North Carolina Press, 2001), chaps. 1–3; Melvin Patrick Ely, *Israel on the Appomattox: A Southern Experiment in Black Freedom from the 1790s through the Civil War* (New York: Random House, 2004), 150–74. Population figures for Savannah's slaves can be found in Richard C. Wade, *Slavery in the Cities: The South, 1820–1860* (New York: Oxford University Press, 1964), 327.

9. Kirkpatrick et al. v. Bank of Augusta et al., January 1860, Georgia Supreme Court, Savannah, case file A-03350, Georgia Department of Archives and History, Morrow.

10. Nehemiah Adams, *A South-Side View of Slavery*, 4th ed. (Boston: Ticknor and Fields, 1860), 12–13.

11. Quoted in James Stirling, *Letters from the Slave States* (London: Parker and Son, 1857), 229–30.

12. The few sources on enslaved teamsters: Ely, *Israel on the Appomattox*, 144–60; Joseph P. Reidy, *From Slavery to Agrarian Capitalism in the Cotton Plantation South: Central Georgia, 1800–1880* (Chapel Hill: University of North Carolina Press, 1992), 71–73; Dunaway, *Slavery in the American Mountain South*, 96–102.

13. Stiles and Fannin to [Governor George R. Gilmer], August 11, 1830, reprinted in the *Milledgeville Georgia Journal*, November 17, 1830, box 32, folder 320, Ulrich B. Phillips Papers, Sterling Library, Yale University (hereafter cited as Phillips Papers).

14. Switzler, *Internal Commerce of the United States*, 261; *Augusta Georgia Courier*, October 11, 1827, box 24, folder 209, Phillips Papers; *Augusta Georgia Courier*, 27 Nov. 1828, box 24, folder 208, Phillips Papers; Frederick Law Olmsted, *Journeys and Explorations in the Cotton Kingdom of America: Based upon Three Former Volumes of Journeys and Investigations by the Same Author*, 2 vols. (London: Sampson, Low, Son, 1861), 1:367; Joseph Holt Ingraham, *The South-West* (New York: Harper and Bros., 1835), 2:169–70.

15. Anderson, *Report of Edward C. Anderson*, 12.

16. J. B. D. De Bow, *The Industrial Resources, etc., of the Southern and Western States*, 3 vols. (New

Orleans: Office of De Bow's Review, 1853), 144–45; Report of the Annual Meeting of the Stockholders, April 6, 1835, *Savannah and Ogeechee Canal Company, Minute Book, 1826–1840*, Central of Georgia Railway, Georgia Historical Society.

17. First Report of President of the Charleston & Savannah Railroad, 1855, box 256, folder 27, Phillips Papers; *Savannah Daily Republican*, November 14, 1849; Marrs, *Railroads in the Old South*, 6, 55–57.

18. William Grimes, *The Life of William Grimes, the Runaway Slave: Written by Himself* (New York: [W. Grimes], 1825), 22–51, available at Documenting the American South, http://docsouth.unc.edu/neh/grimes25/grimes25.html.

19. Emily Burke, *Pleasure and Pain: Reminiscences of Georgia in the 1840's* (Savannah: Beehive, 1978), 10.

20. Charles Manigault to Louis Manigault, February 21, 1856, in *Life and Labor on Argyle Island: Letters and Documents of a Savannah River Rice Plantation, 1822–1867*, ed. James M. Clifton (Savannah: Beehive, 1978), 208–10.

21. Annette Gordon-Reed, *The Hemingses of Monticello: An American Family* (New York: Norton, 2008), chaps. 7–18.

22. Seth Rockman, "Slavery and Abolition along the Blackstone," in *Landscape of Industry: An Industrial History of the Blackstone Valley*, ed. Worcester Historical Museum (Lebanon, N.H.: University Press of New England, 2009), 110–31.

23. On the travel of Lowcountry domestic servants more generally, see Daina Ramey Berry, *Swing the Sickle for the Harvest is Ripe: Gender and Slavery in Antebellum Georgia* (Urbana: University of Illinois Press, 2007), 48–51.

24. Edward J. Thomas, *Memoirs of a Southerner, 1840–1923* (Savannah: n.p., 1923), 8–9.

25. See the slave manifests of W. C. Berry, July 28, 1860; W. C. Berry, August 4, 1860; J. R. Schenk, August 4, 1860; and M. S. Woodhull, August 11, 1860, all in the Vertical History File, folder 15, Georgia State Archives. For an accounting of the slaves who embarked as passengers from Savannah's harbor, see Richard McMillan, "Savannah's Coastal Slave Trade: A Quantitative Analysis of Ship Manifests, 1840–1850," *Georgia Historical Quarterly* 78 (Summer 1994): 354–57.

26. Grimes, *Life of William Grimes*, 8. For more on the domestic slave trade, see Steven Deyle, *Carry Me Back: The Domestic Slave Trade in American Life* (New York: Oxford University Press, 2005).

27. For a useful entry into the literature on slave hire, see Jonathan D. Martin, *Divided Mastery: Slave Hiring in the American South* (Cambridge, Mass.: Harvard University Press, 2004), 7–9; for slave hiring as experienced in the Georgia Lowcountry, see Berry, *Swing the Sickle*, chap. 5.

28. R. M. Dickson to My Very Dear Sister, December 18, 1852, William G. Dickson Papers, Southern Historical Collection, University of North Carolina, Chapel Hill (hereafter cited as Dickson Papers), quoted in Charles B. Dew, *Slavery in Ante-Bellum Southern Industries* (Bethesda, Md.: University Publications of America, 1993), series B, reel 4. (Hereafter *SASI*.)

29. S. M. McDowell to My Dear Uncle, February 21, 1853, Dickson Papers.

30. See, for example, the "Shipping Intelligence" column of February 28, 1849, *Savannah Daily Republican*.

31. Burke, *Pleasure and Pain*, 17.

32. Susan Eva O'Donovan, *Becoming Free in the Cotton South* (Cambridge, Mass.: Harvard University Press), 21.

33. Grimes, *Life of William Grimes*, 24–25.

34. Charles Hoffman and Tess Hoffman, *North by South: The Two Lives of Richard James Arnold* (Athens: University of Georgia Press, 2009), 168.

35. Louis H. Russell to Dear Uncle, December 30, 1847, Hawkins Family Papers, Southern Historical Collection, University of North Carolina, Chapel Hill (SASI, ser. B, reel 11).

36. Louis A. Chamerovzow, ed., *Slave Life in Georgia: A Narrative of the Life, Sufferings, and Escape of John Brown, a Fugitive Slave, Now in England* (London: Watts, 1855), 31–36.

37. Susan Eva O'Donovan, "Universities of Social and Political Change: Slaves in Jail in Antebellum America," in *Buried Lives: Incarcerated in Early America*, ed. Michele Lise Tarter and Richard Bell (Athens: University of Georgia Press, 2012).

38. Frederick Law Olmsted, *A Journey in the Seaboard States with Remarks on Their Economy* (New York: Mason Brothers, 1861), 676–84.

39. William H. Robinson, *From Log Cabin to the Pulpit; or, Fifteen Years in Slavery* (Eau Claire, Wis.: James H. Tifft, 1913), 12–13, available at Documenting the South, http://docsouth.unc.edu/fpn/robinson/robinson.html.

40. Burke, *Pleasure and Pain*, 23–24; Houston Holloway Hartsfield, "Autobiography," 41–42, Houston Holloway Hartsfield Papers, 1894–1932, Manuscript Divisions, Library of Congress.

41. Hartsfield, "Autobiography," 77–78.

42. Rafe (a slave) v. State, June 1856, Georgia Supreme Court, Savannah, case file A-01844, Georgia State Archives.

43. William and Ellen Craft, *Running a Thousand Miles for Freedom; or, the Escape of William and Ellen Craft from Slavery* (London: William Tweedie, 1860), 53–80.

44. Peter P. Hinks, *To Awaken My Afflicted Brethren: David Walker and the Problem of Antebellum Slave Resistance* (University Park: Pennsylvania State University Press, 1997), chap. 5.

45. Samuel Berry to John Buford, 16 Jan. 1855, John Buford Papers, 179901898, Rare Books, Manuscripts, and Special Collections Library, Duke University, quoted in *Records of Ante-Bellum Slave Plantations*, ed. Kenneth M. Stampp (Bethesda, Md.: University Publications of America, 1987), series F, part 3, reel 34.

46. William Webb, *The History of William Webb, Composed by Himself* (Detroit: Egbert Hoekstra, 1873), 1–8, available at Documenting the South, http://docsouth.unc.edu/neh/webb/webb.html.

47. C. Vann Woodward, ed., *Mary Chesnut's Civil War* (New Haven, Conn.: Yale University Press, 1981), 225; Susan Griffin, "The Yellow Mask, the Black Robe, and the Woman in White: Wilkie Collins, Anti-Catholic Discourse, and the Sensation Novel," *Narrative* 12 (January 2004): 55–73. I am indebted to Julia Stern of Northwestern University for this reference.

48. Wm. Capers to Charles Manigault, September 23, 1859, box 27, folder 254, Phillips Papers.

49. William Kauffman Scarborough, ed., *The Diary of Edmund Ruffin*, vol. 1: *Toward Independence: October, 1856–April, 1861* (Baton Rouge: Louisiana State University Press, 1972), 269; on the *Wanderer*, see Tom Henderson Wells, *The Slave Ship "Wanderer"* (Athens: University of Georgia Press, 1968), chap. 4; for an entry point into the debate about reopening the transatlantic slave trade, see Ronald T. Takaki, *Pro-Slavery Debate: The Movement to Reopen the African Slave Trade* (Berkeley and Los Angeles: University of California Press, 1967).

50. Kimberly R. Kellison, "Toward Humanitarian Ends? Protestants and Slave Reform in South Carolina, 1830–1865," *South Carolina Historical Magazine* 103, no. 3 (July 2002): 221; Clarke, *Dwelling Place*, 247–51.

51. Fraser, *Savannah in the Old South*, 314–17.

Chapter 4.

TO "VENERATE THE SPOT"

OF "AIRY VISIONS"

I gratefully acknowledge the advice, criticism, and assistance offered by Daina Ramey Berry, Christine Jacobson Carter, Leslie M. Harris, Charles Johnson, the exceptionally knowledgeable staff of the Telfair Museum of Art, and the anonymous reviewers who reported to the University of Georgia Press. Ryan Curran, a former student of mine at Georgia Southern University, conducted research on the Telfair plantations that sparked my interest in Mary Telfair's role in managing her family's slaveholding interests.

1. Mary Telfair to Mary Few, June 9, 1828, in Betty Wood, ed., *Mary Telfair to Mary Few: Selected Letters, 1802–1844* (Athens: University of Georgia Press, 2007), 80–81; unless otherwise noted, subsequent references to the Telfair-Few correspondence are cited by page numbers in this volume. Although the carriage ran over the driver's legs when he fell from his seat, he survived the incident without serious injury.

2. On the rise of proslavery thought in the nineteenth century, see, in particular, Lacy K. Ford, *Deliver Us from Evil: The Slavery Question in the Old South* (Oxford: Oxford University Press, 2009), chap. 3.

3. Jeffrey Robert Young, *Domesticating Slavery: The Master Class in Georgia and South Carolina, 1670–1837* (Chapel Hill: University of North Carolina Press, 1999), 80, 127, 107 (quotations).

4. For Telfair's life story, see the meticulously researched biography by Charles J. Johnson Jr., *Mary Telfair: The Life and Legacy of a Nineteenth-Century Woman* (Savannah: Beil, 2002), and Wood's introduction to *Mary Telfair to Mary Few*, xi–xxxix. For the role of slavery in early national politics, see Matthew Mason, *Slavery and Politics in the Early American Republic* (Chapel Hill: University of North Carolina Press, 2006).

5. Wood, *Mary Telfair to Mary Few*, xiv–xv. Quotations are from William Few to Edward Telfair, June 30, 1804, in the Gilder Lehrman Document Collection, GLC04842.05, courtesy of the Gilder Lehrman Institute of American History. Despite this attack on the poor judgment of Georgia slaveholders, Few regretted that the northern agenda would undermine the compromises on which the Constitution had been framed. He also, for good measure, sought compensation for one of his former slaves who had improperly been

claimed by another person. For the political debate over the question of the African slave trade, see Ford, *Deliver Us from Evil*, chaps. 1–2.

6. Telfair to Few, January 26, 1840, 197.

7. Telfair to Few, August 4 [1813], 10–11.

8. "Barren wastes" is from ibid.; subsequent quotations are from Telfair to Few, June 1, 1818, 37.

9. Telfair to Few, December 3, 1823, 49.

10. First part of the quotation is from ibid.; "Yankee" quotations are from Telfair to Few, August 14, 1836, 161.

11. The "*sable* tribe" quotation is from Telfair to Few, October 19, 1812, 7; other quotations are from Telfair to Few, January 17, 1815, 22, and Telfair to Few, January 30, 1836, 157.

12. Telfair to Few, n.d., 263; Telfair to Few, April 23, c. 1834, 283.

13. Telfair to Few, December 15, c. 1840, 293; Telfair to Few, c. 1841–42, 296; and Telfair to Few, July 4, 1827, 67. For the extent to which fears of a slave insurrection rippled through the Savannah community as a whole, see Thomas Usher Pulaski to Edward Telfair, 16 November 1806, Edward Telfair Papers, folder 3, Georgia Historical Society, Savannah.

14. Telfair to Few, c. 1826, 62. For the role played by romanticism in southern literary and intellectual life, see Michael O'Brien, *Conjectures of Order: Intellectual Life and the American South, 1810–1860*, 2 vols. (Chapel Hill: University of North Carolina Press, 2003). Telfair's taste in authors was hardly unusual in Savannah during this period. George Welshman Owens, for example, placed busts of Scott and Byron in the front entry of his Regency mansion; see Tania June

Sammons, *The Owens-Thomas House* (Savannah: Telfair Books, 2009), 18.

15. Telfair to Few, November 12, c. 1828, 256; Telfair to Few, March 15, 1820, 42; Telfair to Few, October 28, 1814, 17.

16. For the issues raised by Telfair's spinsterhood, see Christine Jacobson Carter, "Indispensable Spinsters: Maiden Aunts in the Elite Families of Savannah and Charleston," in *Negotiating Boundaries of Southern Womanhood: Dealing with the Powers That Be*, ed. Janet L. Coryell et al. (Columbia: University of Missouri Press, 2000), 110–34, and Carter's excellent monograph on this topic, *Southern Single Blessedness: Unmarried Women in the Urban South, 1800–1865* (Urbana: University of Illinois Press, 2006).

17. Telfair to Few, March 27, c. 1828, 79; Telfair to Few, January 30, 1835, 151.

18. Young, *Domesticating Slavery*, 133–40.

19. See, for example, Telfair to Few, October 19, 1812, 6–7; Telfair to Few, January 25, 1828, 72; Telfair to Few, February 5, 1828, 75.

20. Telfair to Few, October 19, 1812, 7; Telfair to Few, 13 December [1836], quoted in Johnson, *Mary Telfair*, 122; Telfair to Few, 27 March [1829], 89.

21. Telfair to Few, August 20, 1811, 3.

22. Telfair to Few, January 29, [c. 1831], 102. The quotation is from Shakespeare, *The Tempest*, 4.1.151.

23. Telfair to Few, June 12, [1813], 8. As Mary Telfair's generation had already realized, this epic, part of the Ossian cycle, was actually the work of an eighteenth-century author, James Macpherson; see Hugh Trevor-Roper, *The Invention of*

Scotland: Myth and History (New Haven, Conn.: Yale University Press, 2009).

24. On the disasters besetting Savannah during the early national era, see Walter J. Fraser Jr., *Savannah in the Old South* (Athens: University of Georgia Press, 2003), chap. 5.

25. Telfair to Few, September 18, 1819, 39; Telfair to Few, January 4, c. 1833, 114.

26. Telfair to Few, July c. 1814, 15; Telfair to Few, January 14, c. 1814, 253.

27. Telfair to Few, March 30, 1839, 191. Telfair actually associated these words of mourning with a suffering widow, Mrs. Phillips. The lines are loosely quoted from Byron's *Childe Harold's Pilgrimage*.

28. Telfair to Few, July 9, 1833, 122–23.

29. Quoted in Johnson, *Mary Telfair*, 259.

30. For "airy visions" and Telfair's inclination to "venerate the spot" associated with "Times of yore," see Telfair to Few, January 17, 1815, 20. The other quotations were excerpted by Telfair from Selleck Osborn's poem "The Ruins"; see the Commonplace Book, c. 1816, Telfair Family Papers, box 6, folder 57, item 255, Georgia Historical Society.

31. Telfair to Few, May 26, c. 1823, 254. The Few quotation is from Johnson, *Mary Telfair*, 154.

32. Telfair to Few, January 26, 1843, 235; Telfair to Few, March 5, c. 1841, 212–13.

33. Telfair to Few, January c. 1836, 155; Telfair to Few, May 23, 1838, 183. For Telfair's agrarian hostility to urban corruption, see Telfair to Few, August 4, [1813], 11. Telfair did on one occasion reverse the sectional stereotype, characterizing "the Southward" residents as being "only fit *for money*

making Genius" (Telfair to Few, June 1, 1818, 37). More characteristic was her condemnation of the Yankee influence in Savannah; see Telfair to Few, November 26, 1814, 18.

34. Telfair to Few, c. 1841–42, 295.

35. Telfair to Few, December 12, [1842], 232.

36. Telfair to Few, November 16, c. 1838, 289; Telfair to Few, May 27, 1840, 207.

37. See, for example, Frederick Douglass, *Narrative of the Life of Frederick Douglass, an American Slave, Written by Himself* (Boston: The Anti-Slavery Society, 1845), appendix, in which he decries how the supposedly religious slaveholder could claim to be the "warm defender of the sacredness of the family relation" when he really "is the same that scatters whole families,—sundering husbands and wives, parents and children, sisters and brothers,—leaving the hut vacant, and the hearth desolate."

38. Mary Telfair to William Neyle Habersham, October 8, 1841, Telfair Family Papers, box 19, folder 174, Georgia Historical Society.

39. Telfair to Few, June 1, [1834], 138–39.

40. For Telfair's condemnation of Channing, see Telfair to Few, February 24, c. 1835, 286. She very much approved of the proslavery tract *Remarks on Dr. Channing's Slavery* (Boston, 1835), written by James Trecothick Austin in response to Channing's *Slavery* (Boston, 1835). The relationship between evangelical Christianity and proslavery thought can be seen in Elizabeth Fox-Genovese and Eugene D. Genovese, *The Mind of the Master Class: History and Faith in the Southern Slaveholders' World View* (Cambridge: Cambridge University

Press, 2005); Sylvia R. Frey and Betty Wood, *Come Shouting to Zion: African American Protestantism in the American South and British Caribbean to 1830* (Chapel Hill: University of North Carolina Press, 1998); and Jeffrey Robert Young, ed., *Proslavery and Sectional Thought in the Early South, 1740–1829: An Anthology* (Columbia: University of South Carolina Press, 2006).

41. For Telfair's perspective that the missions were improving slaves' religious sensibilities, see Telfair to Few, July 28, 1833, 125. Contrast this with the more pessimistic appraisal she made in Telfair to Few, March 27, [1829], 90.

42. Telfair to Few, February 10, 1843, 238. There was, however, a dynamic, progressive strand of proslavery thought surfacing in other slaveholders' correspondence during this era; see Eugene D. Genovese, *The Slaveholders' Dilemma: Freedom and Progress in Southern Conservative Thought, 1820–1860* (Columbia: University of South Carolina Press, 1992).

43. James Vernon McDonough, "William Jay: Regency Architect in Georgia and South Carolina" (PhD diss., Princeton University, 1950), chaps. 4–5; Hanna Hryniewiecka Lerski, *William Jay: Itinerant English Architect, 1792–1837* (Lanham, Md.: University Press of America, 1983), chap. 4; Page Talbott, *Classical Savannah: Fine and Decorative Arts, 1800–1840* (Savannah: Telfair Museum, 1995), 70–73.

44. *The Octagon Room* (Savannah: Telfair Academy of Arts and Sciences, 1982), quotation 9.

45. Telfair to Few, March 27, c. 1828, 78. For the extent to which the scandalous conduct of her great-niece contributed to her decision to bequeath considerable funds to the academy, see Johnson, *Mary Telfair*, chap. 1, and Carter, "Indispensable Spinsters," 125–29.

46. Quoted in Johnson, *Mary Telfair*, 330–31.

47. For evidence of the slaves' impatience with the paternalistic proslavery myth, see Harriet Jacobs, *Incidents in the Life of a Slave Girl* (Boston, 1861).

Chapter 5.

SLAVE LIFE IN SAVANNAH

1. Freeman Walker to Alexander Telfair, February 10, 1822, in Alexander Telfair Papers, MS 790, Georgia Historical Society, Savannah; *Biographical Dictionary of the United States Congress, 1774–Present*, s.v. "Walker, Freeman (1780–1827)," http://bioguide.congress.gov; Josephine Mellichamp, "Freeman Walker," in *Senators from Georgia* (Huntsville, Ala.: Strode, 1976), 85–90; Mary Carter Winter, "Dorothy Camber Walton," *Augusta Chronicle*, September 5, 1954; *New Georgia Encyclopedia*, s.vv. "George Walton (c. 1749–1804)" and "Telfair Family," http://www.georgiaencyclopedia.org.

2. Walker to Telfair, February 10, 1822.

3. For a fundamental definition of slavery, see Orlando Patterson, *Slavery and Social Death: A Comparative Study* (Cambridge, Mass.: Harvard University Press, 1985).

4. William Andrew Byrne, "The Burden and Heat of the Day: Slavery and Servitude in Savannah, 1733–1865" (PhD diss., Florida State University, 1979), chap. 3, especially 64, 70–79; Betty Wood, *Slavery in Colonial Georgia, 1730–1775*

(Athens: University of Georgia Press, 1984), 80–86, 112–30.

5. Glenn McNair, *Criminal Injustice: Slaves and Free Blacks in Georgia's Criminal Justice System* (Charlottesville: University of Virginia Press, 2009), 5; Richard C. Wade, *Slavery in the Cities: The South, 1820–1860* (New York: Oxford University Press, 1967), 180–83.

6. Byrne, "Heat of the Day," 254–63.

7. Ibid., 200–202.

8. Ibid., 189, 301.

9. Antonio's case in ibid., 103–4.

10. Ibid., 105.

11. Ibid., 189–90.

12. Whittington B. Johnson, *Black Savannah, 1788–1864* (Fayetteville: University of Arkansas Press, 1996), 126–31; Betty Wood, ed., *Mary Telfair to Mary Few: Selected Letters, 1802–1844* (Athens: University of Georgia Press, 2007), 125.

13. For David Walker's appeal in Milledgeville, Georgia, see Glenn McNair, "The Elijah Burritt Affair: David Walker's Appeal and Partisan Journalism in Antebellum Milledgeville," *Georgia Historical Quarterly* 83 (1999): 448–78.

14. "Jail Records 1855–1873," Chatham County, City Archives, Savannah, Georgia; see also Betty Wood, "Some Aspects of Female Resistance to Chattel Slavery in Low Country Georgia, 1763–1815," *Historical Journal* 30 (1987), 611, 618–22, and Wade, *Slavery in the Cities*, 183–97.

15. E. K. Love, *History of the First Baptist Church, from Its Organization, January 20th, 1788, to July 1st, 1888, including the Centennial Celebration, Addresses, Sermons, Etc.* (Savannah: Morning News Print, 1888), 2, available at Documenting the American South, http://docsouth.unc.edu/church/love/love.html; James M. Simms, *The First Colored Baptist Church in North America, Constituted at Savannah, Georgia, January 20, A.D. 1788, with Biographical Sketches of the Pastors* (Philadelphia: Lippincott, 1888), 20, available at Documenting the American South, http://docsouth.unc.edu/church/simms/simms.html.

16. Johnson, *Black Savannah*, 7–9; Simms, *First Colored Baptist Church*, 20–22; Andrew Marshall, letter dated July 19, 1790, in "Letters Showing the Rise and Progress of the Early Negro Churches of Georgia and the West Indies," *Journal of Negro History* 1 (1916): 77–78.

17. Simms, *First Colored Baptist Church*, 22–23.

18. Albert Raboteau, *Slave Religion: The "Invisible Institution" in the Antebellum South* (New York: Oxford University Press, 1978).

19. On the success of these congregations generally, see Johnson, *Black Savannah*, 1–35; on the population of these congregations, 22.

20. Wade, *Slavery in the Cities*, 75–79; Johnson, *Black Savannah*, 139–40; Byrne, "Heat of the Day," 119–22.

21. Charles Grandison Parsons, *An Inside View of Slavery, or A Tour among the Planters* (Boston: John P. Jewett and Company, 1855), 25–28.

22. Wade, *Slavery in the Cities*, 325–30.

23. See "Inventory of the Estate of George W. Owens, December 1856," Chatham County Court, folder 0-55, Wallace and Owens Family Papers, 1766–1885, #747, Southern Historical Collection, The Wilson Library, University of North Carolina at Chapel Hill.

24. Joseph K. Menn, "The Large Slaveholders

of the Deep South, 1860," 2 vols. (PhD diss., University of Texas at Austin, 1964).

25. Parsons, *Inside View*, 14–15.

26. See George S. Owens to his sister Sarah, 22 July 1857, Owens and Thomas Family Papers, Georgia Historical Society, and Page Talbott's unpublished manuscript "The Owens Family Occupancy: A Report of Furnishing the Owens-Thomas House, c. 1834" (2003).

27. Daniel T. Elliott, *Archaeological Investigations at Tabbies 1 and 2, North End Plantation, Ossabaw Island, Georgia*, Report 108 (Savannah: Lamar Institute, 2007).

28. George S. Owens to George Welshman Owens, July 13, 1852, in box 8, folder 74, National Society of the Colonial Dames of America in the State of Georgia Historical Collections, MS 965, Georgia Historical Society, Savannah. For the Houstouns, see Edith Duncan Johnston, *The Houstouns of Georgia* (Athens: University of Georgia Press, 1950), 310–11; Buddy Sullivan, *Early Days on the Georgia Tidewater: The Story of McIntosh County and Sapelo* (Darien, Ga.: Darien News, 1990), 238–39. Details of the murder are in the Owens letter and in "The Execution of Five Negroes for the Cruel Murder of Their Master," in James Holmes, M.D., Delma Eugene Presley, ed., *"Dr. Bullie's" Notes: Reminiscences of Early Georgia and of Philadelphia and New Haven in the 1800s* (Atlanta: Cherokee, 1976), 158–63.

29. McNair, *Criminal Injustice*.

30. An Act to Ameliorate the Criminal Code, and Conform the Same to the Penitentiary System, December 1811.

31. Giles v. State of Georgia, opinion of J. Ste-

phens, *Reports of Cases in Law and Equity*, 28: 465.

32. *Daily Georgian*, May 16, 1854.

33. Byrne, "Heat of the Day," 149–50; *Savannah Republican*, December 15, 1856.

34. "Cemeteries," in *A Digest of All the Ordinances of the City of Savannah*, ed. Charles S. Henry (Savannah: Purse's Print, 1854), 42–56. For information about Torlay, see John Walker Guss, *Savannah's Laurel Grove Cemetery* (Charleston: Arcadia, 2004), 18.

35. Johnson, *Black Savannah*; Genealogical Committee of the Georgia Historical Society, *Laurel Grove Cemetery, Savannah, Georgia*, vol. 1 (Savannah: Georgia Historical Society, 1993), 315–404.

Chapter 6.

FREE BLACK LIFE IN SAVANNAH

1. Ira Berlin, *Slaves without Masters: The Free Negro in the Antebellum South* (New York: Pantheon, 1974), 215, 280–81.

2. Janice L. Sumler-Edmond, *The Secret Trust of Aspasia Cruvellier Mirault: The Life and Trials of a Free Woman of Color in Antebellum Georgia* (Fayetteville: University of Arkansas Press, 2008), 13; Whittington B. Johnson, *Black Savannah, 1788-1864* (Fayetteville: University of Arkansas Press, 1996), 62.

3. Berlin, *Slaves without Masters*, 192–95.

4. Glenn McNair, *Criminal Injustice: Slaves and Free Blacks in Georgia's Criminal Justice System* (Charlottesville: University of Virginia Press, 2009), 40, 56; Johnson, *Black Savannah*, 38–40.

5. Sumler-Edmond, *Secret Trust*, 4.

6. Ibid., 3; McNair, *Criminal Injustice*, 56–57, 116–17.

7. Edward G. Wilson, ed., *A Digest of All the Ordinances of the City of Savannah* (Savannah: John M. Cooper, 1858), 175.

8. Wilson, *Ordinances of Savannah*, 174–75, 184; Oliver H. Prince, ed., *A Digest of Laws of the State of Georgia* (Milledgeville: Grantland & Orme, 1822), 459–560.

9. Johnson, *Black Savannah*, 108–9; Sumler-Edmond, *Secret Trust*, 10–11.

10. Tax Digests for Chatham County, 1806–14; see Parish Register of the Church of St. John the Baptist, 1796–1816 (microfilm, Georgia Department of Archives and History; hereafter cited as Parish Register of St. John). The Parish Registers of the Church of St. John the Baptist for 1796–1816 and 1816–1838 are housed within the sacramental records of the archives of the Roman Catholic Diocese of Savannah.

11. Parish Register of St. John. Church records indicate that Louis Mirault served as godfather for infants who were baptized; he served in that capacity for ceremonies on March 6, 1803, and on March 29, 1807. See also the Tax Digests for Chatham County, 1810, 1811, 1812.

12. Johnson, *Black Savannah*, 109; Account of Jessie S. (Grant) Stiles, #1354, and the Account of Eliza Ann (Grant) Habersham and the Account of Josiah H. Grant, #1605, all in the Registers of Signatures of Depositors in Branches of the Freedman's Savings and Trust Company, 1865–74, National Archives, Washington, D.C.; Tax Digests for Chatham County, 1819–1820.

13. Johnson, *Black Savannah*, 9–10, 79–80; Loren Schweninger, *Black Property Owners in the South, 1790–1915* (Chicago: University of Illinois Press, 1990), 65–66.

14. Austin D. Washington, "The Dollys: An Antebellum Black Family of Savannah, Georgia," *Faculty Research Edition of the Savannah State College Bulletin* 26 (1972): 101–3; Benjamin Quarles, *The Negro in the American Revolution* (New York: Norton, 1973), 144–45.

15. Washington, "The Dollys," 102. Ira Berlin discusses the practice of blacks purchasing their relatives in *Slaves without Masters*, 55–56.

16. Records of the Dolly baptism and the Cruvellier-Redding wedding are in the Parish Register of St. John.

17. Prince, *Laws of Georgia*, 465.

18. Larry Koger, *Black Slaveowners: Free Black Slave Masters in South Carolina, 1790–1860* (Columbia: University of South Carolina Press, 1995), 80–101.

19. Wilson, *Ordinances of Savannah*, 175; Wilma King, *The Essence of Liberty: Free Black Women during the Slave Era* (Columbia: University of Missouri Press, 2006), 80.

20. U.S. Census, 1850; Johnson, *Black Savannah*, 79–80; King, *Essence of Liberty*, 76, 78–79; Tax Digests for Chatham County, 1806, 1812, 1816, 1837, 1854, and 1855; Sumler-Edmond, *Secret Trust*, 32.

21. Berlin, *Slaves Without Masters*, 55; Sumler-Edmond, *Secret Trust*, 23; Johnson, *Black Savannah*, 184; Richard Wade, *Slavery in the Cities: The South, 1820–1860* (New York: Oxford, 1964), 325–27.

22. Wilson, *Ordinances of Savannah*, 181–82.

23. Walter J. Fraser Jr., *Savannah in the Old South* (Athens: University of Georgia Press, 2002), 149–50.

24. Johnson, *Black Savannah*, 14; Fraser, *Savannah in the Old South*, 150.

25. William Harden, *Recollections of a Long and Satisfactory Life* (Savannah: Review Printing Company, 1934), 26–27, 32; Johnson, *Black Savannah*, 11–12; *Savannah City Directory*, 1859.

26. Fraser, *Savannah in the Old South*, 150.

27. Quoted in Thomas Paul Thigpen, "Aristocracy of the Heart: Catholic Lay Leadership in Savannah, 1820–1870" (PhD diss., Emory University, 1995), 571.

28. No. 231, Estate Records of Louis Mirault, May 1828, Court of the Ordinary, Chatham County Superior Court Records Department, Savannah, Georgia; Tax Digests for Chatham County, 1809–1810; Johnson, *Black Savannah*, 62; see also the Register of the Free People of Color for the City of Savannah, Chatham County, Ga., 1817–1829.

29. Tax Digest for Chatham County, 1827.

30. Sumler-Edmond, *Secret Trust*, 14; Whittington B. Johnson, "Free African American Women in Savannah: Affluence and Autonomy Amid Adversity," *Georgia Historical Quarterly* 76 (Summer 1992): 165; Registers of Free Persons of Color, 1817–1829, 1828–1835. Suzanne Lebsock, *The Free Women of Petersburg: Status and Culture in a Southern Town, 1784–1860* (New York: Norton, 1984), includes a chapter on free women of color in Virginia.

31. Johnson, *Black Savannah*, 127–128.

32. Wilson, *Ordinances of Savannah*, 182–83.

33. Johnson, *Black Savannah*, 128; Sumler-Edmond, *Secret Trust*, 49; U.S. Census of 1850 for the state of Georgia, Chatham County.

34. Lucius Q. C. Lamar, ed., *A Compilation of the Laws of the State of Georgia, 1810–1819* (Augusta: W. S. Hannon, 1821), 815; Schweninger, *Black Property Owners*, 63–65; McNair, *Criminal Injustice*, 168–69.

35. Prince, *Laws of Georgia*, 458–59; Johnson, *Black Savannah*, 47; Sumler-Edmond, *Secret Trust*, 5, 44, 46; Thigpen, "Aristocracy of the Heart," 274.

36. Berlin, *Slaves without Masters*, 94; Sumler-Edmond, *Secret Trust*, 6–7.

37. Immediately following the Civil War, there were six fire companies manned by blacks. Four were still using hand engines, and two were called axe companies. The fire apparatus of the white companies included steam engines (either first, second or third class); see F. D. Lee and J. L. Agnew, *Historical Record of the City of Savannah* (Savannah: J. H. Estill, 1869), 153–54; Wilson, *Ordinances of Savannah*, 174; Johnson, *Black Savannah*, 120; Harden, *Recollections of a Long Life*, 19.

38. Sumler-Edmond, *Secret Trust*, 7–8.

39. Prince, *Laws of Georgia*, 469; Johnson, *Black Savannah*, 15, 73–74, 82.

40. Sumler-Edmond, *Secret Trust*, 21, 85–86; *Oliver v. Swoll*, in 61 *Georgia Reports* 248 (1878).

41. Johnson, *Black Savannah*, 80–81.

42. Wilson, *Ordinances of Savannah*, 173, 181.

43. Ibid., 180–81.

44. Johnson, *Black Savannah*, 46–47; Sumler-Edmond, *Secret Trust*, 15.

Chapter 7.

WARTIME WORKERS, MONEYMAKERS

1. See the front pages of the *Savannah Republican* for January 1863; Jacqueline Jones, *Saving Savannah: The City and the Civil War* (New York: Alfred A. Knopf, 2008).

2. Mills Lane, ed., *"Dear Mother: Don't Worry About Me. If I Get Killed, I'll Only Be Dead": Letters from Georgia in the Civil War* (Savannah: Beehive, 1990), 15, 39, 82–88, 93–115.

3. On the white Sheftalls, see Mark I. Greenberg, "Becoming Southern: The Jews of Savannah, Georgia, 1830–1870," *American Jewish History* 86 (1998): 55–75; Saul Jacob Rubin, *Third to None: The Saga of Savannah Jewry, 1733–1983* (Savannah: S. J. Rubin, 1983); David T. Morgan, "The Sheftalls of Savannah," *American Jewish Historical Quarterly* 63 (June 1973): 348–61; Malcolm H. Stern, "The Sheftall Diaries: Vital Records of Savannah Jewry, 1733–1808," *American Jewish Historical Quarterly* 54 (March 1965): 242–77.

4. Jackson B. Sheftall's grandson was named Jackson Benjamin Sheftall; see Rubin, *Third to None*, 89. Biographical information comes from the 1860 federal manuscript census for Savannah, Chatham County, Georgia, and from Report #9, office 623, Records of the U.S. House of Representatives, 1871–1880, *Claims Disallowed by Commissioners of Claims* (Southern Claims Commission), Record Group 233, National Archives, Washington, D.C. (hereinafter cited as J. B. Sheftall file, *Claims Disallowed*).

5. J. B. Sheftall file, *Claims Disallowed*.

6. Ibid. The quotation is from R. B. Avery, one of the claims commissioners assigned to Sheftall's case.

7. J.B. Sheftall file, *Claims Disallowed*; Dylan C. Penningroth, *The Claims of Kinfolk: African-American Property and Community in the Nineteenth-Century South* (Chapel Hill: University of North Carolina Press, 2003); Philip D. Morgan, "The Ownership of Property by Slaves in the Mid-Nineteenth Century Low Country," *Journal of Southern History* 49 (August 1983): 399–420.

8. J. B. Sheftall file, *Claims Disallowed*.

9. Robert Manson Myers, ed., *The Children of Pride: A True Story of Georgia and the Civil War* (New Haven, Conn.: Yale University Press, 1971), 523–25; Timothy J. Lockley, "Trading Encounters between Non-elite Whites and African Americans in Savannah, 1790–1860," *Journal of Southern History* 66 (February 2000): 25–48.

10. "reign": *New York Times*, September 1, 1861; "anarchical": George Mercer Diary, February 9, 1861, 55, in Mercer Family Papers, Georgia Historical Society, Savannah (hereafter cited as Mercer Diary).

11. See the mayors' annual reports for 1862 and 1863: "Report of Thomas Purse (Savannah, 1862) and "Report of Thomas Holcombe" (Savannah, 1863).

12. See William C. Davis, *Look Away! A History of the Confederate States of America* (New York: Free Press, 2003).

13. "Negroes wanted": *Savannah Republican*, September 4, 1862; city council minutes, December 19, 1861.

14. "are as": *New York Times*, January 16, 1861;

"It is": *Savannah Republican,* June 11, 1861; city council minutes, January 5, 1862; Jones, *Saving Savannah,* 135–36.

15. "impertinent": *New York Times,* January 16, 1861; "intelligent . . . enemy": Petition on behalf of "Committee of Citizens of 15 Dis. Lib. County," in *Freedom: A Documentary History of Emancipation, 1861–1867,* series 1, vol. 1: *The Destruction of Slavery,* ed. Ira Berlin, Barbara J. Fields, Thavolia Glymph, Joseph P. Reidy, and Leslie Rowland (Cambridge: Cambridge University Press, 1985), 795–98.

16. See the National Park Service, "The Civil War: Soldiers and Sailors Database," accessed March 1, 2011, http://www.itd.nps.gov/cwss/sailors_index.html.

17. City of Savannah, clerk of council, Registers of Free People of Color, drawer 81, reel 4, Georgia Archives, Morrow, Georgia.

18. Joseph E. Brown [governor] to John Screven, Esq. (filled-out form dated March 2, 1861), in Arnold and Screven Family Papers, Collection #3419, folder 72, Georgia Historical Society; city council minutes, October 23, 1861, and June 3, 1863.

19. Mercer Diary, August 19, 1862, 50; Clarence L. Mohr, *On the Threshold of Freedom: Masters and Slaves in Civil War Georgia* (Athens: University of Georgia Press, 1986), 121, 175–76; Susan E. O'Donovan, *Becoming Free in the Cotton South* (Cambridge, Mass.: Harvard University Press, 2007), 78–82; Myers, ed., *Children of Pride,* 878–82.

20. Mohr, *On the Threshold of Freedom,* 182.

21. "Report of Thomas Holcombe" (1863), 4–5.

22. "kept . . . selling it": scc Claim of Sarah Ann Black, #18222 (hereinafter, name of claimant and number of Chatham County claim); "he": Celia Boisfeillet, #3751.

23. "the business . . . dray": Toby Adams, #3928; "common . . . dray": David Moses, #15448; Charles Verene, #13364.

24. Rachel Brownfield, #13361; "I hired": Stephen Geldersleeve, #20083; James Custard, #16978.

25. "I was": James Custard, #16978; Thomas Garrett, #1290; John Hammond Moore, "Notes and Documents: Sherman's 'Fifth Column': A Guide to Unionist Activity in Georgia," *Georgia Historical Quarterly* 68 (Fall 1984): 382–409.

26. J. B. Sheftall file, *Claims Disallowed.*

27. Diana Cummings, #18901; Anthony Owens, #18095; "All": *Savannah Republican,* January 4, 1865.

28. See Jones, *Saving Savannah.*

29. Biographical information comes from the 1860 and 1870 federal manuscript censuses for Savannah; signature cards of the Savannah branch of the Freedman's Savings and Trust Company, 1865–74; and deposit ledgers in the branches of the Freedman's Savings and Trust Company, 1865–74, Records of the Bureau of Refugees, Freedmen, and Abandoned Lands, Record Group 105, National Archives.

30. Thomas Garrett, #1290; Sandy Small, #3931; Georgiana Guard Kelley, #15586; J. B. Sheftall, *Claims Disallowed.*

31. "on account": Abraham Johnson, #3930; "doubtful": Harriet Dallas, #15213; "Some doubt": Toby Adams, #3928.

32. Georgiana Guard Kelley, #15586; "I was a Union": claim of Madison Smith, testimony of James D. Polite, Report #9, Office 628, *Claims Disallowed*.

33. "I don't": April Walford, #16007; "He": Madison Smith, Report #9, Office 628, *Claims Disallowed*; "I don't owe my old master": Peter Miller, #18904.

34. For the list of eighty interrogatories, see "The Southern Claims Commission Papers: Question Sheet Used in Depositions," accessed December 18, 2011, http://vshadow.vcdh.virginia.edu/claims/SCC_questions.html.

35. Claim of J. B. Sheftall, *Claims Disallowed*.

36. Ibid.

37. Ibid., testimony of Andrew McDowell.

38. Federal manuscript censuses for Savannah, 1870 and 1880. On Jackson B. Sheftall and his family, see the *Savannah Tribune*, March 17, 1894; July 15, 1893; August 26, 1899; and April 7, 1900.

Chapter 8.

"WE DEFY YOU!"

1. F. D. Lee and J. L. Agnew, *Historical Record of the City of Savannah* (Savannah: J. H. Estill, 1869), 99–100.

2. For an example of criticism of the city's surrender, see the *Savannah Republican*, March 6, 1865, quoting the *Augusta Constitutionalist*.

3. John F. Marszalek, *Sherman: A Soldier's Passion for Order* (New York: Free Press, 1995), 312–15; William Tecumseh Sherman, *Memoirs of General W. T. Sherman* (New York: Appleton, 1875, 1886; reprint, New York: Library of America, 1990), 722–25.

4. Sherman, *Memoirs*, 725.

5. *The War of the Rebellion: A Compilation of the Official Records of the Union and Confederate Armies*, 130 vols. (Washington: 1880–1901), series 1, vol. 47, part 2, 37–41; Sherman, *Memoirs*, 725–27; James M. Simms, *The First Colored Baptist Church in North America* (Philadelphia: Lippincott, 1888), 137–38. Simms did not attend, but he remembered the meeting; however, he dated it incorrectly.

6. William A. Byrne, "'Uncle Billy' Sherman Comes to Town: The Free Winter of Black Savannah," *Georgia Historical Quarterly* 79, no. 1 (Spring 1995): 111–13; *Savannah Republican*, January 23, 1865; *Savannah Daily Herald*, January 24, 1865. In *Saving Savannah: The City and the Civil War* (New York: Alfred A. Knopf, 2008), Jacqueline Jones suggests that Special Field Order No. 15 was simply an attempt to deal with the military problem of refugees. Sherman himself argued that all he intended was to "make temporary provisions for the freedmen and their families" (*Memoirs*, 730).

7. Byrne, "'Uncle Billy' Sherman," 112; *Savannah Daily Herald*, February 3, 1865.

8. The best account of the Sherman Reservation can be found in Paul A. Cimbala, *Under the Guardianship of the Nation: The Freedmen's Bureau and the Reconstruction of Georgia, 1865–1870* (Athens: University of Georgia Press, 1997), 166–92; for President Johnson's nullification of Special Field Order No. 15, see 173.

9. Jones, *Saving Savannah*, 225–26; *Statistics of the Population of the United States, Ninth Census*, vol. 1 (Washington, D.C.: Government Printing Office, 1872), 20–22, 100.

10. Sherman, *Memoirs*, 713–14.

11. See Michael P. Johnson, *Toward a Patriarchal Republic: The Secession of Georgia* (Baton Rouge: Louisiana State University Press, 1977) for a well-crafted account of how white elites used secession to enhance their power. There is not space in this essay to explain the continuity of city offices from 1865 to 1869, but for an account of how the mayor and city council remained virtually unchanged during that period, see Thomas Gamble Jr., *A History of the City Government of Savannah, Ga., from 1790 to 1901* (Savannah, 1900), 249–52, 261–67. See also Jones, *Saving Savannah*, 242–43, and Lisa L. Denmark, "At the Midnight Hour: Economic Dilemmas and Harsh Realities in Post-Civil War Savannah," *Georgia Historical Quarterly* 90, no. 2 (Fall 2006), 358, 363. An interesting discussion on the question of "Negro suffrage" appears in the *Savannah Daily Herald*, November 28, 1865.

12. *Savannah Republican*, May 29, July 3, and July 5, 1867; for an excellent account of the political and social struggles though 1867, see Jones, *Saving Savannah*, 213–301.

13. *The Condition of Affairs in Georgia: Statement of Hon. Nelson Tift to the Reconstruction Committee of the House of Representatives, Washington, February 18, 1869* (Freeport, N.Y.: Books for Libraries Press, 1971), 176; for an extended discussion of not just the law of slavery but also the late-antebellum racial justifications for slavery, see T. R. R. Cobb, *An Inquiry into the Law of Negro Slavery in the United States of America* (Philadelphia and Savannah, 1858).

14. *Savannah Daily News and Herald*, October 1 and 2, 1867.

15. *Savannah Daily News and Herald*, October 2, 22, 28, and 29, 1867; November 3 and 4, 1867; March 27 and 28, 1868; April 21, 22, 23, 24, and 29, 1868.

16. *Savannah Daily News and Herald*, August 31, 1868.

17. *Savannah Morning News*, October 28, 1868.

18. *Savannah Morning News*, October 28 and 29, 1868. The story of the New Orleans race riot of 1866 is told best in James G. Hollandsworth Jr., *An Absolute Massacre: The New Orleans Race Riot of July 30, 1866* (Baton Rouge: Louisiana State University Press, 2001).

19. *Savannah Morning News*, October 22, 23, and 27, 1868; *Savannah Daily Republican*, October 23, 1868; Georgia Constitution of 1868, Art. 1, sec. 29, and Art. 2, sec. 2.

20. *Savannah Morning News*, October 22, 23, 27, and 28, 1868; emphasis in the original.

21. James M. Simms's testimony, quoted in *Condition of Affairs in Georgia*, 7; Amherst Stone, quoted in *Condition of Affairs in Georgia*, 45. For voting strictures at the courthouse, see the *Savannah Morning News*, October 27, October 29, and November 2, 3, and 4, 1868; *Savannah Republican*, November 2, 3, and 4, 1868; *Condition of Affairs in Georgia*, 6–10, 38–39, 42–48, 49–50, 55–56.

22. *Condition of Affairs in Georgia*, 7, 44–50.

23. *Condition of Affairs in Georgia*, 7–8; *Sa-*

vannah Morning News, November 2 and 3, 1868; *Savannah Republican*, November 3, 1868.

24. *Savannah Morning News*, November 4, 1868; *Savannah Republican*, November 4, 1868.

25. *Savannah Morning News*, November 4 and 5, 1868; *Savannah Republican*, November 4 and 7, 1868; *Condition of Affairs in Georgia*, 8, 38, 50.

26. *Savannah Morning News*, November 4 and 5, 1868; *Savannah Republican*, November 4 and 7, 1868, *Condition of Affairs in Georgia*, 8, 55.

27. *Savannah Morning News*, November 4, 6, and 7, 1868; *Savannah Republican*, November 7, 1868.

28. *Savannah Morning News*, November 4–8, 1868; *Condition of Affairs in Georgia*, 137.

29. *Condition of Affairs in Georgia*, 55.

30. *Savannah Morning News*, November 4, 1868; *Condition of Affairs in Georgia*, 55.

31. *Savannah Morning News*, November 5, 1868; *Condition of Affairs in Georgia*, 39.

32. *Savannah Morning News*, November 4 and 5, 1868; *Savannah Republican*, November 4, 5, and 6, 1868.

33. *Savannah Morning News*, April 3, April 4, August 13, and August 31, 1869; Jones, *Saving Savannah*, 337, 338.

34. *Savannah Morning News*, October 4, 6, 9, 11, 12, 13, and 14, 1869.

35. The Freedmen's Bureau documented 336 "murders and assaults with intent to kill committed upon freed people in the State of Georgia from January 1, 1868, to November 15, 1868" (*Condition of Affairs in Georgia*, 123–39); see also Numan V. Bartley, *The Creation of Modern Georgia* (Athens: University of Georgia Press, 1990), 68; Edmund L. Drago, *Black Politicians and Reconstruction in Georgia: A Splendid Failure* (Baton Rouge: Louisiana State University Press, 1982), 55, 56, 148, 149; Jones, *Saving Savannah*, 342, 356, 357.

36. *Savannah Morning News*, July 29 and 30, 1872; Jones, *Saving Savannah*, 387, 389; Charles Lawanga Hoskins, *Yet with a Steady Beat: Biographies of Early Black Savannah* (Savannah: Gullah Press, 2001), 24, 117.

37. For the best account of the post–World War II struggle for civil rights in Savannah, see Stephen G. N. Tuck, *Beyond Atlanta: The Struggle for Racial Equality in Georgia, 1940–1980* (Athens: University of Georgia Press, 2001).

38. *Condition of Affairs in Georgia*, 9, 40.

Chapter 9.
"THE FIGHTING HAS NOT BEEN IN VAIN"

1. *Savannah Tribune*, January 7, 1893.

2. Ibid., January 6, 1893; June 4, 1892; October 16, 1892.

3. Ibid., April 29, 1893.

4. *Savannah Tribune*, July 13, 1912; *Macon Weekly Telegraph*, February 7, 1871, November 8, 1870; *Savannah Tribune*, January 25, 1913.

5. Whittington Johnson, *Black Savannah, 1788–1864* (Fayetteville: University of Arkansas Press, 1996); Jacqueline Jones, *Saving Savannah: The City and the Civil War* (New York: Alfred Knopf, 2008), 53, 217, 257, 378–79; Heather Andrea Williams, *Self-Taught: African American Education in Slavery and Freedom* (Chapel Hill: University of North Carolina Press, 1996), 28; *Augusta Chronicle*, July 31, 1872; *Savannah Tribune*, November 16, 1895; E. K. Love, *History of the*

First African Baptist Church, (Savannah: Morning News Print, 1888), 165; James M. Simms, *The First Colored Baptist Church in North America Constituted at Savannah, Georgia, January 20, A.D. 1788* (Philadelphia: Lippincott, 1888), 33–137; *New Orleans Tribune*, April 13, 1867.

6. *Macon Telegraph*, October 16, 1868.

7. U.S. House of Representatives, *Condition of Affairs in Georgia*, 40th Cong., 3rd sess. (1869), Misc. Doc. 52, 7–10; *New York Tribune*, March 20, 1869; *New York Times*, January 30, 1869; *Independent*, February 4, 1869; *Atlanta Constitution*, March 26, 1869.

8. *Savannah Tribune*, March 11, April 1, April 8, and April 15, 1876.

9. *Macon Telegraph*, April 5, 1882; Jones, *Saving Savannah*, 359, 392; *Savannah Tribune* November 9, 1895; Johnson, *Black Savannah*, 12, 127–28; Willard Gatewood, *Aristocrats of Color: The Black Elite, 1880–1920* (Bloomington: Indiana University Press, 1990), 91–92; Charles J. Elmore, *A Historical Guide to Laurel Grove Cemetery South* (Savannah: King-Tisdell Cottage Foundation, 1998), 27; *Savannah Tribune*, June 10, 1876.

10. *Savannah Tribune*, December 4, 1875; June 3, 1876.

11. *Christian Recorder*, April 3, 1884; *Savannah Echo*, quoted in the *Western Recorder*, August 31, 1883.

12. *The Colored Tribune*, June 10, 1876.

13. *Savannah Tribune*, March 19, 1892; John Matthews, "Studies in Race Relations in Georgia, 1890–1930" (PhD diss., Duke University, 1970), 80–81.

14. *Savannah Tribune*, November 18, 1899; *Augusta Chronicle*, November 4, 1899.

15. *Atlanta Constitution*, December 22, 1897; *Savannah Tribune*, December 25, 1897.

16. *Washington Bee*, January 18, 1908.

17. E. K. Love, *Wait on the Lord: A Discourse* (Augusta: Georgia Baptist Book and Job Print, 1882).

18. E. K. Love, *Oration Delivered on Emancipation Day, January 2nd 1888*, (Savannah: Savannah Tribune, 1888), 5–7.

19. *Macon Telegraph*, January 31, 1888; *Augusta Chronicle*, January 31, 1888; *Macon Telegraph*, January 25, 1888; Donald L. Grant, *The Way It Was in the South: The Black Experience in Georgia* (New York: Birch Lane, 1993), 134–35.

20. Cornel West and Eddie Glaude, *African American Religious Thought: An Anthology* (Louisville, Ky.: Westminster John Knox, 2003), 424; *Washington Bee*, November 9, 1889.

21. E. K. Love, *Emancipation Oration! Delivered by Rev. E. K. Love, D.D., Savannah, Ga., at the Emancipation Celebration, at Augusta, Georgia, January 1st, 1891* (Augusta: Georgia Baptist Job Press, 1891), 4–8.

22. *Savannah Tribune*, January 2, 1899.

23. *Atlanta Constitution*, January 2, 1897.

24. *Savannah Tribune*, June 6, 1896; June 24, 1899; July 22, 1899; November 2, 1899; May 6, 1899; July 17, 1897; June 27, 1903.

25. Wright to Grimke, April 27, 1899, in Carter G. Woodson, ed., *The Works of Francis J. Grimke* (Washington, D.C.: Associated Publishers, 1942), 60–61.

26. *Savannah Tribune*, June 16, 1906.

27. "Resolutions of Protest Against Negro

Disfranchisement, July 19, 1907," in Long-Rucker-Aiken Papers, box 17, Misc. Folder, Atlanta History Center; *Savannah Tribune*, August 3, 1907.

28. *Augusta Chronicle*, September 24, 1907.

29. *Savannah Tribune*, September 8, 1906; January 6, 1906.

30. Ibid., September 16, 1899; November 18, 1899.

31. *Savannah Morning News*, September 14, 1906; *Savannah Tribune*, April 20, 1907.

32. Linda O. Hines and Allen W. Jones, "A Voice of Black Protest: The Savannah's Men's Sunday Club, 1905–1911," *Phylon* 35 (1974): 194.

33. *Savannah Tribune*, May 20, 1905; May 27, 1905; June 17, 1905; June 24, 1905; July 1, 1905; July 8, 1905; August 26, 1905; September 2, 1905; Linda O. McMurry, *Recorder of the Black Experience: A Biography of Monroe Nathan Work* (Baton Rouge: Louisiana State University Press, 1985), 27–31; *Savannah Tribune*, February 27, 1909.

34. *Savannah Tribune*, February 23, 1917.

35. Ibid., February 24, 1917; April 14, 1917.

36. Ibid., February 24, 1917.

37. Ibid., September 15, 1917.

38. Ibid., April 20, 1918.

39. *Crisis*, April 1917, 285.

40. *Crisis*, April 1917, 285; May 1917, 18; *Savannah Tribune*, June 8, 1918; February 5, 1921; February 12, 1921; February 26, 1921; September 7, 1922.

41. *Savannah Tribune*, June 8, 1918; June 26, 1920; April 4, 1921; August 4, 1921.

42. In Elizabeth Lindsay Davis, *Lifting as They Climb* (Washington, D.C.: National Association of Colored Women, 1933), 245–46. The Savannah Federation of Negro Women's Clubs, established in 1918, met in the summer of 1921 at the St. Paul CME Church; see the program of the 3rd Annual Meeting of the Savannah Federation of Negro Women's Clubs, July 29, 1921; *Jet*, December 18, 1958.

43. *Savannah Tribune*, June 8, 1918.

44. Ibid., October 16, 1922; *Atlanta Daily World*, May 16, 1948.

45. *National Notes*, September 1927, 7–12; Adele Oltman, *Sacred Mission, Worldly Ambition: Black Christian Nationalism in the Age of Jim Crow* (Athens: University of Georgia Press, 2008), 102.

46. *Savannah Tribune*, December 11, 1920.

47. Ibid., April 7, 1917.

48. *Chicago Defender*, March 20, 1954.

49. Ibid., January 28, 1950; May 29, 1954; September 9, 1954; *Jet*, December 18, 1958.

Further Reading

SAVANNAH AND GEORGIA HISTORY

Allen, Patrick ed. *Literary Savannah*. Athens, Ga.: Hill Street, 1998.

Blassingame, John W. "Before the Ghetto: The Making of the Black Community in Savannah, Georgia, 1865–1880." *Journal of Social History* 6, no. 4 (Summer 1973): 463–88.

"Cemeteries." In *A Digest of All the Ordinances of the City of Savannah*, edited by Charles S. Henry, 42–56. Savannah: Purse's Print, 1854.

Clifton, James, ed. *Life and Labor on Argyle Island: Letters and Documents of a Savannah River Plantation, 1833–1867*. Savannah: Beehive Press, 1978.

Coleman, Kenneth. *A History of Georgia*. Athens: University of Georgia Press, 1991.

Cook, James F. *The Governors of Georgia, 1754–1995*. Rev. ed. Macon: Mercer University Press, 1995.

Fraser, Walter J., Jr. *Savannah in the Old South*. Athens: University of Georgia Press, 2002.

Granger, Mary, ed. *Savannah River Plantations*. Georgia Writer's Project. Savannah: Georgia Historical Society, 1947.

Grant, Donald Lee, and Jonathan Grant. *The Way It Was in the South: The Black Experience in Georgia*. Athens: University of Georgia Press, 2001.

Greenberg, Mark I. "Becoming Southern: The Jews of Savannah, Georgia, 1830–1870." *American Jewish History* 86 (1998): 55–75.

Guss, John Walker. *Savannah's Laurel Grove Cemetery*. Charleston, S.C.: Arcadia, 2004.

Haunton, Richard H. "Savannah in the 1850s." PhD diss., Emory University, 1968.

Hoskins, Charles Lwanga. *Out of Yamacraw and Beyond: Discovering Black Savannah*. Savannah: Gullah Press, 2002.

Johnson, Whittington B. *Black Savannah, 1788–1864*. Fayetteville: University of Arkansas Press, 1996.

Jones, Carmie M., ed. *Historic Savannah: A Survey of Significant Buildings in the Historic Districts of Savannah, Georgia*. 3rd ed. Savannah: Historic Savannah Foundation, 2005.

Lane, Mills B. *Savannah Revisited: History and Architecture*. 5th ed. Savannah: Beehive Press, 2001.

Morgan, David T. "The Sheftalls of Savannah." *American Jewish Historical Quarterly* 63 (June 1973): 348–61.

Morgan, Philip, ed. *African American Life in the Georgia Lowcountry: The Atlantic World and the Gullah Geechee*. Athens: University of Georgia Press, 2010.

Rubin, Saul Jacob. *Third to None: The Saga of Savannah Jewry, 1733–1983*. Savannah: S. S. Rubin, 1983.

Russell, Preston, and Barbara Hines. *Savannah: A History of Her People since 1733*. Savannah: Frederic C. Beil, 1992.

Simms, James M. *The First Colored Baptist Church in North America*. 1888; reprint, New York: Negro Universities Press, 1969.

Stern, Malcolm H. "The Sheftall Diaries: Vital Records of Savannah Jewry, 1733–1808." *American Jewish Historical Quarterly* 54 (March 1965): 242–77.

Vanstory, Burnette. *Georgia's Land of the Golden Isles*. 1956; reprint, Athens: University of Georgia Press, 1981.

NATIVE AMERICAN HISTORY

Miles, Tiya. *Ties That Bind: The Story of an Afro-Cherokee Family in Slavery and Freedom*. Berkeley and Los Angeles: University of California Press, 2005.

———. *The House on Diamond Hill: A Cherokee Plantation Story*. Chapel Hill: University of North Carolina Press, 2010.

Perdue, Theda. *Cherokee Women: Gender and Culture Change, 1700-1835*. Lincoln: University of Nebraska Press, 1998.

Saunt, Claudio. *A New Order of Things: Property, Power, and the Transformation of the Creek Indians, 1733-1816*. Cambridge: Cambridge University Press, 1999.

———. *Black, White, and Indian: Race and the Unmaking of an American Family*. New York: Oxford University Press, 2005.

Snyder, Christina. *Slavery in Indian Country: The Changing Face of Captivity in Early America*. New York: Harvard University Press, 2010.

COLONIAL ERA

Berlin, Ira. *Many Thousands Gone: The First Two Centuries of Slavery in Mainland North America*. Cambridge, Mass.: Harvard University Press, 1998.

Coleman, Kenneth. *Colonial Georgia: A History*. New York: Scribner, 1976.

Coulter, E. Merton. "The Acadians in Georgia." *Georgia Historical Quarterly* 47 (Spring 1963): 68–75.

Davis, Harold E. *The Fledgling Province: Social and Cultural Life in Colonial Georgia, 1733-1776*. Chapel Hill: University of North Carolina Press, 1976.

Gallay, Alan. *The Formation of a Planter Elite: Jonathan Bryan and the Southern Colonial Frontier*. Athens: University of Georgia Press, 1989.

Jackson, Carl Harvey H. and Phinizy Spalding, eds. *Forty Years of Diversity: Essays on Colonial Georgia*. Athens: University of Georgia Press, 1984.

Lambert, Frank. *James Habersham: Loyalty, Politics, and Commerce in Colonial Georgia*. Athens: University of Georgia Press, 2005.

Morgan, Philip D. *Slave Counterpoint: Black Culture in the Eighteenth-Century Chesapeake and Lowcountry*. Chapel Hill: University of North Carolina Press, 1998.

Pressly, Paul. *On the Rim of the Caribbean:*

Colonial Georgia and the British Atlantic World. Athens: University of Georgia Press, 2013.

Snyder, Holly. "A Tree with Two Different Fruits: The Jewish Encounter with German Pietists in the Eighteenth-Century Atlantic World." *William and Mary Quarterly*, 3rd ser., 58 (October 2001): 855–82.

Weeks, Solana. *Savannah in the Time of Peter Tondee*. Columbia, S.C.: Summerhouse Press, 1997.

Wood, Betty. *Slavery in Colonial Georgia, 1730–1775*. Athens: University of Georgia Press, 1984.

REVOLUTIONARY ERA

Coleman, Kenneth. *The American Revolution in Georgia, 1763–1789*. Athens: University of Georgia Press, 1958.

Frey, Sylvia. *Water from the Rock: Black Resistance in a Revolutionary Age*. Princeton, N.J.: Princeton University Press, 1991.

Gottschalk, Louis. *Lafayette between the American and the French Revolution*. Chicago: University of Chicago Press, 1950.

Hall, Leslie. *Land and Allegiance in Revolutionary Georgia*. Athens: University of Georgia Press, 2001.

Jackson, Harvey H. *Lachlan McIntosh and the Politics of Revolutionary Georgia*. Athens: University of Georgia Press, 1979.

Levy, B. H. *Mordecai Sheftall: Jewish Revolutionary Patriot*. Savannah: Georgia Historical Society, 1999.

Nell, William C. *The Colored Patriots of the American Revolution*. Boston: Wallcut, 1855.

Price, Richard, ed. *Maroon Societies: Rebel Slave Communities in the Americas*. 2nd ed. Baltimore: Johns Hopkins University Press, 1979.

Quarles, Benjamin. *The Negro in the American Revolution*. Chapel Hill: University of North Carolina Press, 1961.

TRANSATLANTIC AND
DOMESTIC SLAVE TRADE

Calonius, Erik. *The Wanderer: The Last American Slave Ship and the Conspiracy That Set Its Sails*. New York: St. Martin's, 2006.

Doesticks, Q. K. Philander. "Great Auction Sale of Slaves at Savannah, Georgia, March 2d and 3d, 1859." *New York Tribune*, March 9, 1859.

Eltis, David. *The Rise of African Slavery in the Americas*. Cambridge: Cambridge University Press, 1999.

Johnson, Walter, ed. *The Chattel Principle: Internal Slave Trades in the Americas*. New Haven, Conn.: Yale University Press, 2004.

McMillan, Richard. "Savannah's Coastal Slave Trade: A Quantitative Analysis of Ship Manifests, 1840–1850." *Georgia Historical Quarterly* 78 (Summer 1994): 339–59.

McMillin, James. *The Final Victims: Foreign Slave Trade to North America, 1783–1810*. Columbia: University of South Carolina Press, 2004.

Wax, Darold D. "'New Negroes Are Always in Demand': The Slave Trade in

Eighteenth-Century Georgia." *Georgia Historical Quarterly* 68 (Summer 1984): 193–220.

Wesley, Charles H. "Manifests of Slave Shipments along the Waterways, 1808–1864." *Journal of Negro History* 27 (April 1942): 155–74.

SLAVERY

Bell, Malcolm, Jr. *Major Butler's Legacy: Five Generations of a Slaveholding Family.* Athens: University of Georgia Press, 1987.

Bellamy, Donnie D., and Diane E. Walker. "Slaveholding in Antebellum Augusta and Richmond County, Georgia." *Phylon* 48 (1987): 165–77.

Berry, Daina Ramey. *Swing the Sickle for the Harvest Is Ripe: Gender and Slavery in Antebellum Georgia.* Urbana: University of Illinois Press, 2007.

Byrne, William A. "The Hiring of Woodson, Slave Carpenter of Savannah." *Georgia Historical Quarterly* 77 (Summer 1993): 245–63.

Chaplin, Joyce. *An Anxious Pursuit: Agricultural Innovation and Modernity in the Lower South, 1730–1815.* Chapel Hill: University of North Carolina Press, 1993.

———. "Creating a Cotton South in Georgia and South Carolina, 1760–1815." *Journal of Southern History* 57 (May 1991): 171–200.

———. "Tidal Rice Cultivation and the Problem of Slavery in South Carolina and Georgia, 1760–1815." *William and Mary Quarterly,* 3rd ser., 49 (January 1992): 29–61.

Clarke, Erskine. *Dwelling Place: A Plantation Epic.* New Haven, Conn.: Yale University Press, 2005.

Dusinberre, William. *Them Dark Days: Slavery in the American Rice Swamps.* New York: Oxford University Press, 1996.

Flanders, Ralph Betts. *Plantation Slavery in Georgia.* Chapel Hill: University of North Carolina Press, 1933.

Goldin, Claudia Dale. *Urban Slavery in the American South, 1820–1860: A Quantitative History.* Chicago: University of Chicago Press, 1976.

Gomez, Michael A. *Exchanging Our Country Marks: The Transformation of African Identities in the Colonial and Antebellum South.* Chapel Hill: University of North Carolina Press, 1998.

Harris, J. William. *Plain Folk and Gentry in a Slave Society: White Liberty and Black Slavery in Augusta's Hinterlands.* Middletown, Conn.: Wesleyan University Press, 1985.

Jennison, Watson W. *Cultivating Race: The Expansion of Slavery in Georgia, 1750–1860.* Lexington: University of Kentucky Press, 2012.

Joyner, Charles. *Remember Me: Slave Life in Coastal Georgia.* Atlanta: Georgia Humanities Council, 1989.

Lafayette College. *Lafayette and Slavery.* academicmuseum.lafayette.edu/special /specialexhibits/slaveryexhibit/onlineexhibit/ opener3.htm.

Lee, Anne S., and Everett S. Lee. "The Health of Slaves and the Health of Freedmen: A Savannah Study." *Phylon* 38 (1977): 170–80.

Little, Thomas J. "George Liele and the Rise of Independent Black Baptist Churches in the Lower South and Jamaica." *Slavery and Abolition* 16 (1995): 188–204.

Mason, Matthew. *Slavery and Politics in the Early American Republic*. Chapel Hill: University of North Carolina Press, 2006.

Morgan, Philip. "The Ownership of Property by Slaves in the Mid-Nineteenth Century Low Country." *Journal of Southern History* 49 (August 1983): 399–420.

———. "Work and Culture: The Task System and the World of Lowcountry Blacks, 1700 to 1880." *William and Mary Quarterly*, 3rd ser., 39 (October 1982): 563–99.

Olwell, Robert. *Masters, Slaves, and Subjects: The Culture of Power in the South Carolina Low Country, 1740–1790*. Ithaca, N.Y.: Cornell University Press, 1998.

Smith, Julia Floyd. *Slavery and Rice Culture in Low Country Georgia, 1750–1860*. Knoxville: University of Tennessee Press, 1985.

Starobin, Richard. *Industrial Slavery in the Old South*. New York: Oxford University Press, 1970.

Stewart, Mart A. *"What Nature Suffers to Groe": Life, Labor, and Landscape on the Georgia Coast, 1680–1920*. Athens: University of Georgia Press, 1996.

Twining, Mary A., and Keith E. Baird, eds. *Sea Island Roots: African Presence in the Carolinas and Georgia*. Trenton, N.J.: Africa World Press, 1991.

Wade, Richard. *Slavery in the Cities*. New York: Oxford University Press, 1964.

Wood, Betty. *Women's Work, Men's Work: The Informal Slave Economies of Lowcountry Georgia*. Athens: University of Georgia Press, 1995.

———. "Thomas Stephens and the Introduction of Black Slavery in Georgia." *Georgia Historical Quarterly* 58 (Spring 1974): 24–40.

Wood, Betty, and Ralph Gray. "The Transition from Indentured to Involuntary Servitude in Colonial Georgia." *Explorations in Economic History* 13, no. 4 (1976): 353–70.

Young, Jeffrey Robert. *Domesticating Slavery: The Master Class in Georgia and South Carolina, 1670–1837*. Chapel Hill: University of North Carolina Press, 1999.

ANTEBELLUM ERA

Armstrong, Thomas F. "From Task to Free Labor: The Transition along Georgia's Rice Coast, 1820–1880." *Georgia Historical Quarterly* 64 (Winter 1980): 432–47.

Brandon, Edgar Ewing, ed. *A Pilgrimage of Liberty*. Athens, Ohio: The Lawhead Press, 1944.

Campbell, Edward D. C., Jr., and Kym S. Rice, eds. *Before Freedom Came: African-American Life in the Antebellum South*. Richmond, Va.: Museum of the Confederacy, 1991.

Carey, Anthony Gene. *Parties, Slavery, and the Union in Antebellum Georgia*. Athens: University of Georgia Press, 1997.

Georgia Writers' Project. *Drums and Shadows: Survival Studies among the Georgia Coastal Negroes*. Athens: University of Georgia Press, 1940.

Gillespie, Michele. *Free Labor in an Unfree World: White Artisans in Slaveholding Georgia, 1789–1860*. Athens: University of Georgia Press, 2000.

Levasseur, Auguste. *Lafayette in America in 1824 and 1825, or, Journal of a Voyage to the United States*. Translated by John D. Godman. New York: Research Reprints, 1970.

Lockley, Timothy. *Lines in the Sand: Race and Class in Lowcountry Georgia, 1750–1860*. Athens: University of Georgia Press, 2001.

———. "Trading Encounters between Non-Elite Whites and African Americans in Savannah, 1790–1860." *Journal Southern History* 66, no. 1 (February 2000): 25–48.

Pruneau, Leigh Ann. "All the Time Is Work Time: Gender and the Task System on Antebellum Lowcountry Rice Plantations." PhD diss., University of Arizona, 1997.

Tuttle, Rand Wood. *Weepin' Time: Voices of Slavery in Coastal Georgia*. Bloomington, Ind.: iUniverse, 2010.

ANTEBELLUM FREE BLACKS

Alexander, Adele Logan. *Ambiguous Lives: Free Women of Color in Rural Georgia, 1789–1879*. Fayetteville: University of Arkansas Press, 1991.

Berlin, Ira. *Slaves without Masters: The Free Negro in the Antebellum South*. New York: Pantheon, 1974.

Hoskins, Charles Lwanga. *Yet with a Steady Beat: Biographies of Early Black Savannah*. Savannah: Gullah Press, 2001.

Johnson, Whittington B. "Free African-American Women in Savannah: Affluence and Autonomy amid Adversity." *Georgia Historical Quarterly* 76 (Summer 1992): 260–81.

———. "Free Blacks in Antebellum Savannah: An Economic Profile." *Georgia Historical Quarterly* 64 (Winter 1980): 418–31.

Leslie, Kent Anderson. *Woman of Color, Daughter of Privilege: Amanda America Dickson, 1849–1893*. Athens: University of Georgia Press, 1995.

McNair, Glenn. *Criminal Injustice: Slaves and Free Blacks in Georgia's Criminal Justice System*. Charlottesville: University of Virginia Press, 2009.

Schweninger, Loren. *Black Property Owners in the South, 1790–1915*. Chicago: University of Illinois Press, 1990.

Sumler-Edmond, Janice L. *The Secret Trust of Aspasia Cruvellier Mirault: The Life and Trials of a Free Woman of Color in Antebellum Georgia*. Fayetteville: University of Arkansas Press, 2008.

Sweat, Edward F. "The Free Negro in Ante-Bellum Georgia." PhD diss., Indiana University, 1957.

Walker, Juliet E. K. *The History of Black Business in America: Capitalism, Race, Entrepreneurship*. Vol. 1: *To 1865*. Chapel Hill: University of North Carolina Press, 2009.

CIVIL WAR, EMANCIPATION,
AND RECONSTRUCTION

Avery, I. W. *The History of the State of Georgia from 1850 to 1881*. New York: Brown and Derby, 1881.

Bryant, Jonathan M. *How Curious a Land: Conflict and Change in Greene County, Georgia, 1850–1880*. Chapel Hill: University of North Carolina Press, 1996.

Cimbala, Paul A. *Under the Guardianship of the Nation: The Freedmen's Bureau and the Reconstruction of Georgia, 1865–1870*. Athens: University of Georgia Press, 1997.

Conway, Alan. *The Reconstruction of Georgia*. Minneapolis: University of Minnesota Press, 1966.

Davis, William C. *Look Away! A History of the Confederate States of America*. New York: Free Press, 2003.

Drago, Edmund L. *Black Politicians and Reconstruction in Georgia: A Splendid Failure*. Baton Rouge: Louisiana State University Press, 1982.

Glymph, Thavolia. *Out of the House of Bondage: The Transformation of the Plantation Household*. New York: Cambridge University Press, 2008.

Heard, George Alexander. "St. Simons Island during the War between the States." *Georgia Historical Quarterly* 22 (Sept. 1938): 249–72.

Johnson, Michael P. *Toward a Patriarchal Republic: The Secession of Georgia*. Baton Rouge: Louisiana State University Press, 1977.

Jones, Jacqueline. *Saving Savannah: The City and the Civil War*. New York: Alfred A. Knopf, 2008.

Lane, Mills, ed. *"Dear Mother: Don't Worry About Me. If I Get Killed, I'll Only Be Dead": Letters from Georgia in the Civil War*. Savannah: Beehive Press, 1990.

Lawrence, Alexander A. *A Present for Mr. Lincoln: The Story of Savannah from Secession to Sherman*. Macon, Ga.: Ardivan, 1961.

Mohr, Clarence L. *On the Threshold of Freedom: Masters and Slaves in Civil War Georgia*. Athens: University of Georgia Press, 1986.

Moore, John Hammond. "Notes and Documents: Sherman's 'Fifth Column': A Guide to Unionist Activity in Georgia." *Georgia Historical Quarterly* 68 (Fall 1984): 382–409.

Myers, Robert Manson, ed. *The Children of Pride: A True Story of Georgia and the Civil War*. New Haven, Conn.: Yale University Press, 1972.

Nathans, Elizabeth Studley. *Losing the Peace: Georgia Republicans and Reconstruction, 1865–1871*. Baton Rouge: Louisiana State University Press, 1968.

O'Donovan, Susan Eva. *Becoming Free in the Cotton South*. Cambridge, Mass.: Harvard University Press, 2007.

Osthaus, Carl R. *Freedmen, Philanthropy, and Fraud: A History of the Freedman's Savings Bank*. Urbana: University of Illinois Press, 1976.

Reidy, Joseph P. *From Slavery to Agrarian*

Capitalism in the Cotton Plantation South: Central Georgia, 1800–1880. Chapel Hill: University of North Carolina Press, 1992.

Shadgett, Olive Hall. *The Republican Party in Georgia from Reconstruction through 1900.* Athens: University of Georgia Press, 1964.

Smith, Jennifer Lund. "'Twill Take Some Time to Study When I Get Over': Varieties of African American Education in Reconstruction Georgia." PhD diss., University of Georgia, 1997.

Taylor, Susie King. *Reminiscences of My Life in Camp with the 33rd U.S. Colored Troops.* 1902; reprint, Athens: University of Georgia Press, 2006.

Thompson, C. Mildred. *Reconstruction in Georgia: Economic, Social, Political, 1865–1872.* New York: Columbia University Press, 1915.

AFTER RECONSTRUCTION

Autrey, William Robert. "The Negro Press—Southern Style Militancy: The *Atlanta Independent* and *Savannah Tribune*, 1904–1928." MA thesis, Atlanta University, 1963.

Campbell, Walter E. "Profit, Prejudice, and Protest: Utility Competition and the Generation of Jim Crow Streetcars in Savannah, 1905–1907." *Georgia Historical Quarterly* 70 (1986): 197–231.

Cooper, Jerry. *The Rise of the National Guard: The Evolution of the American Militia 1865–1920.* Lincoln: University of Nebraska Press, 1997.

Dittmer, John. *Black Georgia in the Progressive Era, 1900–1920.* Urbana: University of Illinois Press, 1977.

Duncan, Russell. *Freedom's Shore: Tunis Campbell and the Georgia Freedmen.* Athens: University of Georgia Press, 1986.

Elmore, Charles J. *Richard R. Wright, Sr., at GSIC, 1891–1921: A Protean Force for the Social Uplift and Higher Education of Black Americans.* Savannah: C. J. Elmore, 1996.

Glasrud, Bruce A. *Brothers to the Buffalo Soldiers: Perspectives on the African American Militia and Volunteers, 1865–1917.* Columbia: University of Missouri Press, 2011.

Hall, Clyde W. *One Hundred Years of Education at Savannah State College, 1890–1990.* East Peoria, Ill.: Versa Press, 1991.

Hines, Linda O., and Allen W. Jones. "A Voice of Black Protest: The Savannah Men's Sunday Club, 1905–1911." *Phylon* 35 (1974): 193–202.

Hoskins, Charles Lwanga. *The Trouble They Seen: Profiles in the Life of Col. John H. Deveaux, 1848–1909.* Savannah: St. Matthews Church, 1989.

Johnson, Charles, Jr. *African American Soldiers in the National Guard: Recruitment and Deployment during Peacetime and War.* Westport, Conn.: Greenwood, 1992.

Kousser, J. Morgan. *The Shaping of Southern Politics: Suffrage Restriction and the Establishment of the One-Party South, 1880–1910.* New Haven, Conn.: Yale University Press, 1974.

Patton, June O. "Major Richard Robert Wright, Sr., and Black Higher Education in Georgia,

1880–1920." PhD diss., University of Chicago, 1980.

Perdue, Robert E. *The Negro in Savannah, 1865–1900*. New York: Exposition Press, 1973.

Proctor, Samuel, and Louis Schmeir, eds. *Jews of the South: Selected Essays from the Southern Jewish Historical Society*. Macon, Ga.: Mercer University Press, 1984.

Wright, Richard R. *A Brief Historical Sketch of Negro Education in Georgia*. Savannah: Robinson Printing House, 1894.

Wright, Richard R. Jr. *Eighty-Seven Years Behind the Black Curtain: An Autobiography*. Philadelphia: Rare Book Company, 1965.

OWENS-THOMAS HOUSE

Coleman, Feay Shellman. *Nostrums for Fashionable Entertainment: Dining in Georgia, 1800–1850*. Savannah: Telfair Academy of Arts and Sciences, 1992.

Costen, Ralph. "George Welshman Owens: Attorney, Planter, Politician, Family Man, 1786–1856." In *Savannah Biographies: A Collection of Unedited Biographies Written by History Students at Armstrong State College, Savannah, Ga.*, vol. 12, 1985.

Goff, John H. "Across Georgia with LaFayette." *Georgia Review* 17 (Summer 1963): 193–205.

Sammons, Tania June. *The Owens-Thomas House*. Savannah: Telfair Books, 2009.

TELFAIR FAMILY

Coulter, E. Merton. "Edward Telfair." *Georgia Historical Quarterly* 20 (June 1936): 99–124.

Johnson, Charles J., Jr. *Mary Telfair: The Life and Legacy of a Nineteenth-Century Woman*. Savannah: Frederic C. Beil, 2002.

Wood, Betty, ed. *Mary Telfair to Mary Few: Selected Letters, 1802–1844*. Athens: University of Georgia Press, 2007.

Contributors

JENIFER L. BARCLAY is a visiting assistant professor at Washington State University. She received her PhD in 2011 from Michigan State University. She is a former University of Virginia Carter G. Woodson Institute predoctoral fellow and Case Western Reserve University postdoctoral fellow in African American Studies. Her current book project, "The Mark of Slavery: The Stigma of Disability, Race and Gender in Antebellum America," examines the social relations of disability among enslaved people, as well as the metaphorical intersection of disability, race, and gender in antebellum law, medicine, politics, and popular culture.

KAREN COOK BELL is an assistant professor of African American history at Bowie State University. Her scholarship has appeared in the *Journal of African American History*; *Georgia Historical Quarterly*; *U.S. West-Africa: Interaction and Relations*; *Before Obama: A Reappraisal of Black Reconstruction Era Politicians*; and *Converging Identities: Blackness in the Contemporary Diaspora*. Her research interests include gender and labor history.

DAINA RAMEY BERRY is an associate professor of history and African and African diaspora studies and is the George W. Littlefield Fellow in American History at the University of Texas at Austin. She is the author of *Swing the Sickle for the Harvest is Ripe: Gender and Slavery in Antebellum Georgia* and editor in chief of the award-winning *Enslaved Women in America: An Encyclopedia*. Her current book project, "The Price for Their Pound of Flesh," is a comprehensive study of slave valuation in the South.

TRACEY JEAN BOISSEAU is director of Women's Studies and associate professor of U.S. women's history at Purdue University. She is the author of *White Queen: May French Sheldon and the Imperial Origins of American Feminist Identity* and the coeditor of *Gendering the Fair*; *Feminist Legal History*; and "New Orleans: A Special Issue on Gender and the Politics of Place and Displacement" for the *National Women's Studies Association Journal*. Boisseau has published her research on Susie King Taylor in *thirdspace: a Journal of Feminist Theory and Culture*. Additional research appears in *Signs: Journal of Women in Culture and Society*; *Gender and History*; and *Women's History Review*.

JONATHAN M. BRYANT teaches history at Georgia Southern University. He is the author of *How Curious a Land: Conflict and Change in Greene County, Georgia, 1850–1885*. His new book, *Dark Places of the Earth: The Voyage of the Slave Ship Antelope*, will be published in 2014.

ERIK CALONIUS is a former foreign correspondent for the *Wall Street Journal* and writer for *Fortune* magazine. He is the author of several books, including *The Wanderer: The Last American Slave Ship and the Conspiracy that Set Its Sails.*

FEAY SHELLMAN COLEMAN teaches in the History Department at the University of Cincinnati. She previously served as the chief curator of the Telfair Museum of Art. Her research centers on Savannah's art, architecture, and culture. Publications on Savannah topics include *William E. Wilson: Deep South Photographer*; *The Octagon Room*; *Christopher P. H. Murphy (1869–1939): A Retrospective*; "Melchers and the Telfair Academy: The Evolution of a Collection" in *Gari Melchers: A Retrospective Exhibition*, *Nostrums for Fashionable Entertainments*; *Dining in Georgia, 1800–1850*; *Looking Back: Art in Savannah, 1900–1960*; and *Picturing Savannah: The Art of Christopher A. D. Murphy.* She is currently completing a manuscript titled "'The Palmy Days of Trade': Anglo-American Culture in Savannah, 1735–1835."

ALISHA M. CROMWELL is a PhD candidate at the University of Georgia. She is currently conducting archival research funded by the 2013 Gregory Research Grant for her dissertation, which will focus on how enslaved women assimilated West African marketing techniques into southern market spaces.

KWESI DEGRAFT-HANSON graduated in 2013 with a PhD in interdisciplinary studies from the Graduate Institute of the Liberal Arts at Emory University. His research explores intersections of African American history, culture, and literature in colonial and antebellum slavery in the American South. His focus is on what he terms "hidden landscapes of slavery"—places and spaces, such as some former plantations and slave auction sites in the American South, that are unmarked and without commemoration. He researches historical and contemporary maps and texts for spatial, architectural, and cultural information to facilitate remapping and reimaging their landscapes and recreates them as virtual sites that allow commemorative attention toward the enslaved persons who inhabited them. His most recent publication, "Unearthing the Weeping Time: Savannah's Ten Broeck Race Course and 1859 Slave Sale," was published in *Southern Spaces.*

BOBBY J. DONALDSON is an associate professor of history, the faculty principal of Preston Residential College, and the director of the African American Documentary Initiative at the University of South Carolina–Columbia. In addition to teaching and publishing articles and essays on African American education, religion, and civil rights, Donaldson has served as a curator and consultant for numerous museum exhibitions, historic preservation projects, oral histories, documentary films, and archival collections. He is the author of the forthcoming *In Our Defense: Black Intellectuals in the Jim Crow South.*

MARK R. FINLAY was a professor of history at Armstrong Atlantic State University. His book *Growing American Rubber: Strategic Plants and the Politics of National Security* won the Agricultural History Society's Theodore Saloutos Memorial award as the best book published in the field in

2009. His other publications examined various issues at the intersection of industrial and environmental history, including a study of the Savannah Ogeechee Canal.

WALTER J. FRASER JR. is professor and chair emeritus at Georgia Southern University and has also taught at The Citadel. His numerous books include *Savannah in the Old South* and *Charleston! Charleston! The History of a Southern City*. He is currently at work on "Savannah in the New South."

HILARY N. GREEN is an assistant professor of history at Elizabeth City State University, where she teaches undergraduate courses in African American history, the American Civil War, Reconstruction, and world history. She has a forthcoming essay in *The Urban South During the Civil War Era*, edited by Andrew L. Slap and Frank Towers. She is currently at work on a book manuscript on the development of African American public schools in Richmond, Virginia, and Mobile, Alabama, and an article on the role of tourism in legitimating African American public schools in Richmond, Virginia, 1865–1885.

CORRIE HAND is a student at Georgia State University, where she is pursuing her PhD in eighteenth- and nineteenth-century U.S. history. Her research centers on political, vigilante, and racial violence in the American South.

LESLIE M. HARRIS is associate professor of history and African American studies and Winship Distinguished Research Professor at Emory University. She is the author of the award-winning *In the Shadow of Slavery: African Americans in New York City, 1626–1863* and coeditor with Ira Berlin of *Slavery in New York*, which accompanied the groundbreaking New-York Historical Society exhibition of the same name.

DAWN HERD-CLARK is an associate professor of history at Fort Valley State University, where she teaches African American history. Her forthcoming publications include the introduction to *T. Thomas Fortune's "After War Times": An African American Childhood in Reconstruction Era Florida* and the coauthored "The Troubled Asset Relief Program (TARP): What Has It Accomplished in the Obama Era?" in a special issue of *Race, Gender & Class*.

ALAN R. HOFFMAN, a practicing attorney, holds a BA in history from Yale University, where he studied under Edmund Morgan, and a JD degree from Harvard Law School. He is the translator of the first unabridged English translation of *Lafayette en Amérique en 1824 et 1825* by Auguste Levasseur, Lafayette's private secretary, who accompanied him on his farewell tour of America. He currently serves as president of the American Friends of Lafayette and the Massachusetts Lafayette Society and has lectured on Lafayette at the Owens-Thomas House in Savannah, in venues in fifteen of the twenty-four states that Lafayette visited, and in the District of Columbia.

JACQUELINE JONES is Mastin Gentry White Professor of Southern History and Walter Prescott Webb Chair in History and Ideas at the University of Texas at Austin, where she teaches courses in American southern history. She is the author of *Saving Savannah: the City and the Civil War* and *A Dreadful Deceit: The Myth of Race from the Colonial Era to Obama's America.*

TIMOTHY LOCKLEY is director of the Humanities Research Centre and associate professor of history and comparative American studies at the University of Warwick. He has published widely on race relations, slavery, and poverty in the antebellum South. Major publications include *Lines in the Sand: Race and Class in Lowcountry Georgia, 1750–1860*; *Welfare and Charity in the Antebellum South*; and *Maroon Communities in South Carolina.*

JAMES A. MCMILLIN is the associate director of Bridwell Library of the Perkins School of Theology at Southern Methodist University. His book *The Final Victims: Foreign Slave Trade to North America, 1783–1810* received honorable mention in the 2004 North American Society for Oceanic History's John Lyman Book Award for United States Maritime History. He contributed to *Warm Ashes: Issues in Southern History at the Dawn of the Twenty-First Century.*

GREGORY MIXON is the author of *The Atlanta Riot: Race, Class, and Violence in a New South City.* He has published articles in three journals and is currently working on a new book project examining Georgia's black militia companies, 1865–1905. He is an associate professor of history and affiliated with the Africana Studies Department at the University of North Carolina at Charlotte.

SUSAN EVA O'DONOVAN is an associate professor of history at the University of Memphis. She is a former member of the Freedmen & Southern Society Project, where she coedited the documentary histories *Land & Labor, 1865* (2008); and *Land & Labor, 1866–1867* (forthcoming). She is the author of *Becoming Free in the Cotton South*, for which she received the James A. Rawley Prize from the Organization of American Historians. She is currently coeditor of *American Nineteenth Century History*, and is writing a political history of slaves in antebellum America.

PAUL PRESSLY is director of the Ossabaw Island Education Alliance, a partnership between the Georgia Board of Regents, the Department of Natural Resources, and the Ossabaw Island Foundation. He holds a DPhil from the University of Oxford and is the author of *On the Rim of the Caribbean: Colonial Georgia and the British Atlantic World.*

ANNE ROISE is a project development and strategic planning consultant in Savannah, Georgia, and was previously a trustee of the Historic Savannah Foundation. She is the coordinator for the Mother Mathilda House Project—an interpretive site that will honor the life and work of Mother Mathilda Beasley.

TANIA SAMMONS is the senior curator of decorative arts and historic sites for Telfair Museums. Sammons oversees the reinterpretation of the museums' two National Historic Landmark buildings, the Telfair Academy of Arts and Sciences and the Owens-Thomas House. She also produces original exhibitions and related materials on decorative and fine arts and history. Her publications include exhibition catalogues *The Story of Silver in Savannah: Creating and Collecting Since the 18th Century*; "The Art of Kahlil Gibran," in *The Art of Kahlil Gibran*; *The Owens-Thomas House*; and *Daffin Park: The First One Hundred Years*. Recent originally curated exhibitions include *Sitting in Savannah: Telfair Chairs and Sofas*; *Journey to the Beloved Community: Story Quilts by Beth Mount*, and *Beyond Utility: Pottery Created by Enslaved Hands*.

CHRISTINA SNYDER is an associate professor of history and American studies at Indiana University. She is the author of *Slavery in Indian Country: The Changing Face of Captivity in Early America*, which won several awards, including the Berkshire Conference of Women Historians Book Prize, the James H. Broussard Prize, and the John C. Ewers Prize. Her current book project, supported by an ACLS Fellowship, is a transnational study of race, class, and sovereignty in the era of Indian removal.

JANICE L. SUMLER-EDMOND is a professor of United States history and the director of the W. E. B. Du Bois Honors Program at Huston-Tillotson University in Austin, Texas. She is the author of *The Secret Trust of Aspasia Cruvellier Mirault, the Life and Trials of a Free Women of Color in Antebellum Georgia* (2008). Her current research examines the writings of nineteenth-century African American women activists.

JERMAINE THIBODEAUX is a doctoral student in the Department of History at the University of Texas at Austin. He is an Americanist whose focus is on gender, slavery, and southern history.

PAULETTE THOMPSON is the assistant curator of history for Telfair Museums and is an instructor of history at Armstrong Atlantic State University, where she teaches undergraduate courses in American and World History.

JEFFREY ROBERT YOUNG is a senior lecturer in the Department of History at Georgia State University. His books *Domesticating Slavery: The Master Class in Georgia and South Carolina* and *Proslavery and Sectional Thought in the Early South: An Anthology*, explore the connections between household relationships and sectional politics in the slaveholding South. He is currently researching the literary foundations for the expression of American nationalism in the Revolutionary Era.

Index

Page references in *italics* refer to illustrations.